CISTERCIAN FATHERS SERIES: NUMBER SEVENTY-SIX

THE FIRST LIFE OF
BERNARD OF CLAIRVAUX

CISTERCIAN FATHERS SERIES: NUMBER SEVENTY-SIX

The First Life of Bernard of Clairvaux

by
William of Saint-Thierry, Arnold of Bonneval, and
Geoffrey of Auxerre

Translated by
Hilary Costello, OCSO

α

Cistercian Publications
www.cistercianpublications.org

LITURGICAL PRESS
Collegeville, Minnesota
www.litpress.org

A Cistercian Publications title published by Liturgical Press

Cistercian Publications
Editorial Offices
161 Grosvenor Street
Athens, Ohio 45701
www.cistercianpublications.org

In the absence of a critical edition of Recension B of the *Vita Prima Sancti Bernardi*, this translation is based on Mount Saint Bernard MS 1, with section numbers inserted from the critical edition of Recension A (*Vita Prima Sancti Bernardi Claraevallis Abbatis, Liber Primus*, ed. Paul Verdeyen, CCCM 89B [Turnhout: Brepols Publishers, 2011]).

Scripture texts in this work are translated by the translator of the text.

The image of Saint Bernard on the cover is a miniature from Mount Saint Bernard Abbey, fol. 1, reprinted with permission from Mount Saint Bernard Abbey.

1   2   3   4   5   6   7   8   9

Library of Congress Cataloging-in-Publication Data

Vita prima Sancti Bernardi. English
    The first life of Bernard of Clairvaux / by William of Saint-Thierry, Arnold of Bonneval, and Geoffrey of Auxerre ; translated by Hilary Costello, OCSO.
        pages.   cm. — (Cistercian Fathers series ; Number seventy-six)
    Includes bibliographical references and index.
    ISBN 978-0-87907-176-9 — ISBN 978-0-87907-692-4 (ebook)
    1. Bernard, of Clairvaux, Saint, 1090 or 1091–1153.   2. Christian saints—France—Biography.   I. William, of Saint-Thierry, Abbot of Saint-Thierry, approximately 1085–1148?   II. Arnaldus, Abbot of Bonneval, –approximately 1156.   III. Geoffrey, of Auxerre, active 12th century.   IV. Title.

BX4700.B5V563   2015
271'.1203—dc23
[B]   2015024945

Contents

Acknowledgments

Dr. James France has helped me and encouraged me in this translation. Most of the footnotes, apart from the scriptural quotations, are due to him. He has also helped me considerably with the Latin text, which it was necessary for me to establish before I could undertake the English translation.

If any scholars or any readers desire to see the Latin text, I have a bound copy of it at Mount Saint Bernard Abbey; the manuscript itself is of course kept safely in the archives but could be consulted with permission from the abbot. Br. Martin Horwath took the photographs of the manuscript; these too are available to anyone who wishes to see them.

Fr. Hilary Costello
Mount Saint Bernard Abbey

Introduction

When Bernard, abbot of Clairvaux, died on August 20, 1153, his former secretary, Geoffrey of Auxerre, had already begun to create a *vita* to make the case for Bernard's canonization. Having compiled notes about Bernard's early life and monastic beginnings, Geoffrey arranged for William of Saint-Thierry to incorporate them into a narrative of Bernard's early life and monastic beginnings. After William died in 1148, Arnold, abbot of Bonneval Abbey, took the story further, focusing on Bernard's advocacy for Pope Innocent II in the papal contest with Peter Leonis, Anacletus II. Geoffrey himself then completed the *vita*, writing three books about Bernard's extensive miracles, activities as a peacemaker in Italy and France, and death and burial at Clairvaux.

But the final five-part *vita*—the *Vita prima Sancti Bernardi*, or the *First Life of Bernard of Clairvaux*—did not lead at once to Bernard's canonization. Geoffrey had pinned his hopes on Pope Eugenius III, a former monk of Clairvaux and then a Cistercian abbot before becoming pope in 1145. In part because Eugenius died a month before Bernard, on July 8, 1153, another decade, another pope, and a significant revision of the *vita* intervened before Bernard's canonization. But in 1174, after Geoffrey submitted his revised version of the *Vita prima*, Pope Alexander III named Bernard a saint.

The work that follows here is the first English translation of Geoffrey's revised *Vita prima* (Recension B), the one on which Alexander relied in his canonization decision. The first, longer version (Recension A) received two English translations before Paul Verdeyen prepared his 2011 critical edition.[1] But Geoffrey's shorter Recension

---

[1] William of St. Thierry, et al., *St. Bernard of Clairvaux: The Story of His Life as Recorded in the* Vita Prima Bernardi *by Certain of His Contemporaries, William of St. Thierry,*

B has until now been available only in manuscript witnesses, one of which—the exemplar of this translation—is a treasured possession of the English Cistercian abbey of Mount Saint Bernard.

THE MANUSCRIPT

All those who have held an ancient manuscript in their hands know the feeling of awe that comes over them when they realize that this book written with such care and love by a monk eight hundred years ago is now in their own hands. That was the feeling I had when first I held our manuscript.

The manuscript contains two works: the *Vita prima Sancti Bernardi* and Bernard's *Vita Sancti Malachiae*. It was acquired by Mount Saint Bernard Abbey in 1950 from a bookseller, Bernard Quaritch, who had bought it for £120. Fr. John Morson, who was librarian of the monastery at the time, has given the background of its coming to Mount Saint Bernard:

> Bertram, fourth Earl of Ashburnham (ob. 1878), collected the famous Ashburnham library which was dispersed in the eighteen-nineties. *Appendix* 232, having as its chief content the Life of St. Bernard, was labelled fifteenth century, and was sold at Sotheby's on 1 May 1899 for £3 12s. 6d. It was soon recognized that the writing should be dated about 1200, and that the miniature portrait of the saint, heading the work, had been produced in the life-time of those who had known him. The manuscript passed through the hands of several booksellers, was acquired by the late Mr. James Lyell, then at the dispersal

---

Arnold of Bonnevaux, Geoffrey and Philip of Clairvaux, and Odo of Deuil, trans. Geoffrey Webb and Adrian Walker (London: A. R. Mowbray, 1960); William of St. Thierry, et al., *Bernard of Clairvaux: Early Biographies, Volume 1 by William of St. Thierry*, trans. Martinus Cawley, Guadalupe Translations (Lafayette, OR: Abbey of Our Lady of Guadalupe, 2000); William of Saint-Thierry, et al., *Vita prima Sancti Bernardi Claraevallis Abbatis*, ed. Paul Verdeyen, CCCM 89B (Turnhout: Brepols Publishers, 2011), cited below as VP.

of his collection in 1951 returned to its probable origin, the Order of Cîteaux.[2]

Fr. Morson continues with a description of the portrait of Saint Bernard that begins the work:

The portrait makes this unique among manuscripts of the Life.[3] Crude and rubbed as it is, it may seem at first glance to tell us nothing, but when it is compared with others it appears as one of a family, indeed as an ancestor. It can hardly be doubted that the artist had reflected upon the description of St. Bernard's outward appearance given by Geoffrey.[4] There are the frail body, moderate stature, slightly flushed cheeks, auburn beard. Over the undecorated alb, or possibly monastic cowl, is a bell-shaped chasuble, blue as was often used by the Cistercians. . . . Stole, orphrey and footwear, are of gold. Such decorations were forbidden under St. Bernard's influence and in his life-time.[5] The artist is making the best use of the colours at his disposal, putting on to the vestments the gold which St. Bernard would have shunned, just as he places a golden aureole behind the head. What at first seems to be a low mitre is in fact an exaggeration of the monastic tonsure. Cistercian abbots did not have mitre or ring in the twelfth century, and St. Bernard himself reproved all abbots who sought such privileges.[6] There

---

[2] John Morson, "Some Manuscripts of the Life of St. Bernard," *Bulletin of the John Rylands Library* 37 (1955): 476–502, here 485.

[3] My fuller discussion of the manuscript and portrait is in *The Life of the Spirit* (November 1953), and in *Collectanea Ord. Cist.* (1954), 30–4, 214–21 . . . [Morson note, abbreviated].

[4] Book 3, n1: Migne, P. L. 185, 303 [Morson note].

[5] First statutes of the General Chapter, st. 10. The date (formerly given as 1134) and origin of these statutes are discussed at length by J. A. Lefèvre in *Collectanea Ord. Cist.* (1954), 157–82, 241–66 [Morson note]. For the statute itself, see Chrysogonus Waddell, *Narrative and Legislative Texts from Early Cîteaux*, Studia et Documenta, vol. 9 (Cîteaux: Commentarii Cistercienses, 1999), 320, under the heading "Quid liceat uel non liceat nobis habere de auro, argento, gemmis et serico. X."

[6] *De Officio Episcoporum*, n36. Migne, P. L. 182, 832 [Morson note].

are no insignia but the crozier held in the left hand, the right being raised to teach, as so often in the early portraits.[7]

He then goes on to describe the manuscript itself and the inferences that can be made about its date, provenance, and textual value:

> The book contains 163 vellum sheets, edges slightly planed, measuring 10 by 7 inches, each ruled with twenty-nine or thirty lines, rebound between the original boards with their clasp. The unskilled and hasty writing, coming probably from a newly founded scriptorium, indicates about 1200 as a likely date and provenance rather Flemish than French. The errors of the illiterate scribe are many, but behind them one can recognize an accurate dictation, resulting in an early and useful sample of recension B. These characteristics, possibly also the marking of accents and frequent punctuation, suggest a Cistercian origin.[8]

Although Fr. Morson considered the manuscript to be of Flemish provenance, others argue that it is French. Adriaan H. Bredero, for example, lists it in his register of manuscripts of Recension B as "prov[enance]. Abbaye cistercienne en France (?)."[9] As far as I can tell, it is the only manuscript of the *Vita prima sancti Bernardi* in a library of the Cistercian Order. For that reason it is a valuable manuscript for Mount Saint Bernard Abbey and for the Order. The

---

[7] Morson, "Some Manuscripts," 485–86. Morson reproduces the portrait in black and white on p. 480.

[8] Morson, "Some Manuscripts," 486–87. Adriaan H. Bredero, who has studied the manuscript history of the *Vita Prima*, suggests that the MSB manuscript (hereafter MSB 1) could be earlier than was previously thought; he groups it with eleven other manuscripts of Recension B from the twelfth or thirteenth century; see his "Études sur la 'Vita Prima' de Saint Bernard," *Analecta* 17, nos. 1, 2 (1961): 3–72, 215–60, and 18, no. 3 (1962): 3–59, here 17:23–24. Jean Leclercq identifies it as a manuscript of the twelfth century ("Études sur Saint Bernard et le texte de ses écrits," *Analecta* 9 [1953]: 3–245, here 43). The image is reproduced on the cover of this book and in James France, *The Cistercians in Medieval Art* (Thrupp, UK: Sutton Publishing, 1998), 40; and in James France, *Medieval Images of Saint Bernard of Clairvaux*, CS 210 (Kalamazoo, MI: Cistercian Publications, 2007), 73.

[9] Bredero, "Études," 17:24.

scribe who wrote it is unknown, but he or she writes with a strong, clear, firm hand, despite mistakes here and there, showing some lack of familiarity with Latin. In a sense those mistakes make the text even more personal. It is clear that behind them lies an accurate text, one containing an early witness to Recension B of the *Vita prima*.[10]

But there it was, lying in our archives for sixty years, and no one had much interest in it. That is why I decided to translate the Latin into English. Fr. Morson ended his article with the hope that some scholar would make a critical edition of Recension B. To do that one would have to collate at least the eighteen twelfth- and thirteenth-century surviving manuscripts that Bredero has identified. This translation is much less adventurous than a critical edition would be, but it does introduce the only manuscript of the *Vita prima* that belongs to a Cistercian monastery.

In 1163, when Geoffrey submitted the original, longer, version of Bernard's *vita*, Alexander III was in the process of redefining the traditional canonization process, with canonization requests now not to be submitted during a synod or council but at a different time, so that those evaluating the request would have the time to verify the facts—and specifically the miracles—reported in the *vita* accompanying the request. Bredero explains the implications for the *vita* as Geoffrey perceived them:

> This requirement implied that the stories in a *vita* about virtuous deeds and miracles were to fit the more or less stereotypical scheme that corresponded with the position of the candidate-saint in the world of church and society during his life.
>
> As a result of these changes in procedure, a *vita* now had to satisfy paradoxical requirements. On the one hand, a stereotypical *Life* of a saint, characterized by piety, was required;

---

[10] This title refers to the fact that the five books of the *Vita* (or, in some manuscripts, six) constitute the first of three hagiographical lives of Bernard. Bredero describes it as "the oldest, the most important, and the most extensive description of Bernard's life that has been preserved in many manuscripts. Both other lives are significantly less comprehensive and, to a large extent, depend for their content on this *vita prima*" (*Bernard of Clairvaux: Between Cult and History* [Grand Rapids, MI: William B. Eerdmans Publishing Company, 1996], 25).

on the other hand, information was to be provided with
regard to authentic facts. This paradox forced the hagiogra-
pher to select and disguise his facts in such a way that veri-
fication would be difficult, if not impossible. Such selectivity
was of special importance when the candidate-saint had been
a well-known figure during his lifetime, or, at least, while it
was still possible to hear people tell about the reported miracles. If Geoffrey of Auxerre was aware of these changes in
procedure, this may have prompted him, as the only author
who was still able to do so, to change the text of the *vita prima*
accordingly.[11]

As a result, Bredero continues, "Geoffrey's revision of this *vita* . . .
concerns mainly abridgments or elimination of passages, as well as
some stylistic and factual improvements."[12]

THE AUTHORS OF THE *VITA PRIMA*

William of Saint-Thierry, the first of the three authors, was a
learned theologian (probably more learned than Bernard himself)
and spiritual writer. But in this book he appears more simply and
humbly as a friend of Saint Bernard, whom he probably met in 1128
in a hut on the grounds of Clairvaux Abbey, when both men were
seriously ill. He was five years older than Bernard, having been born
at Liège in 1085. After beginning his monastic life at Saint Nicaise in
Reims, in 1119 or 1120 he was elected abbot at the nearby Abbey of
Saint-Thierry. But in 1135, after seven years of wishing to become a

---

[11] Bredero, *Bernard of Clairvaux*, 33–52, here 45–46; see also Adriaan H. Bredero,
"The Canonization of Saint Bernard and the Rewriting of His Life," in *Cistercian
Ideals and Reality*, ed. John R. Sommerfeldt, CS 60 (Kalamazoo, MI: Cistercian
Publications, 1978), 80–105.

[12] Bredero, *Bernard of Clairvaux*, 46. For more on changes from the first to the
second version, see Bredero, *Bernard of Clairvaux*, 46–52. To facilitate comparison
of the two versions of the *Vita*, I have inserted the critical edition's section numbers, bracketed, into my translation and used them for references in the two indices. At the beginning of each book of the translation I also note the extended
passages that Geoffrey deleted from Recension A.

Cistercian, he resigned his abbacy and entered the Cistercian monastery of Signy, in the Ardennes, where he died in about 1148, five years before Bernard.[13]

The second author, Arnold of Bonneval, became a monk of the Benedictine monastery of Marmoutier in 1138 and was elected abbot of Bonneval, in the diocese of Chartres, in about 1141. He resigned the abbatial office before 1156 and probably died at Marmoutier soon afterward. He was friendly with the Cistercians but probably did not know Bernard well personally. Unable to come to Clairvaux while Bernard was dying, he reportedly sent him a gift of delicacies. Geoffrey of Auxerre reports that Bernard made a final effort to write a short letter of thanks to Arnold, mentioning his inability to eat or sleep and signing it in his own hand; that final letter appears as part of Geoffrey's narrative of Bernard's death in the last book of the *vita* (bk. 5.9–10).[14]

Scholars have questioned the authenticity of this final letter, but to me their arguments seem inadequate.[15] Even if Arnold was not very close to Bernard, he was certainly friendly with many of the friends of Clairvaux. If the letter is authentic, it must have been written in August 1153, within the fortnight before Bernard died, for Geoffrey says Bernard dictated it "a very few days before his sacred passing from us" (bk. 5.9).

Since Arnold was well known to the monks of Clairvaux, Geoffrey asked him to complete the work that William had not been able to finish. Although Arnold initially declined, he later undertook the

---

[13] For a recent study of the relationship of William and Bernard, see E. Rozanne Elder, "Bernard and William of Saint Thierry," in *A Companion to Bernard*, ed. Brian Patrick McGuire (Leiden: Brill Academic Publishers, 2011), 108–32, here 116. Elder points to the joint efforts of the two men in encouraging monastic reform and to William's initiative in drawing Bernard into the pursuit of Abelard for heresy (119–22).

[14] Bernard, Ep 310 (SBOp 8:230; *The Letters of St Bernard of Clairvaux*, trans. Bruno Scott James [London: Burns and Oates, 1953], #469, p. 521).

[15] For challenges to the letter, see, e.g., Richard Upsher Smith, "Arnold of Bonneval, Bernard of Clairvaux, and Bernard's Epistle 310," *Analecta* 49 (1993): 273–318; and Bredero, *Bernard of Clairvaux*, 104–8.

work, tracing Bernard's life from the time of the papal schism, which began in 1130, until about 1148.

Geoffrey of Auxerre, the author of the last three books of the *Vita prima*, probably also initiated the entire work. He must have entered Clairvaux soon after 1140, but before that he had been a student in Paris under Peter Abelard, studying theology. He could have had a brilliant career in the church, but when Bernard preached to the clerics of Paris in what became his *On Conversion to Clerics*, Geoffrey was so overcome by Bernard's words that he changed his whole way of life and became a monk of Clairvaux.[16] Bernard soon made the young monk his traveling companion and secretary; in that role, Geoffrey began in 1145–1147 to record his observations of Bernard's activities, especially his miracles, with the aim of writing a life of Bernard.

When Geoffrey revised the finished five-book work to meet the new papal requirements for canonization, his alterations apparently offended some members of the Order who had helped to shape the first version in its final form. Although in 1162 the monks of Clairvaux elected him abbot, the fourth successor to Saint Bernard, in 1165 he was forced to resign, partly because of his editorial work on the *Vita prima*.[17]

The Role of the *Fragmenta Gaufridi* in the *First Life* of *Saint Bernard*

The *Fragmenta Gaufridi* are the most ancient biographical witness to Saint Bernard. Two editions appeared in 2011, both based on the manuscript at the Cistercian monastery of Tamié. Christine Vande Veire first prepared a critical edition of the text, collating the Tamié manuscript with two other manuscripts copied from it and with

---

[16] *Ad Clericos ad Conversione* (SBOp 4:69–116); on Geoffrey's conversion, see Bredero, *Bernard of Clairvaux*, 94–95.

[17] Bredero, *Bernard of Clairvaux*, 49–50.

various printed editions. A little later Fr. Raffaele Fassetta, OCSO, a monk of Tamié, again edited the work.[18]

The Tamié manuscript of the *Fragmenta* was originally at Clairvaux. After being lost for some time during the French Revolution, it came to the monastery of Orval and then eventually to Tamié. The manuscript has two parts. The first part, which the editors title *Fragmenta* II, contains five short passages relating to the childhood of Bernard, to his father, Tescelin, and to his mother, Aleth, here incorrectly called Elizabeth. The second, much longer, part (known as *Fragmenta* I) consists of sixty passages, again relating the childhood of Bernard from his birth in 1090 up to his encounter with the heretics of Toulouse and his healing of a hysterical woman in 1145.

Geoffrey of Auxerre has for many years been recognized as the author of the second part of the *Fragmenta*.[19] He wrote his longer portion of the *Fragmenta* during his years as Bernard's secretary, taking notes on the events he witnessed with the purpose of later writing a full account of Bernard's life. The author of the shorter part is more difficult to determine. Both Vande Veire and Fassetta follow Ferruccio Gastaldelli, who in 1989 persuasively conjectured that the author was Raynaud, another monk of Clairvaux.[20] After entering Clairvaux in 1117, in 1121 Raynaud was sent by Bernard to become abbot of Foigny. In 1131, however, he left Foigny and returned to

---

[18] *Fragmenta Gavfridi*, ed. Christine Vande Veire, in *Vita Prima Sancti Bernardi Claraevallis Abbatis,* ed. Paul Verdeyen (Turnhout0: Brepols Publishers, 2011), 235–307; see also Geoffroy d'Auxerre, *Notes sur la vie et les miracles de saint Bernard; Fragmenta I,* [*Précédé de*] *Fragmenta* II by Raynaud de Foigny, ed. and trans. Raffaele Fassetta, SCh 548 (Paris: Éditions du Cerf, 2011). Vande Veire places the longer portion before the shorter to reflect the chronological order of the two portions and so labels them *Fragmenta* I and II (see *Fragmenta* 254–55 and 254n41). Fassetta agrees with Vande Veire in numbering the longer portion as *Fragmenta* I and the shorter as *Fragmenta* II, but he begins his edition with *Fragmenta* II.

[19] For a discussion of the origins, purpose, and dating of the *Fragmenta,* see Vande Veire, *Fragm,* 254–61; and Ferruccio Gastaldelli, "La più antiche testimonianze biografiche su San Bernardo. Studio storico-critico sui *Fragmenta Gaufridi,*" *Analecta* 45 (1989): 3–80; reprinted in Ferruccio Gastaldelli, *Studi su San Bernardo e Goffredo di Auxerre,* Millennio Medievale, 30; Reprint, 3 (Florence: Sismel. Edizioni del Galluzzo, 2001), 43–127. See also Bredero, "Études," 218–19.

[20] Ferruccio Gastaldelli, "La più antiche testimonianze."

Clairvaux, serving Bernard as secretary until replaced by Geoffrey. It seems likely that Geoffrey then sent both parts of the *Fragmenta* to William of Saint-Thierry as a basis for the life of Bernard.

William certainly relied extensively on the *Fragmenta* in book 1 of the *Vita prima*, using in his narrative all the earlier part by Raynaud and just over half of the second part—sections 1–39. But as a highly skilled author, he wove these materials on Bernard's life into an original narrative, combining the sources he had at hand with his own reminiscences of close friendship with Bernard, gathered during the time the two of them had lived together in the little hut on the grounds of Clairvaux, where Bernard had been sent to recover from a severe illness. William thus rewrote the narrative in his own words, making hardly any explicit reference to the words in the *Fragmenta*. In writing book 4, Geoffrey also used the *Fragmenta* extensively, but, unlike William, he often repeated the words verbatim, expanding the story while incorporating his own earlier notes from the *Fragmenta*.

Unlike William and Geoffrey, Arnold of Bonneval appears to have worked almost entirely without reference to the *Fragmenta*, including only two episodes found there, Bernard's encounter with Peter of Pisa and the death of Peter Leonis—and perhaps he takes even those from another source.[21] In fact I can find only one sentence taken in part from *Fragm* I.39 about the death of Peter Leonis: "For *this foolish pontiff*, the heir to Peter Leonis, came to the man of God in secret, and he, Bernard, *brought him to the feet of the lord Innocent* after he had rid himself of *the insignia that he had usurped*" (*et ipse ridiculus pontifex . . . usurpatis insignibus . . . ad domini Innocentii pedes adduxit*) (VP 2.47).[22] The absence from this book of other quotations from the *Fragmenta* points to Arnold's use of other sources.

---

[21] Bredero suggests that Arnold relied on Raynaud de Foigny for his discussion of Bernard's 1136 visit to Milan and used information about the papal schism received from Arnulf of Séez, who had been the archdeacon of Bishop Geoffrey de Lèves of Chartres, and probably additional material from a source at Clairvaux, perhaps Geoffrey d'Auxerre himself (see Bredero, *Bernard of Clairvaux*, 114–15).

[22] In the translation, phrases taken directly from the *Fragmenta* are italicized (*Fragm* I.39: *ipse ridiculus pontifex temerariae usurpata insignia ponens, cum omnibus fautoribus suis procidens* [sic] *ad pedes domini Innocentii papae*).

THE WORK

The *Vita prima* contains the story of Saint Bernard's life from his mother's dream about him before he was born in 1090 until his death at Clairvaux at the age of 63 in 1153; it also includes a few events from just after his death. To that extent it can be understood as what Thomas Heffernan calls a sacred biography.[23] The events it relates appear chosen and presented to advance Bernard's canonization. Michael Casey, discussing the importance of the biographer's recognizing the work as hagiography, comments on what that genre means for its portrayal of Bernard:

> The fundamental assertion of the *Vita prima* is that Bernard of Clairvaux was a holy man. The single most important fact which this work mediates is that some of his contemporaries thought sufficiently highly of him to present his career from this perspective. . . . What is certain is that the *Vita prima* is not principally concerned with conserving objective data for the use of future historians. Facts it certainly contains, but they are elaborated selectively. There is a case to present; if suitable facts are available they are exploited. If not they can be expanded or glossed; incidents can be leaned on to yield a favorable interpretation. Where cooperative events are lacking, legends may be used.[24]

The writers were men of their time, accepting the religious traditions of the period and the teaching of the church while it was undergoing profound changes such as the rise of scholasticism, which became dominant in the following century. Their pens were tipped

---

[23] Thomas Heffernan, *Sacred Biography: Saints and Their Biographers in the Middle Ages* (New York: Oxford University Press, 1988); see also Bredero, "The Canonization of Saint Bernard," 80–83.

[24] Michael Casey, "Towards a Methodology for the *Vita prima*: Translating the First Life into Biography," in Bernardus Magister: *Papers Presented at the Nonacentenary Celebration of the Birth of Bernard of Clairvaux, Kalamazoo, Michigan*, ed. John R. Sommerfeldt, CS 135 (Kalamazoo, MI: Cistercian Publications, and Cîteaux, 1992), 55–70, here 57.

with fine Latin, with rhetoric playing a prominent part under the influence of classical writers such as Virgil, Cicero, and Seneca. To this tradition was added Bernard's own genius for poetic phrases and ability to invest almost every sentence with an apt scriptural quotation. Bernard was also gifted with great charm, combined with a deep sense of humility that captivated everyone he met. This charm, this charisma, manifested itself especially when as a young man he decided to exercise his zeal for the religious life within his own family and then reached out toward a widening group of social peers and church prelates and even, after the schism of 1130, the highest dignitaries in the church, including archbishops, cardinals, and the supreme pontiff.

All these traits are apparent in Bernard's better-known books, such as *On Loving God* or his most influential work, the *Sermons on the Song of Songs*. But for an understanding of how they began and developed, it is necessary to read the *Vita prima* and to read it with discretion. It is not a totally objective narrative, not history as we know it today. The three writers tend, for example, to underplay the weaknesses of their hero. Undoubtedly Bernard had weaknesses, yet this compelling *Life* conveys not only his force of character and spiritual power but the deep admiration and affection of those who knew him well.

BOOK 1

William of Saint-Thierry's book, which begins the *Vita prima*, introduces Bernard as a man of extraordinary charisma who gradually impressed and stimulated everyone with whom he came into contact. William also shows Bernard as the fulfillment of prophecy, becoming as an adult the gifted preacher foreseen in his mother's dream of him as a barking dog. During his life, indeed, the numbers of those he influenced rapidly multiplied, many of them becoming some of the most powerful figures of their age.

William portrays the young Bernard as precocious, exceeding all his siblings in his natural genius, progress in studies, and prodigious memory, as seen in his ability to memorize the Scriptures. William reports that as a young man Bernard spoke to the members of his family with words of fire, predicting their future and drawing them with him into Cîteaux, the home of the most severe monastic life of the time. There was apparently no resisting his impassioned, powerful overtures. Every member of the family fell under his spell, even though at first they opposed him. So, for example, William tells of Bernard's brother Gerard, who mocked him for his behavior. But when one of Bernard's prophecies came true, Gerard dared not oppose Bernard any longer; willingly though unwillingly he joined the group, eventually becoming one of Bernard's most fervent disciples.

This first book thus shows Bernard as a man of forceful enthusiasm who drew his friends and family into a circle of monks. In 1113, Bernard entered Cîteaux; such was his compelling energy that two years later his abbot, Stephen Harding, sent him and his family members who had joined him at Cîteaux to found its third daughter house, Clairvaux.[25] There, by his own example, Bernard taught the young community to live in austerity and poverty, blazing a trail that drew noblemen and peasants alike to become disciples, living the most austere life of any age.

Stories of Bernard's healing both members of his own family and strangers he met on his travels became so well known that Bernard's reputation as a miracle worker quickly spread, as William conveys in lyrical prose. Bernard's preaching was also so powerful and his faith so firmly rooted that William described his work, in the language of 1 Corinthians 13:2, as equivalent to "moving mountains," with such a powerful effect that "what this little-known and ailing man, at death's door and strong only in speech, did in this life was a greater miracle than all his other miracles" (bk. 1.61). Gradually men came to Clairvaux to partake of its spiritual riches, and within a short space of time it became a large community with many members. As a result, after a while it became necessary for Clairvaux to found other monasteries, so that Bernard's influence began to spread to many places in France and beyond.[26]

---

[25] For a discussion of the relationship between Stephen and Bernard, see Joël Regnard, "Saint Bernard and the New Monastery," CSQ 49, no. 4 (2014): 431–53.

[26] Louis Lekai credits the quick Cistercian expansion in the twelfth century to Bernard's "dynamic character and energy"; he counts 331 Cistercian houses

William shows that influence as not limited to monks and monasteries, however. When in 1115, as the new abbot of the small unknown monastery of Clairvaux, Bernard needed to be ordained to the
priesthood, he approached the bishop of Châlons-sur-Marne, William
of Champeaux. Almost immediately Bishop William saw the young
abbot as holding the key to the future of the church and became
closely knit with him in a deep spiritual friendship. Soon afterward,
William of Saint-Thierry himself met Bernard; so great became their
friendship that Bernard told William the details of his early life and
many other things that William included in the *Vita prima*.

William's book thus contains a number of significant stories about
Bernard's life, including the deathbed repentance of Lord Josbert,
Bernard's famous letter to his cousin Robert, written in pouring
rain but undampened, the onslaught of the legendary flies of Foigny,
Bernard's determination to guard his chastity against repeated onslaught, and his recurring health problems.[27] These stories witness
to Bernard's growing influence on his contemporaries, the growth
of his authority, and the magnetism of his person and his words.

This book also includes stories of some of William's own encoun-
ters with Bernard, giving more personal insight into William himself
than does any other surviving work. He tells, for example, of his first
visit to the ailing Bernard, his shock at the circumstances in which
Bernard was housed, and his own longing to remain there with
Bernard. He also writes of his later extended stay at Clairvaux as an
invited guest of Bernard when both were sick and isolated from the
community. On this occasion, William relates, Bernard supervised
William's own slow recovery to health, even attempting to govern
William's dietary decisions.

---

existing across Europe in 1151 and estimates a total population of over 11,600
monks. See *The Cistercians: Ideals and Reality* (Kent, OH: Kent State University
Press, 1977), 34, 44.

[27] On the flies of Foigny, see Anselme Dimier, "Le miracle des mouches de
Foigny," *Cîteaux* 8 (1957): 57–62. On Bernard's poor health, see E. Rozanne Elder,
"Making Virtues of Vexing Habits," in *Studiosorum Speculum: Studies in Honor of
Louis J. Lekai, O. Cist*, ed. Francis Swietek and John R. Sommerfeldt, CS 141 (Ka-
lamazoo, MI: Cistercian Publications, 1993), 75–94.

The book William wrote looks deeply into the heart of Bernard, describing in simple yet elegant words the humility, charity, and gentleness of this great man and superb orator. This book is thus imbued with William's enthusiasm for his friend and spiritual guide. It is no wonder that this first portion of the *Vita prima*, ablaze with William's admiration for Bernard, is the most personal portion of the work. It focuses much more on Bernard the man, the monk, and the abbot than on Bernard the public figure; it contains some miracles but mostly tells the human stories that are still best known and loved about the young Bernard, who so shaped William's own life and thought.

Book 2

After William died, leaving his work unfinished, Arnold of Bonneval wrote a second book. While the Benedictine Arnold was apparently also a friend of Bernard's, at least according to Bernard's Epistle 310, he was older and less concerned with the force of Bernard's individual personality than William had been. Instead, he focused on Bernard's role in resolving the papal schism, which divided the church in the West between two popes, both claiming supreme power and authority and both supported by a powerful clique. Innocent II was the wiser but more diffident, while Peter Leonis—Anacletus II—was much more powerful, much more overbearing; it was up to the bishops of Europe to choose which to accept as the supreme pontiff. Because Anacletus was dangerously powerful in Rome, Innocent sailed north to Pisa, calling a council of bishops to meet in Étampes to discuss the crisis.

When the king of France, Louis VI (r. 1108–1137), summoned Bernard to the council, the bishops agreed that the matter should be put to him to resolve—that the business of God should be decided by the servant of God. Bernard reluctantly undertook the task and, after some inquiries, named Innocent pope. This decision placed Bernard at the center of church politics, quickly establishing him as the most influential person of the twelfth century. It was, I suppose, unprecedented in the checkered history of the papacy that an abbot, not even a prelate in the church, should choose the pope, yet as Arnold tells it, such was the charisma of Bernard that he did it and did it very well.

Arnold's deep interest in the events of the papal conflict sometimes caused him to digress from his overview of Bernard's life and public role. So although Arnold describes the disruption caused by an apparently mentally disturbed monk during Innocent's visit to Clairvaux and Bernard's healing of the man, he at once turns to Innocent's long journey back to Rome and his forcing his way into the Lateran Palace, where he was greeted by many of the Roman nobility and people. He goes on to explain that because of the still too-powerful forces of Anacletus, Innocent then once again left Rome and set up court at Pisa. From there he called on Bernard to go to Milan to quell the schism started by Archbishop Anselm, a follower of Anacletus.

At this point, though, Arnold remembers his purpose, turning once again to Bernard, who, accompanied by two cardinals, Guy and Matthew, crossed the Apennines and entered Milan. The enthusiasm among the Milanese for his coming was so great that as he approached, still seven miles away, they went out in large numbers to greet him: "Those going before the abbot and those following cheered him with mighty acclamations of joy, and . . . he was for a long time delayed by the dense crowd" (bk. 2.9). The story concludes with peace restored to the city through Bernard's sanctity.

At this point, instead of continuing with the theme of Bernard's social and political authority, Arnold for a while considers Bernard's spiritual power, inserting three miracles of healing that show both Bernard's authority over those possessed by the devil and his popularity among ordinary people, popularity that preceded him as far as Milan and was soon recognized throughout France, Germany, Italy, Spain, and England. But Arnold also notes Bernard's anxiety about the effect of his charisma and the popular confidence in his power to heal:

> The people's faith would not allow the least hesitation in the
> man of God, and, because of his impressive humility, he did
> not presume to put to the test these unaccustomed requests or

to be embarrassed when the people made them. If he obstinately resisted the loving-charity of those asking, . . . he would seem to offend God, and if his own faith might dissent from the faith of the people, he would be seen by his diffidence to cast a shadow over God's omnipotence. He burned within himself over this, and although he thought it necessary to do these signs not so much for the faithful as for the unbelievers, he committed his bold efforts to the Holy Spirit and, relying on prayer, putting his trust in the power coming from heaven, with the spirit of fortitude he rebuked Satan, who fled from him. (bk. 2.9)

Arnold even suggests Bernard to be a close equivalent to Jesus, saying that the people's veneration "went beyond what was due to a mortal man" (bk. 2.14) and that "everywhere people were saying that *a great prophet has arisen who is mighty in deed and in word*" (bk. 2.15; Luke 7:16; 24:19). Arnold's enthusiasm for Bernard's popularity knows no bounds: "From the castles nearby, from the villages and cities, the multitudes flocked to Milan to follow the holy man, both strangers and citizens. They sought his blessings, they listened to his words, they watched his wonderful works, and they delighted beyond belief in his teaching and miracles" (bk. 2.15).

Arnold's narrative here again turns back from this public acclaim, for a time showing Bernard as an abbot and a man of simplicity and personal restraint. For as soon as Bernard returned to Clairvaux from this journey, he found that his monks were waiting to confront him with a problem that he had not foreseen, one a direct result of his public role: the original monastery had already become too small to house the ever-growing number of recruits gained by his preaching and charisma. At first he was reluctant to do anything to replace the original buildings, because the community had so recently spent a considerable amount of money and effort on the first enterprise; he voiced his fear that "the men of the world" would judge the community of being either "fickle and changeable" or wealthy if they so soon undertook to build a larger monastery (bk. 2.29). But he was quickly forced to change his mind at the urgent request of the seniors, who pointed out the desperate need of a more extensive place. Thus a new building project got underway; it was soon achieved with the generous support of many noble lords and the vigorous work of the young monks and lay brothers. Clairvaux rapidly arose to completion in the place where it now stands.

After this episode, however, Arnold shows Bernard as once again turning away from his monastic obligations to resume his role as a public figure. In 1137, Roger, the king of Sicily, a follower of Anacletus, called a council and instructed Cardinal Peter of Pisa, a man of remarkable eloquence and learned in canon law, to defend the cause of the antipope. Roger was convinced that Cardinal Peter would easily obliterate all opposition by his forceful rhetoric. Indeed, he nearly did so before Bernard's spirited refutation: "But the man of God, understanding the matter to be not one of words but of the power of the kingdom of God, spoke"—and at length proclaimed the disaster that would befall the church and the world if the schism did not quickly come to an end (bk. 2.45). Bernard's reply to the cardinal went down in history as one of the most remarkable of his glorious career.

After the end of the papal schism, the death of Anacletus in 1138, and the restoration of peace, Arnold enlarges his lens to subsequent events, sketching briefly the rapid spread of the Cistercian Order and the European bishops who emerged from the Order, including the election of Eugenius III in 1145, a former monk of Clairvaux and the first Cistercian pope. After briefly writing of Bernard as "a man with a pure heart and mind" (bk. 2.51), he introduces another outbreak of hostility, now between Count Theobald of Blois and the king of France, now Louis VII, with Bernard resolving it through his intervention, "as a solicitous mediator, the holy abbot." So Arnold concludes his book, insisting that the efficacy of Bernard as a public figure throughout those long years had resulted from his holiness as a monk and abbot. His book thus ends with the resumption of "tranquility and the desired serenity of peace," achieved by Bernard (bk. 2.55).

BOOK 3

Now Geoffrey, Bernard's secretary, takes up the story in a book considerably shorter than the two previous ones. It turns somewhat sharply from Bernard's public role to a focus on "the way of life and the teaching of this blessed father" (bk. 3.Prol). After praising Bernard's spiritual stature, Geoffrey describes his physical appearance, his clothing, and his bearing at table, marked by austere discipline at meals. This book contains so much detail that one can visualize Bernard at home in his monastery with his monks. Even when away from Clairvaux, Geoffrey shows, Bernard was above all a monk and a man of devotion. To emphasize his intensity of interior meditation even while traveling, Geoffrey inserts Bernard's visit to Hugh of Grenoble and the Carthusians. He draws a picture of the man he admires, a holy man, kind and gentle, a man of deep recollection, one not given to the frivolities of ordinary men and women, one who loved his monastery and his monks and who, therefore, despite his greatness in the eyes of the world, declined every effort to make him accept the dignities of ecclesiastical preferment.[28]

When Geoffrey does turn in this book to Bernard's public life, he concentrates not on Bernard's role in the papal schism and his work to settle regional and ecclesiastical crises, but on the Second Crusade, Bernard's opposition to Peter Abelard, and his encounter with Gilbert de la Porrée. Geoffrey presents Bernard's involvement in the Second Crusade as resulting directly from papal pressure, including Pope Eugenius's calling on Bernard to preach the crusade. At first reluctant to do so but eventually moved, says Geoffrey, by "a general edict from the supreme pontiff" (bk. 3.9), Bernard forfeited his own opinion and obeyed the pope, with enormous success. As Henri Daniel-Rops writes, "His burning words spoken at Vézelay on Easter Sunday, 1146, kindled a flame that seemed at first to outshine the fervour of Clermont fifty years before."[29] Geoffrey praises Bernard's involvement and quotes his powerful words of encouragement, but it is clear that Bernard was unwise to get involved in something he

---

[28] Casey writes, "The Bernard we learn about from the *First Life* is one who conforms to Geoffrey's vision. Bernard's sanctity is presented according to the way in which Geoffrey perceived holiness. . . . Geoffrey's Bernard is a serious man without much in the way of lightheartedness or spontaneity" (Casey, "Towards a Methodology," 61).

[29] Henri Daniel-Rops, *Cathedral and Crusade*, trans. John Warrington (London: J. M. Dent and Sons, 1957), 453.

was powerless to influence, as Geoffrey underlines by his effort to explain Bernard's participation. The intrigues and deceits among the leaders of the crusade ended in disaster not only for the church but also for Bernard's reputation.

Geoffrey also somewhat briefly surveys Bernard's opposition to Peter Abelard, which resulted in Abelard's condemnation at the Council of Sens in 1141.[30] Geoffrey refers to Abelard, his own former master, as "a famous and celebrated teacher" but one whose teaching was "full of serious blasphemies" (bk. 3.13). Abelard was an astute thinker, a champion of reason, a man who, as he wrote in his *Historia Calamitatum*, "preferred the weapons of dialectic to all the other teaching of philosophy" and who based his teaching on question, argument, and conclusion.[31] In this he was easily the greatest master of his time, preparing the way for Albert the Great and Thomas Aquinas in the following century.

Geoffrey's judgment of Abelard's teaching as blasphemous reflects his adherence to Bernard's views, prompted by William of Saint-Thierry's warnings of dangerous teachings in Abelard's writings. William was particularly disturbed by the fact that Abelard's lectures were sowing widespread skepticism among the students of Europe.[32] As Geoffrey reports, the matter came to a head at the Council of Sens, where Bernard argued against Abelard's theological errors, despite an original reluctance to attend."[33] As a result, the council condemned Abelard. Though Geoffrey commends Bernard for his

---

[30] Although the council has traditionally been dated to 1140, Constant J. Mews has established the correct date as 1141, in "The Council of Sens (1141): Abelard, Bernard, and the Fear of Social Upheaval," *Speculum* 77, no. 2 (2002): 342–82.

[31] Abelard, "Historia Calamitatum," in *The Letters of Abelard and Heloise*, trans. Betty Radice, rev. Michael Clanchy (1974; rev., London: Penguin Books, 2003), 1–43, here 3.

[32] Sister Edmée [Kingsmill], "Bernard and Abelard," in *The Influence of Saint Bernard*, ed. Benedicta Ward, Fairacres Publication 60 (Oxford: SLG Press, 1976), 89–134.

[33] Mews suggests that the unknown figures who persuaded Bernard to attend and speak against Abelard may have been advisers to King Louis VII, such as Suger of Saint Denis and Joscelin of Soissons, as well perhaps as Samson, archbishop of Reims ("Bernard of Clairvaux and Peter Abelard," in *A Companion to Bernard of Clairvaux*, ed. Brian Patrick McGuire [Leiden: Brill Academic Publishers, 2011], 133–68, here 167).

role in bringing about the condemnation, Sr. Edmée Kingsmill rightly notes the cost to Bernard's reputation: "In most modern studies Bernard is presented (if more implicitly than explicitly) as the villain of the piece whose reactionary zeal cut down a veritable Socrates."[34]

Constant J. Mews argues, however, that the issue went beyond both theology and philosophy, that while William and Bernard responded explicitly to what they saw as theological error in Abelard's teaching, the operative cause of their response was fear that Abelard's increasing influence among former supporters of the schismatic Pope Anacletus II might lead to a new schism within the church: "If sympathizers of Anacletus II were sympathizing with Abelard in questioning the full omnipotence of the Trinity, then the authority of the Church and message of Christ himself could be challenged."[35]

Geoffrey also quickly summarizes a similar situation, Bernard's encounter with Gilbert de la Porrée in 1148 at the Council of Reims. Gilbert was one of the most erudite (and apparently frequently incomprehensible) men of his day. According to Otto of Freising, "what he meant was never clear to childlike minds, scarcely even to men of education and learning."[36] He was brought before the council after two of his archdeacons accused his teaching on the Trinity to Pope Eugenius III as heretical. After a drawn-out discussion that wearied even the pope, Gilbert submitted to the will of the council, but only, he said, because his position might cause scandal to the less-learned faithful, who could hardly be expected to understand the subtleties of his arguments. He thereafter maintained that his own orthodoxy should be sufficiently irreproachable in the eyes of men who knew how to reason philosophically.[37]

---

[34] [Kingsmill], "Bernard and Abelard," 90.

[35] Mews, "Bernard of Clairvaux," 160–62, here 161.

[36] Otto of Freising, *The Deeds of Frederick Barbarossa* 1.lii (l), trans. Charles C. Mierow (New York: Columbia University Press, 1953), 88.

[37] For recent studies of Gilbert, see Karen Bollermann and Cary J. Nederman, "Standing in Abelard's Shadow: Gilbert of Poitiers, the 1148 Council of Rheims, and the Politics of Ideas," in *Religion, Power, and Resistance from the Eleventh to the Sixteenth Centuries: Playing the Heresy Card*, ed. Karen Bollermann, Thomas M. Izbicki, and Cary J. Nederman (New York: Palgrave Macmillan, 2014), 13–36;

Toward the end of this book, Geoffrey returns to Bernard's private life, mourning with Bernard over the loss of his brother Gerard in 1138 and telling how Bernard overflowed with grief and sadness, bared his heart before his brethren, and, overcome with tears and anguish, lamented over Gerard, letting all the world grieve with him in his poignant Sermon 26 on the Song of Songs.[38] Geoffrey goes on to speak of his own experience as companion and amanuensis, at Bernard's side as he traveled throughout Europe. For those wishing to know Bernard more deeply, Geoffrey appends a list of Bernard's writings to emphasize his thought and spiritual gifts (bk. 3.29). Finally, Geoffrey ends the book with a heartfelt paean of praise for the man of God, whom he calls "a beautiful olive, a fruitful vine, . . . a solid vessel" (bk. 3.32).

Book 4

In Book 4 the mood changes. Here, Geoffrey relates the miraculous events he and others have witnessed, now clearly preparing for Bernard to be recognized as a miracle worker and saint. In fact, Christopher Holdsworth calls attention to one case in which Geoffrey's agenda is particularly clear. When mentioning Pope Eugenius's presence at the 1147 Cistercian general chapter, Geoffrey neither lingers on Eugenius's extraordinary presence—he was the first pope ever to attend a chapter—nor mentions the business transacted there, despite the fact that at that momentous chapter the abbots incorporated the Savigniac and Obazine Orders into the Cistercian Order, in the filiation of Clairvaux. As Holdsworth points out, Geoffrey's goal here was distinct from the abbots' activities at that chapter,

---

Clare Monagle, "The Trial of Ideas: Two Tellings of the Trial of Gilbert of Poitiers," *Viator: Medieval and Renaissance Studies* 35 (2004): 113–29.

[38] Bernard, *Sermones super Cantica Canticorum* 26.2–27.1 (SBOp 2:311–13; *On the Song of Songs II*, trans. Kilian Walsh, CF 7 [Kalamazoo, MI: Cistercian Publications, 1976], 60–74).

his concern being rather to report something that happened on the evening of the day that the Chapter ended: Bernard's healing of a deaf child. This silence about something that seems to us so important may seem strange, until we recall two things: that Geoffrey's overarching intention was to show Bernard as a man of God, not to give a consecutive account of his life, and that if Geoffrey had said something about the affiliation of Savigny, it could have led him on to mention the problems that immediately followed it, . . . events that might not have redounded to Bernard's reputation.[39]

Indeed, Geoffrey devotes this book to Bernard's role as a man of spiritual gifts, a healer. In it he records nearly two hundred fifty such events, though some of them may also appear elsewhere in the *vita*. Geoffrey expected Bernard's miracles to be attributed to God, effected through the agency of Saint Bernard. His contemporaries would for the most part have taken them in the same sense, though toward the end of Bernard's life there was probably a growing tendency to belittle his holiness and dismiss some of the miracles.

Geoffrey usually groups Bernard's miraculous events under various headings rather than presenting them in chronological order. These groups alternate between gifts that Bernard exercised in proximity to the recipients and those done from a distance, echoing the movement of the *vita* as a whole between Bernard's life at home, as a monk and abbot, and his public journeys and engagement in public crises.

The first and most important group of these events recounts Bernard's spiritual gifts, especially his gift of spiritual predictions. Twelve predictions include several in which Bernard declares that people he has just met—among them Henry, the brother of the king of France, and Andrew, a member of Henry's entourage—will soon become monks of Clairvaux. Coming almost immediately true in Geoffrey's telling, these predictions demonstrate Bernard's prophetic powers and link him with the biblical prophets. Geoffrey narrates these predictions near the

---

[39] Christopher Holdsworth, "The Affiliation of Savigny," in *Truth as Gift: Studies in Medieval Cistercian History in Honor of John R. Sommerfeldt*, ed. Marsha L. Dutton, et al., CS 204 (Kalamazoo, MI: Cistercian Publications, 2004), 43–88, here 49.

beginning of the book, with no explicit time sequence. Here, Bernard appears as a thaumaturge, a man always acting under the inspiration of the Holy Spirit. This inspiration underlies all the other events that Geoffrey narrates.[40]

A second spiritual gift is bilocation, which Geoffrey shows six times at the beginning of book 4, when Bernard, though physically absent, does a marvelous work as if he were present. So, for example, Gerard, the abbot of Mores, sees him circulating among the monks during Vigils while he was actually sick in his room: "At the night hour," Bernard tells Gerard, "I was afflicted with serious physical problems, but even though I was not present in my body, I was there in spirit" (bk. 4.4).

One case in this book demonstrates Bernard's power over the devil, seen in his healing of a deranged person.[41] A man whom Geoffrey describes as troubled by a demon is healed when Abbot Pons comes into the man's cell with a stole previously worn by Bernard; the demon departs, shouting, "I can remain here no longer!" (bk 4.7). Geoffrey calls particular attention to Bernard's humility in hearing of this event, laughing at those who expressed astonishment at the event.

These stories precede a group of seven or more events involving substances blessed by Bernard and working their power at some distance from him. Geoffrey introduces this group with a story about a woman in the territory of Auxerre who experiences such a lengthy labor that she becomes too weak to deliver the child. When Bernard hears of her agony he sends her a gift of blessed water; as soon as she tastes it, she gives birth to a son (bk. 4.23). Numerous stories of blessed bread follow: (1) a great number of people asked for blessed bread from the man of God; (2) a knight in the region of Meaux is healed by swallowing a piece of bread blessed by Bernard; (3) a desperately wounded young man is healed when bread blessed by

---

[40] See André Picard and Pierre Boglioni, "Miracle et Thaumaturgie dans la vie de Saint Bernard," in *Vie et légendes de Saint Bernard de Clairvaux. Création, diffusion, réception (XIIᵉ–XXᵉ Siècles), Actes des Rencontres de Dijon, 7–8 juin 1991*, ed. Patrick Arabeyre, et al. (Brecht and Cîteaux: *Cîteaux: Commentarii Cistercienses*, 1993), 36–59.

[41] A large number of such events also appear in the earlier books.

Bernard is put in his mouth; (4) several loaves remain incorrupt for seven years or more; (5) Gerard and Henry, two Cistercian abbots in Sweden, witness to bread's being incorrupt eleven years after being blessed; (6) others similarly witness to such incorruption; (7) Bernard gently rebukes his great admirer, Archbishop Eskil of Denmark, for double-cooking blessed bread, and Eskil later finds that new bread Bernard blesses and gives him is preserved for three or more years (bk. 4.23–24).

Then Geoffrey turns to physical healings, usually associated with the towns or cities that Bernard visited for church matters from 1145 to 1147. Six kinds of healings are included: (a) forty-nine healings of blindness, (b) twenty-seven healings of deaf or deaf and mute persons, (c) sixty healings of crippled or lame persons, (d) eight healings of paralysis, (e) more than fifty instances of "many other healings," and (f) fifteen special cases. Thus with the other cases already mentioned, in this book Geoffrey reports roughly two hundred thirty-six miracles performed by Bernard, with notable detail included in some cases, suggesting that Geoffrey himself witnessed them or heard about them from reliable witnesses.

Book 5

As Book 4 resonates with Geoffrey's admiration for Bernard's miraculous power, Book 5 is permeated with the sadness of Bernard's death. In this book Geoffrey loses his friend, Clairvaux and its monks lose their abbot, and the church loses its greatest son of the twelfth century. Geoffrey here shows the monks of Clairvaux grieving with an intensity found in no other context in the *Vita prima*: all understand Bernard, so dominant in the history of the time, to be irreplaceable.

In 1153, after being abbot of the monastery for thirty-eight years, Bernard was dying. It seems that his community had been prepared for his death since the beginning of the year, when he, recognizing its approach, began increasingly to withdraw from life. In a letter to his Uncle Andrew during this period, he expressed his awareness that little time remained to him. But as he lingered, on the verge of death, the metropolitan of Metz, Archbishop Hillin of Trier, asked him to intervene in violent events taking place near the city. Amazingly, in response to this request Bernard recovered sufficiently to travel to Metz, over a hundred miles away.

Bernard's behavior here must be recognized as not only remarkable but even somewhat inappropriate. After being away from Clairvaux so often and so long on the business of the church, when he at last returned to Clairvaux, with death approaching, his primary duty was surely to remain with his monks as their abbot. It seems strange that at that point he undertook still another mission, because of the needs of a local church, placing that call above his duty to his own community. But his immediate response to the crisis at Metz reveals a great deal about his character and self-understanding as a servant of the church and a seeker of peace.

The conflict at Metz was between the bishop, Stephen, and Duke Matthew of Lorraine, but the people of the city were caught up in it, with the men of the city having been recently ambushed in a narrow defile of the River Mosel, beneath the height of Froidmont in the direction of Pont-à-Mousson. In this battle on February 28, 1153, more than two thousand men of Metz had perished, some killed by the sword, some by drowning; the city was now preparing to take revenge. In this crisis, Archbishop Hillin begged Bernard to intervene. When Bernard arrived, he found the opposing forces on the banks of the Mosel, with both sides intent on war. After some negotiations, in spite of the aggression on both sides, Bernard predicted that peace would prevail, saying, "It was shown to me in a dream" (bk. 5.4). Eventually, as Geoffrey tells it, through a conference of the leaders on a small island in the Mosel, peace was restored.

By late April or early May, after performing a few miracles at Metz, Bernard was back at Clairvaux. Growing ever more frail, he said to his community, "*These are the words that I spoke* [John 14:10] to you before I fell ill in this winter just past. What you feared has not yet come to us. Summer is near at hand and, believe me, the dissolution of this body" (bk. 5.8). Soon afterward he seems to have become increasingly unaware of what was going on around him. As Geoffrey puts it, "He withdrew his affections and the bonds of his sacred desires, which he had previously showed with such careful attention" (bk. 5.8). So when Bishop Geoffrey of Langres showed up to deal with him and questioned his lack of interest in the urgent matters he raised, Bernard sent him away, saying in the words of Saint John's sacerdotal prayer, "I am not of this world" (John 17:16; bk. 5.8).

On August 20, at almost the third hour of the day—about 9:00 a.m.—Bernard died. In the passage about his death, Geoffrey links him to three groups of people, the visiting prelates who had heard that death was near, the monks chanting the office of Tierce, and the brothers keeping vigil at his side. With this movement Geoffrey moves closer and closer to Bernard's final moment, from the gathering of those from outside the monastery, to the monastic choir singing Tierce, and finally to "those of his sons standing by close to him lamenting with grief and copious tears" (bk. 5.13). So he slowly narrows the lens from those in the outer world who learned the news of Bernard's death and mourned his departure, to the members of the community gathered in prayer, and finally to those few who experienced his last moments with him, weeping at its piercing reality.

Geoffrey concludes his story of Bernard's death with a song of praise for the life of the holy man:

> Happy that soul, so uplifted by the high privileges of his merits,
> Where the desires of his lowly sons follow him,
> Where the sacred desires of the heavenly beings drew him.
>
> Happy and truly serene is that day for him
> On which the resplendent midday, Christ, blazed out—
> A day long awaited by him all the days of his life
> With such longing, sought with sighs,
> Frequented in his meditations,
> Foreshadowed in his prayers.
>
> Happy the transition from labor to rest,
> From waiting till gaining the prize,
> from agony to victory, from death to life,
> From this world to the Father. (bk. 5.13)

Geoffrey goes on to describe what happened after Bernard died, as the community carried his body, clothed in priestly vestments, to the church, where many came to mourn over him. Among them were many women, but, barred from entering the church by Cistercian practice, they remained outside. Bernard lay in state for two days while the vast concourse of people brought a variety of objects to touch to his body as souvenirs and sacred relics. So great was the crush of people and anxiety about its becoming even greater at the time of the burial that the monks buried Bernard somewhat earlier than they had planned, early in the morning two days later, on August 22, before the altar of the Blessed Virgin Mary.

Geoffrey concludes his account with stories he has heard about Bernard's appearances after his death, so emphasizing his rebirth into eternal life. One of those stories, concerning William of Montpellier, appears only in Recension B. In it Bernard appears to William and takes him to a high mountain. There, William composes a eulogy, quoting many verses of Scripture in praise of Bernard's departure from this world (bk. 5.22).

CONCLUSION

As the work of three authors who knew Bernard in different ways and focused on different aspects of his life, the *Vita prima* lacks both a coherent narrative and a single perspective. At the same time, it has a generally chronological structure, beginning before his birth and ending with his death and burial. Nonetheless, Geoffrey's initiation of the project, his provision of the *Fragmenta* to undergird the text, and especially his revisions to Recension B, all aimed at achieving Bernard's canonization, culminated in a powerful book that finally was not only concerned with that canonization but also has introduced Bernard's life and its meaning to generations of readers and hearers.

Bernard was in his own eyes a simple and humble servant of God, but his influence in his own time had no bounds, extending not only to popes, bishops, and secular aristocrats, both men and women, but also to the common people, who everywhere acclaimed him. Yet in the final analysis, Bernard's influence in the centuries since his death has been even more powerful because of his writings. Although they are hardly mentioned in the *Vita prima*, Geoffrey of Auxerre acknowledges them on the final page of Book 4, where he lists Bernard's main treatises and letters, though excluding many of his sermons, such as those on the liturgical year. So he anticipates the enormous impression that these writings have had on the spiritual lives of so many in the eight and a half centuries since Bernard lived.[42]

---

[42] Bernard's letters, published in SBOp 7–8, reveal his widespread interaction with men and women across Europe, personal connections that are almost invisible in the *Vita prima*.

Abbreviations

Analecta	*Analecta Sacri Ordinis Cisterciensis* (1945–1965).
Beginning	*The Great Beginning of Cîteaux: A Narrative of the Beginning of Cîteaux: The* Exordium Magnum *of Conrad of Eberbach.* Translated by Benedicta Ward and Paul Savage. Edited by E. Rozanne Elder. CF 72. Kalamazoo, MI: Cistercian Publications, 2011.
CCCM	Corpus Christianorum, Continuatio Mediaevalis (Turnhout: Brepols Publishers).
CF	Cistercian Fathers series (Cistercian Publications).
Cîteaux	*Cîteaux in der Nederlanden* (1950–1958); *Cîteaux: Commentarii Cistercienses* (1959–present).
CS	Cistercian Studies series (Cistercian Publications).
CSQ	*Cistercian Studies* (1966–1990); *Cistercian Studies Quarterly* (1991–present).
Exordium	*Exordium Magnum Cisterciense sive Narratio de Initio Cisterciensis Ordinis*, ed. Bruno Griesser, CCCM 138 (Turnhout: Brepols Publishers, 1994).
Fragm	*Fragmenta Gaufridi.* Edited by Christine Vande Veire, in *Vita prima Sancti Bernardi Claraevallis Abbatis*, ed. Paul Verdeyen. CCCM 89B. Turnhout: Brepols Publishers, 2011. 235–70.
James	*The Letters of Saint Bernard of Clairvaux.* Translated by Bruno Scott James. London: Burns Oates, 1953.
Notes	Geoffrey D'Auxerre. *Notes sur la vie et les miracles de saint Bernard*: Fragmenta I. (*Précédé de)* Fragmenta II, by Raynaud de Foigny. Edited and translated by Raffaele Fassetta. SCh 548. Paris: Éditions du Cerf, 2011.
PL	Patrologiae cursus completus, series Latina. Ed. J.-P. Migne. 221 volumes. Paris, 1844–1864.
RB	The Rule of Saint Benedict.
SBOp	Sancti Bernardi Opera. Edited by Jean Leclercq and H. M. Rochais. Rome: Editiones Cistercienses, 1957–1963.

SCh   Sources Chrétiennes. Paris: Les Éditions du Cerf.
SSOC   Scriptorum S. Ordinis Cistercienses. Rome: Editiones
           Cistercienses.
VP   *Vita prima Sancti Bernardi Claraevallis Abbatis.* Edited by Paul
           Verdeyen. CCCM 89B. Turnhout: Brepols Publishers, 2011.
           1–233.

Works of Saint Bernard

Apo   *Apologia ad Guillelmum abbatem.* SBOp 3:61–108; "St
           Bernard's Apologia to Abbot William." Translated by Michael
           Casey. In *The Works of Bernard of Clairvaux, 1, Treatises 1.* CF 1.
           Spencer, MA, and Shannon, Ireland: Cistercian Publications,
           1970. 1–69.
Conv   *Ad clericos ad conversione.* SBOp 4:69–116; "On Conversion,
           a Sermon to Clerics." Translated by Marie-Bernard Saïd.
           In Bernard of Clairvaux, *Sermons on Conversion.* CF 25.
           Kalamazoo, MI: Cistercian Publications, 1981. 1–79.
Csi   *De consideratione.* SBOp 3:379–493; *Five Books on
           Consideration: Advice to a Pope.* Translated by John D.
           Anderson and Elizabeth T. Kennan. Bernard of Clairvaux,
           vol. 13. CF 37. Kalamazoo, MI: Cistercian Publications, 1976.
Dil   *De diligendo Deo.* SBOp 3:109–54; *On Loving God.* Translated
           by Robert Walton. CF 13B. 1973; Kalamazoo, MI: Cistercian
           Publications, 1995.
Ep(p)   Epistola(e). SBOp 7–8; *The Letters of St Bernard of Clairvaux.*
           Translated by Bruno Scott James. Introduction by Beverly
           Mayne Kienzle. Stroud, UK: Sutton Publishing Ltd, 1953;
           Kalamazoo, MI: Cistercian Publications, 1998.
Gra   *De gratia et libero arbitrio.* SBOp 3:155–203; *On Grace and
           Free Choice.* Translated by Daniel O'Donovan. In Bernard
           of Clairvaux, *Treatises 3.* CF 19. Kalamazoo, MI: Cistercian
           Publications, 1977. 3–111.
Hum   *De gradibus humilitatis et superbiae.* SBOp 3:1–59; *The Steps
           of Humility and Pride.* Translated by M. Ambrose Conway.
           In Bernard of Clairvaux, *Treatises 1.* CF 13. Kalamazoo, MI:
           Cistercian Publications, 1973. 1–82.
Laud   *De laude novae militiae.* SBOp 3:205–39; *In Praise of the New*

	Knighthood. Translated by M. Conrad Greenia. In Bernard of Clairvaux, *Treatises 3*. CF 19. Kalamazoo, MI: Cistercian Publications, 1977. 113–67.
Miss	*Homiliae super "Missus est" in Laudibus Virginis Matris*. SBOp 4:3–58; *Magnificat: Homilies in Praise of the Blessed Virgin Mary*. Translated by Marie-Bernard Saïd. CF 18. Kalamazoo, MI: Cistercian Publications, 1979. 1–58.
Mor	*Ep de moribus et officiis episcoporum*. SBOp 7:100–31; *On Baptism and the Office of Bishops*. Translated by Pauline Matarasso. CF 67. Kalamazoo, MI: Cistercian Publications, 2004.
Par	*Parabolae*. SBOp 6/2:257–303. *The Parables*. Translated by Michael Casey. In Bernard of Clairvaux, *The Parables and the Sentences*. CF 55. Kalamazoo, MI: Cistercian Publications, 2000. 11–102.
Pre	*De praecepto et dispensatione*. SBOp 3:241–94; "St Bernard's Book on Precept and Dispensation." Translated by Conrad Greenia. In *The Works of Bernard of Clairvaux, 1, Treatises I*. CF 1. Kalamazoo, MI: Cistercian Publications, 1970. 71–150.
SC	*Sermones super Cantica Canticorum*. SBOp 1–2; *Sermons on the Song of Songs 1–4*. Translated by Kilian Walsh and Irene Edmonds. CF 4, 7, 31, 40. Kalamazoo, MI: Cistercian Publications, 1971–1980.
Sent	*Sententia*. SBOp 6/2:1–256. *The Sentences*. Translated by Francis R. Swietek. In Bernard of Clairvaux, *The Parables & the Sentences*. CF 55. Kalamazoo, MI: Cistercian Publications, 2000. 103–458.
VMal	*Vita Sancti Malachiae*. SBOp 3:295–378; *The Life and Death of Saint Malachy the Irishman*. Trans. Robert T. Meyer. CF 10. Kalamazoo, MI: Cistercian Publications, 1978.

Editor's Note

I am grateful to Neil Bernstein, Sr. Joanna Dunham, OCSO, Beverly Kienzle, Constant J. Mews, Gregory Proctor, Dom Mark Scott, OCSO, Tyler Sergent, and Lorraine Wochna for assisting me with editorial questions concerning this important text, and to Elana Harnish, Megan Milano, and Nick Riley for assisting with the preparation of the two indices. MD.

The First Life of
Bernard of Clairvaux

Book 1

by William of Saint-Thierry

*Here begins the Preface of the Lord William,
the Venerable Abbot of Saint-Thierry,
to the Life of Saint Bernard,
Abbot of Clairvaux.*

I am going to write the life of your servant, which
will give honor to your name. This is your gift,
O Lord God, his God, just as you willed that
through him the renewal of the church in our time
has blossomed anew. It now has the former splendor
of grace and power that it had in apostolic times. I
call on your love now to be my helper; that love I
have still to urge me on.

Surely there is no one who has within himself *that
breath of life** from your love, however small it may be,
and who sees your glory and your honor so clearly
and faithfully shining out over this world who would
not take up the work as far as he was able. He could
make the light inflamed by you but lying hidden to
be written down by his pen and made manifest and
put up on high *to shine on all those in your house.**

I myself have wanted for a long time to be of service to him in my position, but I was held back by
awe and timidity, and because the importance of the
material should be reserved to more accomplished

*Gen 2:7

*Matt 5:5

1

writers, it would be better to wait until after his death, for fear that he might be put under pressure by my praise and be safer *from the wiles of men and their abusive words.** But he is still flourishing, still competent; the weaker his body, the stronger and more powerful his actions, which do not prevent him from doing things worthy to be remembered, and always he accumulates more and more noble deeds. Yet he remains silent, and they need to be written down. *But I have not long to live.**

*Ps 30:21

*2 Tim 4:6

While my infirmities are leading me to *the body of death** and all my members are beginning to respond to the close embrace of death, I feel that *I am on the point of departure,** and I fear that what I have put off may be too late, namely, the task that I longed to complete before the last journey.

*Rom 7:24

*2 Tim 4:6

But some of my brothers out of their kindness and respect urge me on and exhort me. They know all about him because they have always been with the man of God and have made careful inquiries about him. They have been with him, have seen and heard many things about him, and have suggested many wonderful things that God has done through his servant while they were present. As they are religious men and in the school of their master, I feel that they are free from every taint of deceit. More than that, they have brought forward as witnesses the authority of proven persons, such as bishops, clerics, and monks. I cannot possibly question the faith in the faithful. It goes without saying that everybody knows these things, that the whole church tells Saint Bernard's virtues. For this reason I have taken upon myself this task as far as I can without vanity on my part but out of the trust I have in a kind friend. I have taken account of the marvelous material the brothers have all offered me in praise of God.

I do not, however, write these things as if I were putting them accurately in order, but rather I have undertaken to bring them together and rewrite them into unity of style, not intending to publish them while he was alive or writing them up while he knew about it. Still, I *have confidence in the Lord** that they will take it up again after me and after his death, do better and more worthily what I myself have attempted, invest the worthy material with another style, and powerfully present *his death, which was precious in the sight of the Lord.** So by writing his life they will commend his death and throw light on his death from his life. Now then, with the Lord's help let us take up the task we have proposed.

*Rom 14:14

*Ps 115:6

Here ends the Preface.
The life of the holy abbot Bernard begins.

BERNARD'S BIRTHPLACE AND FAMILY[1]

[1] Bernard was born in Fontaine, the town of his father, in Burgundy. His parents were upper-class people according to secular standards, but even more noble in dignity according to their devout Christian values. His father, Tescelin,[2] was a military man of long standing, a religious and just man. He acted like John the Baptist, the precursor of the Lord, following the army of the gospel in that he struck no one, was not given to fraud, was content with his wages,* and used them well to do good. So he served his earthly rulers with his counsel and his weapons, and yet he did not neglect to render to the Lord his God what was due

*Luke 3:14

---

[1] The section titles are not present in the manuscript or critical edition but are added in this translation. Section 48 from Recension A is absent from this text.

[2] Called Ginger or Redhead because of the color of his hair, which Bernard inherited (*Notes* II.1).

to him.[3] Bernard's mother, Aleth,[4] was from a castle called Montbard. She followed in her own way the rule of the apostle and maintained her household* in the fear of the Lord under her husband,* intent on works of mercy and guiding her children with sound discipline.* She had seven children, six boys and one girl, whom she bore not so much to her husband as to God.[5] All her boys eventually became monks, and her girl became a nun. She did not bring them up in a secular fashion, but as soon as they were born she offered each of them to God with her own hands. For this reason she shunned the habit of giving her children to be breastfed by another, but with her own mother's milk she gave them a mother's goodness in a natural way. As they grew up she kept them under her guiding hands, bringing them up in a kind of monastic fashion rather than that of the court. She did not allow them sweet delicate foods but rather common and nourishing food, and so she prepared them, under the Lord's guidance, as if teaching them the way of life of a hermit.

*1 Tim 5:4
*Eph 5:22

*Eph 6:4

HIS MOTHER'S DREAM

[2] Bernard was Aleth's third child. While he was still in her womb she had a dream that presaged

---

[3] Geoffroy d'Auxerre, *Notes sur la vie et les miracles de saint Bernard*: Fragmenta I. (*Précédé de*) Fragmenta II, by Raynaud de Foigny, ed. and trans. Raffaele Fassetta, SCh 548 (Paris: Éditions du Cerf, 2011), 72–75 (hereafter *Notes*); *Fragmenta Gavfridi* (hereafter *Fragm*) I.1, II.1, ed. Christine Vande Veire, in *Vita prima Sancti Bernardi Claraevallis Abbatis* (hereafter VP), ed. Paul Verdeyen, CCCM 89B (Turnhout: Brepols Publishers, 2011), 235–70 (here 273, 305).

[4] In *Fragm* I.1, she is wrongly called Elizabeth because of an error by a copyist.

[5] Guy (b. 1087), Gerard (b. 1088), Bernard (b. 1090), Humbeline (b. 1092), Andrew, Bartholomew, and Nivard.

the future. She saw within her a dog totally white with some red hair on its back, and it was barking. At this she was alarmed; when she consulted a religious man, he immediately foretold with a prophetic insight what David had said about holy preachers: *The tongues of your dogs lick the blood of their enemies.** So he replied to her anxiety and unease, "*Do not be afraid;** all is well. You will be the mother of the best breed of dog. He will be the guardian of God's house, and like a guard dog he will bark against the great enemies of the faith. He will be a famous preacher, and like a good dog gifted with a healing tongue, he will heal souls suffering from many ills."

*Ps 67:24

*Luke 1:30

When the good woman heard this response, she accepted it as a reply from God and was happy about it, and from then on she completely regained her love for her unborn child.[6] She began to think that he should be brought up to be schooled in holy matters according to the manner of the vision and its interpretation, which had been promised to him in such a sublime way. And this is what happened. As soon as he had been happily born, not only did she offer him to God, as was the custom with the others, but she went on to do what holy Anna had done. The mother of Samuel, who had asked for a son from God and had received one, had placed him in the temple for the abiding service of God;* likewise Aleth offered Bernard as an acceptable gift to God in the church.[7]

*see 1 Sam 1:22-28

[3] As soon as she possibly could, she placed him to be taught by the renowned teachers in the church of Châtillon so that he might progress in the things he was best at. Afterward it was recognized that, influenced by Bernard himself, the church of Châtillon

---

[6] *Fragm* I.1, II.2 (VP 273, 305–6; *Notes* 82–83, 74–77).
[7] *Fragm* I.3 (VP 274; *Notes* 76–77).

changed from its secular way of life and joined the
Regular Canons. The boy, filled with grace and gifted
with natural genius, quickly fulfilled his mother's desires for him. For he progressed in his studies above his
age and beyond his peers. In secular studies, however,
he already began to mortify himself and, as it were in
a natural way, looked toward the perfection he would
achieve. He was simple with regard to worldly matters,
loving to be on his own, avoiding the limelight, deeply
thoughtful. *He was obedient to his parents and subject to*

*Luke 2:51

*them.** Kind and gracious to everyone, at home he
tended to be simple and quiet, rarely going out, un-
believably shy. He was never one for speaking much,
though he was devout, so his childhood was childlike.
He gave himself up to his studies, and in this way he
discerned and came to know God in the Scriptures. In
all this he progressed a great deal in a short time and
was highly perceptive in his mental aptitude, as can be
seen from what we are going to recount.

[4] When he was still a boy, he was troubled with
a severe pain in his head and took himself to bed.
A young woman was brought to him with the purpose of mitigating the pain with her singing. When
he became aware that she was coming in with her
musical instruments, with which she used to play
the fool with people, he made an exclamation of
annoyance and rejected her and sent her away. God's
loving mercy was not lacking to the good zeal of the
holy boy; he was continually aware of its strength.
Being moved by the Holy Spirit, he noticed at once
that he had been freed from all the pain in his head.

BERNARD'S DREAM OF JESUS' BIRTH

From then on he progressed considerably in his
faith, and the Lord appeared to him just as *he had*

once appeared to Samuel in Shiloh and revealed his glory to him.* On the solemnity of the Lord's Nativity, when at night they were all getting ready, as was the custom, for solemn Vigils, the Lord came to him. Since the hour for celebrating the Night Office was put off a little, Bernard was sitting there waiting with everyone else, and his head drooped in sleep. Then it happened that the child Jesus revealed himself in his Holy Nativity to the little boy, awakening in him the beginnings of divine contemplation and increasing his tender faith. Jesus appeared to him *like the spouse coming forth from his chamber.** He appeared to him before his very eyes as the wordless Word was being born from his mother's womb, *more beautiful in form than all the children of men.**

Bernard was taken out of himself so that his child-like love was transformed by the holy boy. So persuasive to his mind was this moment that from then on, as he confesses, he believed he was at the very moment of the Lord's birth. From those who often listened to him it is obvious that the Lord showered him with blessings at that time, since he has spoken about this mystery more frequently and delved into its meaning more profoundly.

Afterward he wrote a little book in praise of the Mother of God and her Son and his Holy Nativity among his works or treatises, taking his material from the gospel of Saint Luke, where we read, *The angel Gabriel was sent by God to a city in Galilee** and the following.[8]

We should not be silent about the fact that from his earliest years when he had any money he used to give it in alms secretly. He did this in a shy way. He

*1 Sam 3:21

*Ps 18:6

*Ps 44:3

*Luke 1:26

---

[8] *Fragm* II.5 (VP 307; *Notes* 78–81); *In laudibus Virginis Matris* (SBOp 4:13–58).

performed his acts of piety in accordance to his age,
or rather beyond his age. **[5]** As time went on he progressed *in age and grace with God and men.** Boyhood
soon gave way to adolescence. His mother, Aleth, had
brought up her children in the faith and had done all
that she could to educate them for their future in this
world. She died and went happily to be with the Lord.
We must not pass over the fact that for a long time
she had lived a happy life with her husband. She was a
good and honorable wife in the good and honest ways
of this world and in the catholic faith. For many years
before her death, she brought up her children, insofar
as a woman could who is obedient to her husband's
authority and does not have rights over her own body.*

 In her home, in her married life, in her dealings
with the world around her, she was for the most
part living an eremitic or monastic life, using simple
food and putting aside elaborate dresses and worldly
vanities; as far as she was able, she kept herself away
from secular cares and pursuits. She applied herself
to fasting, vigils, and prayers. There were some things
she could not do without monastic profession, but
she replaced those by almsgiving and various works
of mercy. She persisted in these things daily until her
last days, when, in coming to the end, she migrated
from this world to be perfected in the world to come
by him to whom she went.

 When she was dying, the clergy and those who
had gathered round her were singing the psalms for
the dying, and she joined in, so that when it came to
her last moment and her voice could not be heard,
she could still be seen to move her lips and with her
tongue to praise the Lord. Finally, when it came to
that part of the litany *by your passion and cross free her,
O Lord,** raising her hand she made the sign of the
cross and *gave up her spirit,*† so that her hand that was
raised could not lower itself.‡

*Luke 2:52

*see RB 58.25

*the Office
of the Dead
†Matt 27:50
‡d. Sept. 1, 1103

[6] From now on Bernard began to live his life in his own way. He was spoken of as a young man with high hopes, one elegant in bearing, gracious and pleasing to look at, of charming manners and a keen intellect, and polished in speech. As he began to make his debut into society, many paths were opened to him, so that he was assured of success in whatever he undertook. A future of great promise smiled on him everywhere. Yet he was under pressure from friends whose way of life was very different and whose boisterous friendships aimed at making his way of life like theirs. If this life had gone on and become attractive to him, how bitter would have become the thing dearest to him: the chastity that he loved and held dear in his heart. The *crooked serpent**   *Isa 27:1
spread out its nets of temptation and in various ways *lay in wait for his heel.**   *Gen 3:15

It once happened that when Bernard was looking around, his gaze fell on a woman, but he at once corrected himself, blushed within himself, and blazed with annoyance at himself. A pool of freezing water lay near; he jumped into it and remained there until he was nearly frozen and, by the power of grace, his lust had been cooled. He was then clothed with the love of chastity in the same way as Job, who said, *I made a pact with my eyes that I should not think upon a virgin.**   *Job 31:1

A NAKED GIRL COMES TO HIS BED

[7] Round about this time the devil tried to play a trick on him. While he was sleeping, a naked girl snuck into bed with him. When he became aware of this, he peacefully and silently ceded to her that part of the bed that she had occupied and moved over to the other side and went to sleep. She was miserable

about this and waited expectantly; then she started stroking him and tried to stimulate him. Finally, since he took no notice of her, the impudent girl blushed and, filled with dismay and amazement at his persistence, got up and hurried away.

It also happened that Bernard and some companions were guests at the house of a certain matron. This woman started to think about him, about what a pleasant young man he was, and she allowed her eyes to be ensnared so that she burned with desire. She then made up a special bed for him to honor him above the others. That night she got up and brazenly approached him. When Bernard realized what was afoot, he, never short of ideas, shouted out, "Thieves, thieves!" Hearing this, she fled. The whole family got up, lit their lamps, and looked for the thief, but of course he was not to be found. They all returned to their beds, and silence reigned and darkness once more returned. Everyone else reposed as before, but not this wretched woman. She got up again and sought Bernard's bed, but again he shouted, "Thieves, thieves!" Again they looked for the thief in vain, and as Bernard was the only one who knew what was happening, he kept it to himself. A third time the stupid woman tried and was rejected; she was hardly able to desist, because of either fear of being found out or desperation at his unwillingness. On the following day Bernard's companions took him to task and queried him concerning his dreaming all night about thieves. He answered, "To tell the truth, there was a thief. The hostess was trying to snatch away from me a priceless treasure, my chastity, which no one could restore."

[8] Meanwhile he was thinking to himself and pondering that saying, "It is not safe to sleep close to a serpent or to live long with a snake," so he began to think about flight from the world. He looked around him and saw that the world and the prince of

the world offered him many openings and promised him great opportunities, yet all was false *and vanity of vanities, and all was vanity*.* He listened to the voice of the Truth speaking inwardly, calling out to him and saying, *Come to me, all you who labor and are burdened, and I will refresh you*.* Deciding that the most perfect way was to leave the world, he made inquiries and sought out where he could more certainly and more purely find *rest for his soul** under the yoke of Christ.

*Eccl 1:1

*Matt 11:28-29

*Matt 11:27

Bernard Finds Cîteaux

Making a search for such a place, he came upon the newly founded Cistercian plantation,[9] a new way of monastic life, a great harvest but needing workers, for hardly anyone had gone there seeking the grace of conversion because the way of life there was too austere and poor. For a person *truly seeking God*,* however, it held no terrors, so he set aside all fear and hesitation and turned his mind to Cîteaux in order to melt away and be hidden in *the hiding place of God's face from the disturbance of men and from the contentious tongues*.* It would be for him a flight from vain pride, from his noble lineage, from his own gift of a keen intellect, perhaps even from his growing reputation for holiness.[10]

*RB 58.7

*Ps 30:21

[9] When Bernard's brothers, who loved him in too human a fashion, realized that he was seriously considering entering religious life, they tried their utmost to deflect his mind to literary studies and enmesh him more seriously in secular pursuits through a love for secular learning. As he himself would readily admit,

---

[9] Louis Lekai, "From Molesme to Cîteaux" and "The Fundamentals of Cistercian Reform," chaps. 2–3 in *The Cistercians: Ideals and Reality* (Kent, OH: Kent State University Press, 1977), 11–32.

[10] See *Fragm* I.4 (VP 275; *Notes* 86–89).

their delaying tactics might well have succeeded had it not been for the persistent memory of his holy mother. Again and again he fancied he saw her hurrying toward him, complaining reproachfully that he had not been softly nurtured for this sort of trifling, nor was it with this end in view that she had educated him.

*in 1111

There came a day, as he was riding to join his brothers, who were with the duke of Burgundy engaged in besieging Grancey Castle,* when his anxiety preyed on him more intensely. Passing a church midway on his route, he turned aside and entered. There he prayed with a flood of tears and hands stretched out, pouring out his heart like water before the face of the Lord his God. That was the day that saw his purpose firmly fixed in his heart.

He Begins to Persuade His Brothers

*Rev 22:17

*Ps 82:15

*Aleth's brother

[10] Nor did he turn a deaf ear to the voice that says, "*Let the one* who hears say, 'Come.'"* From that day on, *as fire consumes the forest or the flame sets the mountains ablaze,** running hither and thither and pouncing first on what lies to hand before ranging farther afield, so too the fire that the Lord had purposely kindled in his servant's heart first attacked his brothers, leaving only the last, too young as yet for the religious life, to be a comfort to their aging father, before moving on to kinsmen, comrades, friends—wherever there was the slightest hope of conversion. His uncle Gaudry,* the castellan of Touillon, a man of rank and reputation and renown, was the first to vote with his feet, as the saying goes, and to opt with his nephew for the monastic state.[11] Swift on his heels came Bartholomew,

---

[11] *Fragm* I.4, I.7 (VP 275, 277; *Notes* 86–89, 94–95).

youngest but one of the brothers and not yet knighted, who gave his easy assent to Bernard's words of wisdom. But Andrew, the next in age to Bernard and himself a new-made knight, found it hard to accept his brother's counsel, until suddenly he exclaimed, "I see my mother!" And indeed she appeared to him distinctly, smiling serenely, and approving her son's intention; thereupon, surrendering on the spot, another recruit left the ranks of the world for the army of Christ. Andrew was not alone in seeing his mother rejoicing over her sons: Bernard too confessed to a similar vision.[12]

Guy, the oldest of the brothers, was a man of substance, already married and more firmly established in the world than the rest. Doubtful at first, he reflected long and deeply and then agreed to enter the religious life provided his wife gave her consent, a most unlikely step for a young noblewoman with infant daughters to bring up. Bernard, however, inspired with an unshakeable hope in God's mercy, promptly assured Guy that his wife would either come to share his feelings or die fairly soon.[13]

After a while, as there was no moving her, her magnanimous husband, helped even then by that strength of faith of which he was later to offer so shining an example, conceived at God's prompting the bold plan of abandoning all outward trappings and living a peasant's life, working with his hands to keep himself and his wife, whom he could not put away against her will. Bernard, meanwhile, who was running about, rounding up this man and that, arrived on the scene, and almost at once Guy's wife fell gravely ill. Realizing how it would hurt her *to kick against the goad*,* ***Acts 26:14** she begged forgiveness of Bernard, who had been sent

---

[12] *Fragm* I.8 (VP 278; *Notes* 94–97).
[13] *Fragm* I.3, I.9 (VP 274, 278; *Notes* 86–87; 96–99).

for, and sought assent for her own entry into religion. When she and her husband had been finally parted according to ecclesiastical practice, each taking a vow of chastity, she joined a congregation of women religious, where she serves God devoutly to this day.[14]

GERARD AND THE LANCE

[11] The next in age after Guy was Gerard, a knight active in combat, prudent in counsel, and loved by all for his remarkable courtesy and kindness.[15] Worldly wisdom had him dismissing his brother's quick compliance as mere frivolity, and he was resolute in rejecting Bernard's sound advice and admonishments. Finally Bernard, afire with faith and zeal for his brother's welfare, exclaimed in a fit of exasperation, "I know, I know, that it takes affliction to make a man receptive." Then, putting a finger to Gerard's side, he added, "The day will come, and soon, when a lance will strike you here in your side and will open a road into your heart for the words of salvation you treat with such contempt, and you will fear for your life but not lose it." And as he had said, so it came about.

A little later, outnumbered by enemies and wounded as his brother had predicted, Gerard was taken prisoner in a skirmish and hauled off with a

[14] At Larrey, near Dijon; see *Fragm* I.3 (VP 274; *Notes* 86–87).

[15] Conrad of Eberbach, *Exordium Magnum Cisterciense sive Narratio de Initio Cisterciensis Ordinis* 3.1, ed. Bruno Griesser, CCCM 138 (Turnhout: Brepols Publishers, 1994), 138–43 (hereafter *Exordium*); *The Great Beginning of Cîteaux: A Narrative of the Beginning of Cîteaux: The* Exordium Magnum *of Conrad of Eberbach*, trans. Benedicta Ward and Paul Savage, ed. E. Rozanne Elder, CF 72 (Kalamazoo, MI: Cistercian Publications, 2011), 209–11 (hereafter *Beginning*).

lance head fixed in the very spot to which Bernard had pressed his finger. Fearing death, which seemed imminent, he shouted out loud, "I am a monk, I am a monk of Cîteaux!" This did not, however, prevent his being taken prisoner and shut away. A messenger was sent hotfoot to Bernard, but he did not come: "I knew," he said, "that it would be hard for him *to kick against the goad.** His wound is not mortal, though, but life-giving."* And so it proved. For Gerard, although he recovered from his wound faster than could have been hoped, did not change his resolve, or rather the vow he had made. Now that the love of the world no longer fettered him and only the chains of his enemies prevented him from entering the religious life, God's mercy came swiftly to his aid. His brother arrived and tried to get him freed, but without success. Forbidden even to speak with him, he stood close by the prison wall and shouted, "Brother Gerard! We shall be leaving soon to enter the monastery. As for you, be a monk here since they will not let you out, and rest assured that what you want to do but cannot will be deemed done."

[12] A few days later, while Gerard was fretting more and more, he heard in his sleep a voice saying to him, "Today you will be freed." It was the holy season of Lent. Early that evening, as he was pondering what he had heard, he bent to touch his shackles, and one of the leg irons fell off with a clatter in his hand, so that he was less restricted and could hobble along. But what was he to do? The door was bolted, and there was a crowd of poor people at the gates. He stood up, however, and less out of hope than of the tedium of lying there, and excited too by the idea of trying, he moved across to the door of the undercroft in which he was held in fetters. No sooner had he touched the bolt than the bar came away in his hand and the door opened. With the shuffling gait of a

man in irons he made his way to the church, where
they were singing Vespers.

When the beggars waiting outside saw what was
happening, providentially frightened out of their wits,
they ran off without raising the alarm. As he was hob-
bling churchward, a member of the household, cousin
to the man whose prisoner he was, chanced to come
out, and seeing him make what haste he could toward
the church, called out, "You are late, Gerard!" And as
the other turned pale, "Hurry up," he added, "there's
still some left for you to hear." The man's gaze was held
fixed, and he was quite unaware of what was happening. Not until he had given the still-shackled Gerard
a helping hand up to the steps of the church and the
latter was passing inside did he realize what was going
on and make an unsuccessful effort to detain Gerard.

So it was that Gerard, freed in spirit and body alike
from the world's grip, faithfully fulfilled the vow he
had taken. At the same time the Lord made most
powerfully plain the grace that his servant Bernard had
derived through the holy life he led so perfectly, for
in the spirit of him who made what is to be, Bernard
was enabled to see what was to come as though it had
already taken place. When he placed his finger on the
spot on his brother's side where the wound was soon
to gape, the lance appeared to him in its very actuality,
as he himself later confessed when questioned by those
from whom he could not keep it secret.[16]

BERNARD GATHERS HIS GROUP OF RELATIVES

[13] The others had gathered together in the Spirit
with Bernard. On the morning of the first day when

---

[16] *Fragm* I.2 (VP 273–74; *Notes* 82–85).

they entered the church, they heard the words of the apostle Paul being read out: *God is faithful because the good work he has done in you he will bring to completion at the day of Jesus Christ.** The devout young man had hardly had time to hear these words when they came to him *as a clap of thunder from heaven.** He began to rejoice in the Spirit, for he was now the spiritual father of all those reborn in Christ, his own brothers, and he saw clearly that the hand of the Lord was working with him. From this moment he set himself to assemble whomever he could by the force of words and began *to put on the new man.** With those with whom he used to discuss worldly matters he now talked earnestly about conversion, pointing out to them the joys of flight from the world, the way the miseries of this life would come to a speedy death while life after death was to be forever either in bliss or in wretchedness.

    Could he do more? *As many as were ordained to eternal life** one after another came to believe him and consent to his counsel since the grace of God was working in them. Some at first hesitated but *were cut to the heart,** because God's servant, by his prayers and insistence, the truth in his words, brought them round.

    Lord Hugh of Macon[17] was also among those who joined him. Today he has been snatched away from the community at Pontigny that he had built and is now the bishop of the diocese of Auxerre, which he rules in an admirable and dignified way. When he heard that his dear friend and companion had converted, he lamented the loss, as though Bernard were dead to the world. Where before they used to agree together in their talks, now they lamented with one another for different reasons, different griefs. They

**Phil 1:6

**Acts 2:2

**Eph 4:24

**Acts 13:48

**Acts 2:37

---

[17] Hugh of Macon, who entered Cîteaux with Bernard, was the founding abbot of Pontigny in 1114 and bishop of Auxerre from 1136 to 1151.

spoke with words of disagreement, different points of view. In the course of their friendly words with one another, the Spirit of Truth was gradually infused into Hugh, and they began to face one another with words of mutual understanding. They shook hands in friendly agreement about the new way of life that was more worthy of them, more truly spiritual, so that they had *one heart and one soul in Christ** and became friends once more as of old.

*Acts 4:32

[14] After a few days, however, Bernard learned that Hugh had reneged on his proposal, influenced by his companions. An opportunity arose for Bernard when there was a meeting of the bishops in that area; he hurriedly took it and went to call Hugh back from his straying or, as Saint Paul put it, *to bring him to birth** in Christ. Those who had led Hugh astray noticed that Bernard was there and, keeping an eye on Hugh, stopped Bernard from approaching him, so that he *could not cry out to the Lord* for him.*

*Gal 4:19

*Jdt 9:1

Bernard betook himself to prayer and weeping, and pretty soon there was an immense downpour of rain. They had gathered in a field where the weather was serene and no such change was expected. So they all ran for cover from the storm to the local village. There, Bernard got hold of Hugh. "Stay with me," he said, "out of this shower of rain." They remained together alone, but the Lord was with them. Very soon it became calm, and serenity of soul returned. The pact they had made was renewed and their proposal confirmed, which from then onward would not again be violated. [15] *The wicked saw and were angry, they gnashed their teeth and melted away,*[18] but *the just man put his confidence in the Lord** and *triumphed gloriously** over the world.

*Ps 111:10

*Prov 28:1

*see Exod 15:1

[18] *Fragm* I.6 (VP 275–77; *Notes* 90–95).

From now on, when Bernard spoke either publicly or privately, mothers hid their sons from him, wives kept their husbands away from him, and friends fended off their friends from contact with him, because the Holy Spirit put so much power into his speech that hardly any other love could withstand its force. When the number of those who joined themselves to him and took on this way of life increased, it became like the early church, where we read that *the company of believers had one heart and one soul** in the Lord. *They all dwelt together and none of the rest dared to join them.** They had their own house in Châtillon, where they lived together, and nobody dared join them who was not one of their number. But if someone did enter and saw and heard what they were doing and singing, it was just as the apostle Paul says of the Christians in Corinth: *If all prophesy, anyone entering will be convinced by all and will be called to account by all, and falling down he will adore the Lord and declare that God is truly among them,** and he himself will adhere to them in unity, or if he goes away he will repent with tears because they are so blessed.**

*Acts 4:32

*Acts 5:12-13

*see 1 Cor 14:24-25

*Job 29:11

In those days and in that district it was unheard of for anyone who was still remaining in the world not to have his conversion known to everyone. They kept together for six months in secular dress after their first project so that they could all have time to wind up their business affairs.

The Listless Pair

[16] When some of them began to suspect that the tempter might try to draw one of them away, God revealed what was going to happen concerning this matter. One of them *gazed into the vision of the night,** and he saw them all sitting in one house

*Dan 7:14

in an orderly fashion eating some food, amazingly fresh, gorgeous, and tasty. While most of them were taking their food with hearty appetites, two of them, he noted, remained listless, hardly partaking any of this salutary food. One of them took nothing; the other seemed to take some but scattered it about carelessly. This is how it turned out later. One of them returned to the world before the project had started; the other *began the good work* like the rest but did not *bring it to completion.**

*Phil 1:6

I saw him later in the world, like Cain, *tramping about aimlessly from the presence of the Lord.** As far as I could judge he was a miserable sight, down and out and, to look at, pathetic. In the end, however, he returned to Clairvaux as an invalid and forced by need, even though he was from a good family and well-liked by all his family and friends. When he got there he renounced his properties but not really his own will, and he died among them, not as a brother or one of them, but as *a poor man and beggar,** apart and asking for mercy.

*Gen 4:14

*Ps 39:18

[17] When the time came for Bernard to fulfill his vow and achieve his plans, with his brothers and spiritual children he took leave of his father's dwelling. He was like a father among his brothers, for he had brought them to birth in Christ, *the Word of life.** Guy, the oldest, saw his brother Nivard, the youngest, playing with other boys in the road and said to him, "Hello, Nivard, this whole place of ours is now yours alone." He replied, not like a child, "What? You've got heaven, and leave me earth! That's not a fair deal." Still, when the others had departed he remained at home with his father, but as soon as he could he followed his brothers, and no one could stop him, neither his father nor his acquaintances nor his friends. So it was that all the brothers followed God's will, and there were left in their home their

*Eph 5:26;
1 Cor 4:15

father with his daughter, about both of whom we will talk later.[19]

CÎTEAUX

[18] At that time Cîteaux was still a novelty and just a *little flock** living under venerable Stephen, their abbot.[20] They were beginning to grow dejected because of the lack of vocations, and their hopes for future numbers were fading.[21] It appeared that they could not pass on their inheritance, which was holy poverty, to anyone, because although the holiness of their life was admired by all who saw it, they kept away from that severe austerity. But now, all of a sudden, God visited them* and made them joyful again. It was so unexpected, so sudden. It was as if their house had received this reply from the Holy Spirit: *Shout for joy, you barren woman who bore no children! Break into cries of joy and gladness, you who were never in labor! For the sons of the forsaken one are more in number than the sons of the wedded one,* * and afterward *you will see your children's children unto many generations.**

*Luke 12:32

*i.e., the community at Cîteaux

*Isa 54:1; Gal 4:27

*Tob 9:11

BERNARD ENTERS CÎTEAUX WITH HIS COMPANIONS

[19] In the year 1113 from the Lord's Incarnation, and thirteen years from the founding of Cîteaux,[22] Bernard, the servant of God, who was about

---

[19] *Fragm* I.11 (VP 279; *Notes* 98–101).

[20] Stephen Harding, third abbot of Cîteaux, 1109–1133; d. 1134.

[21] See *Exordium* 1.21 (CCCM 138:79; *Beginning*, 98–99).

[22] David N. Bell, "From Molesme to Cîteaux: The Earliest 'Cistercian' 'Spirituality,' " CSQ 34 (1999): 469–82.

twenty-two years old, entered Cîteaux with more than thirty companions and submitted himself to the sweet yoke of Christ under Abbot Stephen. From then on *the Lord blessed him, and the vine of the Lord of hosts started to give fruit,** extending its branches as far as the sea and its boughs well beyond.** This was the beginning, the holy principles on which the man of God based his life. I consider that no one could adequately tell his manner of life, how his life on this earth somehow reflected the life of heavenly beings. No one could possibly write about the life he lived without living it himself. Only a person who had been given such graces and lived by them would be able to tell how from the very moment of his conversion the Lord filled him with his chosen grace, *how he feasted on the plenty of his house.** He entered the house of the Lord, which was *poor in spirit,** at that time still hidden away and of no importance. He had the intention of dying from the hearts and memory of mankind, with the hope of disappearing *like a lost vase.**[23]

But God had other ideas and was making him ready *as a chosen vessel,** not only to strengthen and expand the monastic order but *to carry his name before kings and Gentiles** to the ends of the earth. Of course he did not apply this teaching to himself or even think about it; rather he had in his heart the need to be constant in following his vocation, so that he constantly said in his heart and even often on his lips, "Bernard, Bernard, *what have you come for?**[24] In the same way as we read about Our Lord—*Jesus began to do and to teach*—*from the moment he entered his cell in the novitiate he himself began to do what he would later teach other people.

*Josh 18:16

*Ps 79:12

*Ps 35:9

*Matt 5:3

*Ps 30:13

*Acts 9:15

*Acts 9:15

*Matt 26:50

*Acts 1:1

---

[23] See *Fragm* I.4 (VP 275; *Notes* 86–89).

[24] Thus Bernard places himself in the role of Judas in Gethsemane, betraying the Lord through his sins.

[20] Afterward, when he became abbot of Clairvaux, he used to tell the novices who had come and were keen to enter, "If you are keen to learn what goes on inside, leave your bodies outside, since you have brought them with you from the world. Only your spirits enter here; *the flesh does not profit at all*."* But when the novices feared the novelty of these words, he showed sympathy for their frailty and added more kindly that only *the desires of the flesh** should be left outside. But he himself while he was a novice in no way spared himself; rather he constantly mortified himself, not only concerning *the desires of the flesh*,* which pertain to the body, but even the body itself by which they are done. But when he began very frequently to experience the sweetness of God's love bestowed on him, because he was being enlightened interiorly with love, he also feared those bodily expressions and hardly allowed them any scope in his life, except for what was needed in his dealings with other people. Since he put this continual mortification into practice as was his custom, it became habitual and second nature for him.

He was totally absorbed in the spirit; his thoughts were often completely directed toward God, as were his spiritual meditations, and his mind was totally occupied with God, so *that what he saw he did not see, what he heard he did not hear*,* nor did he taste what he ate; he felt hardly anything with his bodily senses. For instance, he spent a whole year in the novitiate, yet when he left it he still did not know whether it was a carved roof, which we usually call vaulted, or not. However frequently he went in and out of the church, he thought there was only one window in the east end, whereas there were three.

*John 6:64

*1 John 2:16

*1 John 2:16

*Isa 6:9

BERNARD'S PERSONAL ASCETICISM

He had dampened down all sense of curiosity about such things, so that if perhaps he did happen to see them he did not advert to them because his mind was elsewhere, as they say. Indeed, without memory mere sense perceptions count for nothing. **[21]** In him there was no contradiction between nature and grace, so much so that what was written in Wisdom was fully implemented in him: *I was a boy of happy disposition, and I had received a good soul; or rather, being good, I had entered an undefiled body.** He had endowed with a keen intelligence by nature, and grace enabled him to contemplate spiritual or divine things, for he *had received a good soul*, since by reason of a natural spiritual grace he was strongly able to overcome himself by his innate quality of virtue without a tendency to carnal sensuality or haughty disdain, enjoying his spiritual studies and those things that are of God,* spontaneously leaning toward God in his service and subduing himself to the Spirit. His body was in no way sullied by consent to shameful acts, yet he necessarily took care of it in such a way that he made himself serve the spirit and be a suitable tool in his service of God. But from the gift of prevenient grace and by the help of a natural tendency, and also by the use of a good spiritual discipline, the body in him is such that he could hardly desire anything that worked against the spirit, at least to harm the spirit. The spirit in him overcame the forces of flesh and blood so powerfully, as he yearned to oppose the flesh of the weak animal nature that fell under its burden, that to this day it has not been able to rise again.

What am I to say about the sleep that in other people is accustomed to give rest from work and the senses or recreation for their minds? From then till today he keeps vigil beyond normal human strength.

*Wis 8:19-20

*Heb 5:1

He used to complain that he wasted no time more than when he was asleep. For him the comparison between death and sleep is apt, for those who are asleep seem to be dead as far as humans can see, though to God death is no more than sleep. If he heard a religious snoring out loud while asleep, or if he saw someone lying around in a careless way, he could hardly put up with it but complained that he was sleeping in an unbecoming or worldly way. To his own meager time of sleep he joined his meager ration of food. In neither case did he allow his body its full measure but took just what he considered absolutely necessary. As for vigils, since staying awake was usual for him, it was his custom not to spend the whole night sleepless.

[22] Even today he hardly takes any pleasure in eating but only eats for fear of breaking down. Before he eats anything, just thinking of what he is going to eat seems to be enough for him. So he takes his food as if it were an agony for him. From the first days of his religious life, that is, from the time he left the novitiate, since his physical makeup was extremely frail and delicate, because of his continuous fasting and vigils, because of the cold, and because his stomach was dragged down by hard and continuous labor, it has rejected whatever he takes, and he vomits it raw and undigested. Of course, by the process of nature food passes to the bowels, and that part of his body was so obsessed with distressing sickness that it discharged only with great pain. Whatever is left over to nourish his body is not so much to sustain his life as to defer his death. After a meal he always reckons up how much he has eaten. If he ever catches himself going slightly beyond the usual measure he does not allow it to go unpunished. Even though he would sometimes like to regale himself in a little extra, he finds he can hardly do so.

So from the beginning he was a novice among
novices, a monk among monks, strong spiritually but
frail in body, without allowing himself any relaxation
concerning his rest or his food, or any withdrawal
from the common work or the duties placed on him.
He reckoned everyone else to be holy and perfect
but himself to be still no more than a beginner, a
learner, in no way needing the indulgences or relaxations of those who had become more merito-
rious and more perfect. He needed to be a fervent
novice under the strict rule of the order, under strict
discipline.

[23] As a result, when the brothers were engaged
in manual work that he was not used to, he had
an ardent desire to emulate them in the common
monastic way of life, but he lacked the competence
required for digging, cutting down trees, carrying
things on his shoulders, or taking his turn in any hard
manual work that was equally demanding. When his
strength failed him, he used to turn to more menial
tasks, relying on humility as a compensation.

Now it is remarkable that he who had received
great graces in the contemplation of spiritual things
by God's gift should not only put up with being occupied with such chores but even take great delight
in them. Other people often give themselves over to
manual labor to such an extent because of human
weakness that their minds wander away and become
distracted from the interior unity of the spirit. But
as we have said, Bernard mortified this sensual type
of distraction and was privileged to have a greater
grace *by the power of the Holy Spirit,** so that he could
completely give himself outwardly to his work and
at the same time rest totally with God inwardly. His
conscience was thus satisfied, and so too his devotion.

While he was working he used to pray and meditate without their interfering with his work. His ex-

*Rom 15:19

terior work did not form a barrier to the sweetness
of his interior contemplation. To this day he confesses
that whatever he gains from the Scriptures, whatever
he finds spiritually in them, comes chiefly from the
woods and fields, and he has no teachers besides
the oaks and beeches; he was accustomed to make
a good-humored joke of this among his friends.[25]

[24] At harvest time the brothers were occupied
in reaping with vigor and joy in the Holy Spirit, but
as he was quite unable to do the work, not knowing
how, he was ordered to sit on his own and take some
rest; he was so upset at this order that he found refuge
in prayer. He was so close to tears that he asked God
to give him the grace for harvesting. His simple faith
won him his religious desire. God gave him at once
what he had hoped for. From then on he became so
skilled in the work that he used to relish it, realizing
that he had obtained this gift from God alone, so that
he devoted himself to it more willingly. Whenever he
was free from this work or other jobs, he used either
to pray or read or meditate. If he had the chance
for solitude, he used it for prayer, but wherever he
was, either by himself or with the others, he made
solitude of heart his own, and so he was everywhere
alone with God.

Lectio Divina

He gave himself to frequently reading the Scriptures
in order, simply yet with joy. He said that he understood them better than his own words and that whatever was there enlightened him with truth and power;

---

[25] See Bernard, Ep 106 (SBOp 7:266); #107 in *The Letters
of St Bernard of Clairvaux*, trans. Bruno Scott James (London:
Burns Oates, 1953), 155–56 (hereafter James).

*of wisdom

he affirmed that they impressed on him the original fount* more than he gained from the current commentaries. He read the commentaries of the holy and orthodox teachers and in no way felt that his own interpretation was equal to theirs, but while he adhered faithfully to them and followed them, he himself drew from the same source that they had drunk from. Full of the Spirit who had divinely inspired the whole Holy Scripture, he himself used them with confidence and assurance, as the apostle says, *for teaching, for reproof, for*

*2 Tim 3:16

correction, for training in righteousness. When he preaches the Word of God, he makes every text he expounds plain and enjoyable, and he does this in such a way that even his reproofs are successful. Everyone who listens to him, seculars as well as religious, are struck with astonishment at his teaching and the gracious

*Sir 41:19;
Luke 4:22

words *that proceed out of his mouth.**

Clairvaux Founded: Bernard Becomes Abbot

*Gal 1:15

[25] *When he who had set him apart from** the world and called him to reveal in him his glory with a still greater grace, God brought together *into one* a great

*John 11:52

number of sons *who had been scattered abroad.** God put it into the heart of Abbot Stephen to send these brothers to build a house at Clairvaux. As they were going, Stephen appointed Bernard as abbot over those he sent,[26] surprising those men who were mature in age and had worked hard both in the world and in the religious life. They feared for Bernard because he was a youth of tender age and subject to sickness and also was not used to vigorous manual work.

---

[26] *Exordium* 2.1 (CCCM 138:72–73; *Beginning*, 129).

Clairvaux was in the district of Langres, not far from the river Aube. It was an ancient denizen of thieves and in antiquity was called the Valley of Wormwood, either because of the abundance of bitter wormwood or because of the bitter grief of those who fell into the hands of robbers. In that *place of horror and vast solitude** these meek and virtuous men settled down, making *a den of thieves* into the temple of God and *a house of prayer.** There they served God in simplicity for a time in poverty of spirit, *in hunger and thirst, in cold and exposure, in constant vigils.** Often they had to satisfy their hunger with a gruel made out of beech leaves. Their bread was made out of *barley, millet, and vetches,** as the prophet Ezekiel says. When this bread was put before a religious man who came to the guesthouse, he wept over it, took some of it away secretly, and showed it to everyone, thinking it miraculous that any man could live like this, especially such men as these!

[26] But the man of God was not interested in this matter. His greatest care was for the salvation of many souls. From the first day of his conversion right up to the present time, he was known to have only one thing in his thoughts, namely, to have a mother's love for every soul.[27] Indeed, there was a sort of conflict in his heart between his holy desires and his holy humility. At one moment he confesses that he is dejected that his efforts cannot show any results, but afterward his burning ardor makes him forget himself, and he admits that he finds no other consolation than the salvation of many souls. In the end, charity gives birth to confidence, yet humility keeps it in place.

And so it happened that on one occasion he rose early for Vigils. Then after Vigils there was a long inter-

*Deut 32:10

*Matt 21:13

*2 Cor 11:27

*Ezek 4:9

---

[27] SC 23.1–2 (SBOp 1:139–40; CF 7:26–27).

val before Lauds in the morning, and he went outside.
He walked around close by and was praying to God
that his prayers and those of his brothers might be
acceptable, for he was, as I have said, filled with the
desire for spiritual fruitfulness. All of a sudden, while
he was standing there, he closed his eyes in prayer and
saw on all sides a great multitude of men in diverse
clothing and different walks of life coming down from
the hills close by into the valley below; so many were
they that the valley could not contain them. What this
meant is clear to everyone.[28] The man of God was so
encouraged by this wonderful vision that he exhorted

*RB 4.74   his brothers *never to despair of God's mercy.**

GERARD: THE CELLARER'S COMPLAINT

[27] Before winter started, his brother Gerard,[29]
who was the cellarer of the house, complained
strongly to Bernard about the supplies for the house
and said that the brothers did not have enough to
buy them. Their needs were so pressing that he could
not accept mere verbal encouragement. There was
just not enough to give out.

The man of God inquired from him how much
would be needed for the present shortage. He replied
twelve pounds.[30] Bernard then sent him off and resorted to prayer. A little while later Gerard came back
and told him that a woman from Châtillon was outside
and wanted to speak to him. He went out to see her,
and she fell at his feet, offering him twelve loaves to
obtain his blessing. She implored him to pray earnestly

---

[28] See *Fragm* I.13 (VP 280; *Notes* 102–3).

[29] D. 1138 (*Exordium* 3.1 [CCCM 138:148–51; *Beginning*,
209–14]).

[30] The critical edition has *undecim libras* "eleven pounds."

for her husband, who was seriously ill. Bernard talked with her briefly and sent her off, saying to her, "Go now, and you will find that your husband is healed." She went back home and found it just as he had said. The abbot then comforted his cellarer for his timidity and told him to have *greater trust in the Lord** in the future. To tell you the truth, this did not occur just this once, but whenever a necessity of this sort came up he received help from the Lord from an unexpected source. Because of this event, men who were insightful understood that *the hand of the Lord was with him,** and they were cautious about burdening him with unimportant matters because they knew his mind was tender and still fresh from the delights of heavenly secrets; they only consulted him about interior matters of conscience and the needs of their souls.[31]

*Ps 26:14

*Luke 1:66

[28] For them the situation was similar to what we read about when the Israelites came to Moses after he had conversed with the Lord on Mount Sinai and, coming out of the dark cloud, he went down to the people. His *face was beaming with horns of light and was so awesome that the people fled away from him.** Just so, the holy man Bernard came from the face of the Lord, where in the solitude of the Cistercian life and the sublime height of contemplation he remained in silence, enjoying those blissful moments. He brought with him something miraculous that he had acquired, something of divine purity rather than human. These men who were under his authority and with whom he lived were all almost estranged from him.

*Exod 34:35

Often enough, when he had to preach to them on spiritual subjects and the development of their spiritual lives, *he spoke* to them *with the tongues of angels,** so that they could hardly grasp the meaning. Above

*1 Cor 13:1

---

[31] *Fragm* I.15 (VP 282; *Notes* 106–9).

*Matt 12:34

*Job 6:60

*2 Cor 6:14-15

all, in matters of human behavior, he led them *out of the abundance of his heart** to set them standards so sublime and to demand such perfection of them that *his words seemed hard*,* so little did they understand what was being said to them. Again, when he heard them singly in confession, accusing themselves of the various fantasies to which human thought is prone and which no one can avoid in this life, here, above all, no *fellowship* could be found between *his light and their darkness*,* for he discovered that those he had taken for angels were in this respect ordinary men. Possessed himself of an almost angelic purity and conscious that God had bestowed on him from his youth his singular grace, he jumped naïvely to the conclusion that monks were proof against the temptations to which the frailty of human nature exposes all humankind and could not fall into the mire of such imaginings—or if they did so, they were not monks.

[29] But those who were truly devout and combined piety with prudence revered his teaching even if they did not understand. If they were at times dumbfounded by the novelty of what they heard when confessing their faults (since he seemed to be sowing seeds of despair in men already weak), they still felt that, by admitting their wickedness to him instead of seeking excuses, at least, as Job said, they were not perversely *denying the words of the Holy*

*Job 6:10

*Ps 142:2

One,* inasmuch as *no man living is justified in the sight of God.** So it came about that holy humility became the mistress of both teacher and those being taught. For when the accused humbled themselves before the accuser, he himself began to suspect the zeal of his indignation in the face of their self-abasement. It came to such a point that he felt that his own ignorance was more to blame and regretted having to speak at all since he did not know what to say. He feared, lest by speaking to men not so much of things beyond as of those unworthy of them, he might harm the conscience of his hearers.

And again he realized that he was demanding of simple monks a degree of perfection that he himself had not yet attained. He began to think that they might well think in the silence of their souls *upon better things and more germane to their salvation** than they would hear from him, that they might *work out their salvation* more devoutly and efficaciously on their own than through any example of his, that indeed his preaching might prove more of a stumbling block to them than a way of building up their interior lives. He was disturbed and saddened over this thought, and *questions arose in his heart,** so he decided to withdraw from all activities into himself and *wait*, in solitude of heart and *in silence, on the Lord** until the Lord should, according to his mercy, reveal his will to him in this matter.

*God's mercy was not slow in coming to his aid.** It was only a few days later that Bernard saw in a dream at night a boy standing by him and looking at him with the brilliant light of God, who bade him with great authority to speak confidently whatever words should be put into his mouth, *for it was not he who spoke but the Spirit who spoke within him.**[32] From that time on the Spirit indeed spoke more openly in and through him, giving *greater power to his words** and depth to his *understanding of the Scriptures,** also increasing the appreciation and respect of his hearers and endowing him with a new *understanding of the poor and needy,** *the repentant sinner,** and the seeker for pardon.

[30] Now that he had learned to some degree to take part in ordinary conversation and act in a more humane fashion, he began to enjoy the fruits of their common conversation and living among them on

*Heb 6:9

*Luke 24:38

*Lam 3:26

*Dan 7:12

*Matt 10:20

*Eph 6:19
*Luke 24:45

*Ps 40:12
*Luke 15:7

---

[32] *Fragm* I.13 (VP 280–81; *Notes* 102–3).

their own level. His father also, who had remained alone at home, came to live with his sons and become one of them. After he had lived with them for some time, he died at a good old age.[33]

Humbeline Meets Her Match and Wins

Their sister, who was married and given to a worldly life, became aware of the dangers inherent in riches and the pleasures of worldly living, so in due time God inspired her to visit her brothers. When she came along, intending to see her venerable brother, as she approached the monastery with her retinue, dressed in fine clothes, Bernard utterly refused to go to see her, saying that he despised her appearance and calling her vile, like a snare of the devil trying to capture souls. She heard about these words and was extremely confused and full of regret that none of her brothers would deign to meet her. She found her brother Andrew, who was at the door of the monastery, and when he saw her decked out in fine clothes, he called her "wrapped-up crap,"[34] so she dissolved into tears. "I may be a sinner," she retorted, "but *Christ died for them.** Because I am a sinner, all the more do I need counseling and guidance. If my brother despises my flesh, a true servant of God would not despise my soul. Let him come out here, let him command. Whatever he commands I will do." Holding her to this commitment, Bernard came out to meet her with his brothers.* He could not, however, separate her from her marriage to her husband, so he first of all forbade her all worldly grandeur

*Rom 5:6;
1 Cor 8:11

*probably in
1122

---

[33] Tescelin joined Clairvaux in 1120 and died shortly afterward.
[34] *Ob uestium apparatur stercus inuolutum*

in fashionable dress and every form of ostentation, and he urged her to live in that style of life that her mother had followed for a long time with her husband. He then sent her off. She went back home and, obedient to his demands, immediately changed her ways *according to the power of the Most High.**   *Ps 76:11

Everyone was astonished in the change in this dainty young noblewoman. She changed her way of life in regard to costume and diet and began to live a hermit's life while still in the world. She applied herself to vigils, undertook a regime of fasting, gave herself to continual prayers, and alienated herself from every worldly pursuit. She lived with her husband for two years like this. Then he, especially in the second year, wishing to honor God, did not presume any more to approach *this temple of the Holy Spirit.** Finally, because of the strength of her   *1 Cor 3:16-17 perseverance, he was prevailed upon to free her from her bonds to him and conceded to her the chance of serving God, to whom she had engaged herself, in accordance with the rites of the church. She took advantage of the freedom she had desired and went to the monastery of Jully, where she lived with the nuns who were there and made her vows to God for the rest of her life.* The Lord bestowed on her the   *d. in 1141 grace of holiness, so that she showed herself equal to   at Jully those men of God both in mind and in body.

BERNARD: ORDAINED TO THE PRIESTHOOD

[31] Shortly after Bernard had been sent to Clairvaux, he needed to be ordained into the ministry that he had assumed. But the see of Langres, which had the right to ordain him, was vacant at the time, so the brothers looked for a place where he could be ordained. They soon discovered that the bishop of

Châlons-sur-Marne, the venerable William of Champeaux, was a man of good reputation.[35] They decided
to send him there. And so it came about. He went to
Châlons, accompanied by Elbodo, a monk of Cîteaux.
The younger man entered the house of the bishop,
looking emaciated and deathly pale and clothed in
rags, while the senior monk was well built, physically strong, and elegant. Some of those there smirked
and some mocked, but others, recognizing the reality,
showed him due respect. When they wanted to know
which of the two was the abbot, the bishop was the
first *to have his eyes opened** and perceived the servant
of God, and so received him as such.

*Num 24:16;
Neh 1:6

    As soon as they were in private conversation and by
Bernard's words the bishop discovered the prudence
of the young man, he was more and more impressed
by his humble manner of speaking; so this wise man
understood his guest's arrival as a divine visitation.
His welcome was so warm that they became familiar
friends at once, and their conversation soon became
free and confidential. Their understanding of one
another deepened beyond mere words. What more
can I say? From that moment they became *one heart
and one soul in the Lord.** This fact was so apparent
that they quite often became guests of one another,
so that the bishop made Clairvaux his own home. Indeed, not only was Clairvaux the home of the bishop,
but also the whole of the city of Châlons became a
home to the monks of Clairvaux. Indeed, through
the bishop's influence, the province of Reims and the
whole of Gaul was moved toward a devout reverence
for the man of God. Such was the prestige of the
bishop that many others learned to accept Bernard

*Acts 4:32

---

[35] William of Champeaux taught Abelard at Paris. He
founded the house of Regular Canons at Saint Victor, Paris,
and was bishop of Châlons-sur-Marne from 1113 to 1122.

and revere him *as an angel of God.** It would appear
that this bishop, a man of such great authority, had
such a leaning toward this unknown monk—to be
sure a monk of such humility—that he must have
had some presentiment of the grace that was to blos-
som in him later on.[36]

[32] A little later, when the abbot's illness became
so severe that nothing could be expected except his
death or a life more serious than death, the bishop
paid him a visit.* On seeing Bernard, the bishop asserted that there was still hope not only for his life
but even for his return to health, provided he listened
to his advice and agreed that care should be given to
his body as was required for this type of illness. But
Bernard would not easily be turned away from his
accustomed rigor and usage, so the bishop betook
himself to the Cistercian chapter, where a few of the
abbots had assembled.[37] *He prostrated himself fully on
the ground,** and with humility worthy of a bishop
and the love expected of a priest he asked for and
obtained his request that for a whole year Bernard
should submit himself to him in obedience.

How could they refuse such a humble request from
such an influential person? He returned to Clairvaux
and ordered a small house to be built outside the
cloister and the boundary of the monastery. He then
directed that none of the restrictions of the Order
in the matter of food and drink or anything of that
sort should be laid on Bernard, so that he should not
have any solicitude for the concerns of the house, but
that he should live there in the manner he himself
had laid down for him.

**Acts 27:23;
Gal 4:14*

*Sept. 1119

*RB 53.7

---

[36] *Fragm* I.20 (VP 284–85; *Notes* 114–17).
[37] The abbots of Cîteaux and her daughters La Ferté, Pontigny, and Morimond.

WILLIAM OF SAINT-THIERRY FINDS BERNARD

[33] It was at that time that I began to be a regular visitor at Clairvaux and to see him. While I was there with another abbot[38] visiting him, I found him in a little hut such as lepers often have near public cross-roads. I found him there under obedience to the bishop and the abbots, as I have said, resting from all interior and exterior concern concerning the monastery, free to be with God by himself and as it were rejoicing *in the delights of paradise.** I was *admitted into that royal bedchamber,** and when I pondered over that dwelling and him who dwelt there, I swear to God, the house filled me with such reverence that it seemed as if I were *approaching the altar of God.** I overflowed with such affection for that man, with such a desire to be with him in his poverty and his simplicity, that if I had been given the option that day, I would have desired nothing more than to remain with him forever and be at his disposal.

Since he received us with such great joy, we asked what he was doing, how he was getting on; he smiled at us in his generous fashion and replied, "Wonderfully! Up to now rational men have obeyed me, but now *by God's just judgment** I have been ordered to be obedient to someone, more like an irrational beast." He told us that a rustic, vain man, who knew nothing about the illness that he was suffering, was boasting that he would cure him. He had been handed over to him by the bishop, the abbots, and his brothers under obedience.

When we sat down to eat with him, we realized that he was so ill and needed to be entrusted to such

*Ezek 28:13
*Song 1:3–4

*Ps 42:3

*Wis 16:18

---

[38] Joran, abbot of the Benedictine Abbey of Saint Nicaise in Reims.

care and providence as was necessary. But we saw him, under this doctor, being offered food that even a healthy person could hardly touch unless he was famished. *We saw and we pined away*,* hardly able to contain ourselves even by the silence of the Rule; we were stirred up with anger and outrage at that sacrilegious man, a murderer. But he who put up with these things with indifference ate it all with equal approval, just like one whose senses were so spoilt and virtually dead that he could hardly taste anything. Indeed he was known to have eaten raw grease*[39] given to him for a long time in error instead of butter, to have drunk oil instead of water, and many other like things that were given to him.* He used to say that he liked only water because, when he took it, it cooled his mouth and his throat.

*Ps 118:158

*MSB MS. 1: *sagenam* (dripping or grease)

*see also bk. 3.2

[34] This, then, was how I found him. This was how that man of God lived in his solitude. Yet he *was not alone, for God was with him*,* and he was in the care of the holy angels, and they were his guardians. That truth is demonstrated with very clear indications. One night he was alone attentively pouring out his soul in prayer when he drowsily heard voices that were thin and dream-like coming from a great crowd who were passing by. Getting up, he heard these voices more clearly. He rose up from the cell he was lying in and followed them on their way. Not far away the place was thick with thorns and brambles, though now it is quite changed. On this spot there were choirs standing, spread here and there, singing from side to side, and the holy man heard them

*John 16:32

---

[39] Horstius has *sanguinem* ("blood") here, perhaps deriving from *sagumen*, which the critical edition reports as witnessed by MS. D of Recension A (Bruges Bibl. de la Ville MS. 32). All printed editions of the *Vita prima* through the PL follow Horstius in printing *sanguinem;* the critical edition, however, reads *sartaginem.*

and was deeply moved.[40] At that time he did not at
first recognize the hidden meaning of the vision, but
after some years when the monastery was moved and
the oratory was placed there on that very spot he
discerned the meaning of the voices he had heard.

I remained there with him for a few days, still annoyed, and wherever I looked around me I was be-
witched as if *I saw a new heaven and a new earth,** tracing
the ancient ways of our fathers the Egyptian monks
and in them the blossoming footprints of men of our
time. **[35]** Ah, that was the time to perceive the golden
age of Clairvaux, when those men of virtue who had
once been rich in worldly affairs and honored as such
were now planted in the poverty of Christ and in his
blood, giving glory to the church *in toil and hardship,
in hunger and thirst, in cold and exposure,** *in persecutions
and calamities, in many hardships.** These were the men
who made Clairvaux ready to be the place of plenty
and peace that it is today. They did not think of living
in this way for themselves, but only for Christ and the
brothers who would later serve God there. They gave
no thought to what they themselves lacked, provided
that they could leave after them what was sufficient
and necessary for future arrivals to gain experience of
voluntary poverty for the sake of Christ.

The first thing those who came down from the
hills surrounding Clairvaux would see *was God in
these houses.** This silent valley spoke to them of the
simplicity and humility in the buildings, mirroring
the simplicity and humility of those living there.
Then, in that valley full of men, where none was at
rest, where all were toiling at their work and each
one had a job assigned to him, at midday and at

*Rev 21:1

*2 Cor 11:27
*2 Cor 12:10

*Ps 47:4

---

[40] *Fragm* I.20 (VP 284–85; *Notes* 114–17). See also *Fragm* I.32
(VP 290–91; *Notes* 134–35).

midnight they found silence all round them, save for the sound of work, save for the brothers occupied in the praise of God. Indeed their practice of silence enjoys such renown and has instilled such reverence for their way of life that even among the seculars who come there speech is so respectful that, I aver, they do not chatter idly or talk about trivial matters, but only what is worthy of the place.

Clairvaux: In Shady Woodlands

The solitude of this place, among the shady woodlands and enclosed by the nearby impassable mountains in which the servants of God lie hidden, represented in a fashion that cave where our holy father Saint Benedict lived.* It was there that he was *found by the shepherds,** and these men, who marveled at his life in the cave, seemed also to have imitated his way of living in solitude.[41] Their *love was well ordered* * and made that vale full of men into a solitary place for each of them, because their life was so well ordered—for just as if one person is in disorder, even when alone, so that person is inwardly disturbed, so where unity of spirit and a rule of silence govern a multitude, solitude of heart and an orderly life defends each one.

[36] To live in simple dwellings and simple ways of life was like nourishment to those dwelling there. Their bread seemed to them more like clay than bran. It was produced from the hard labor of the brothers, pressed out of the sterile earth of the desert, and whatever provisions there were had hardly any taste except for their hunger for God, or rather what the love

*Subiaco

*Luke 2:15-16

*Song 2:4

[41] *The Life of St. Benedict by Gregory the Great: Translation and Commentary*, ed. and trans. Terrence G. Kardong (Collegeville, MN: Liturgical Press, 2009), chap. 8, pp. 8–9.

of God could instill into them. And yet the simplicity of these young novices was such that they would
have denied themselves even that taste. They thought
that anything at all that gave them pleasure in eating
was like poison, so much so that they rejected God's
gifts on account of the grace they experienced within
themselves. Anything that had seemed impossible beforehand to people living ordinary lives, they now undertook not only all the time without grumbling but
even with huge pleasure with the help of God's grace,
since their spiritual father's zeal instilled this pleasure
into them. But this pleasure brought with it another
sort of complaint that was all the more dangerous,
because they thought that what they were doing was
spiritual, far distant from mere bodily fitness.

They had persuaded themselves that any pleasure
in the flesh was harmful to the soul; moreover, their
conscience bore witness to this understanding, as did
their memory, faithful to the gospel. It was as if *they*
*Matt 2:12 *departed to their own country by another way,** so they
thought, since because of the delight from the love
within them, they seemed to themselves to be living
enchantingly as hermits and took just as much delight
in nauseating things as the more pleasant. **[37]** In this
matter they held suspect the daily admonitions of
their spiritual father, in that he seemed to be comply-
ing with mundane things rather than with the spirit.

When the bishop of Châlons happened to be passing
that way, this matter was brought to him for his opin-
*Acts 7:22 ion. He was a man *mighty in speech,** and he embarked
on a sermon to them, saying that any man who rejected
the gifts of God on account of the goodness of God
was putting himself at enmity to God's grace and resisting the Holy Spirit. He then quoted the story of Elisha
the prophet and the followers of the prophets who
were leading an eremitical life with him in the desert.
One day when it came to mealtime they found *some*

*bitter deathly herbs in the pot used for their meal.** Through *2 Kgs 4:40-41
God's power and the ministry of the prophet, the food
was sweetened by the flour dropped into it. "So also for
you," he said, "the flour of God's grace working in you
changes bitterness into sweetness. Take it, then, with
thanksgiving; you will be safe in doing so, for though
by nature it is not quite fit for human use, through
God's grace it has become fit for you to use, so you
should use it and eat it. On the other hand, if you still
remain disobedient and incredulous, *you will be resisting the Holy Spirit** and so be ungrateful for his grace." *Acts 7:51

[38] This took place at that period under Bernard,
the abbot, and through his teaching. It was a valley
aglow with light and love, a school of contemplation
and spirituality. Here was fervor for the discipline
of the Rule, and everything was done and ordered *Exod 25:40,
*according to the pattern shown to him on the mountain** Heb 8:5
when he dwelt with God *in the cloud** at Cîteaux, that *Exod 16:10
school of solitude. If only he had kept to those basic
principles of his early way of life and afterward grown
accustomed to live as a man among men and, having
learned how to *understand the needy and the poor,** to *Ps 40:2
have compassion on the weaknesses of men; if only
he had shown these same qualities toward himself as
he had toward others: kindness, discretion, concern!

Bernard's Self-Imposed Rigor, None Too Wise

But as soon as he had become free from the chain of
his novice's year of obedience and had performed its
duties, he returned to his accustomed former ways, like
a bow under tension, and again took up his original
rigorous life, like a cascade of water that has been held
back and suddenly released. He imposed on himself a
punishment for that long period of quiet and a penalty

for the task that had been interrupted. You would have
seen this debilitated and frail man trying to carry out
whatever he could without considering whether he
could do so, solicitous for everyone else while heedless of himself, a model of obedience to everyone yet
hardly ever listening to anyone who was speaking out
of love or with authority about his own welfare. He
was always striving to make greater efforts, thinking
nothing of what he had already done. He would not
spare his own body but had to add vigor to his spiritual gains. His body was undermined by various sicknesses, brought on by his fasting and constant vigils,
and was thus in a weakened state.

[39] During the day and at night he prayed standing
upright until at last *his knees weakened by fasting** and
his feet swollen by his labors could no longer bear the
weight of his body. For a long time and as far as possible
he kept secret the hair shirt next to his skin, but when
it became known, he immediately relinquished it and
went back to the common usage. His food was bread
dipped in milk or water, cooked vegetables, or the soft
mash made for babies. His sickness would not allow
him anything else, or he refused other things for the
sake of frugality. He drank wine only infrequently and
then only a little, since he asserted that water suited his
sickness and also his appetite. In spite of being so weak
and exhausted, he would by no means allow himself
to be excused during the day or at night from the
common work of the brothers or from the duties and
tasks of his ministry. Doctors saw him and his way of
life, and they were amazed. They surmised that nature
had endowed him with such drive that he was like a
lamb linked to the plow and impelled to till the fields.[42]

*Ps 108:24

---

[42] *Agnus ad aratum alligatus arare;* this alliteration is impossible
to render into English. I have tried to emulate it with the letter *l*.

Now when his stomach was so decayed that he vomited up his food undigested, this behavior began to be more and more unacceptable to the brothers, especially when *they were singing in choir,** yet he would not leave the assembly of the brothers but had a receptacle dug into the earth by the place where he was standing, and for quite a while he put up with this painful inconvenience as far as he could. In the end, things became so intolerable that he was forced to leave the common life and live by himself alone, except for the times when he had to take part in meetings of the brothers for the sake of conferences or consoling them or the need for monastic discipline.

[40] This became a sad necessity, for that holy brotherhood was now deprived for the first time of his constant paternal companionship. In this we are saddened, and we weep over this sorry outcome of his sickness, but at least we admire the love he shows in his holy desires and spiritual warmth. The outcome of his sickness, however, should not be a cause for indefinite weeping and sorrowing.

Perhaps God in his wisdom willed this illness *to shame the many strong and great of this world by the weakness of this man.** Nothing, then, has been left undone because of Bernard's sickness that should have been done, for the grace he had received blossomed later. Who else in our time has done anything as great as he? Even though close to death and failing in health, he has done wonders for the honor of God and the profit of the holy church, far more than others with strong physique and in fine fettle. Look at the number of men he has drawn from the world by his words and his example, not only to conversion of life but even to perfection. Just think of the many houses he has set up throughout the whole of Christendom, without a doubt *cities of refuge,** so that whoever has

*RB 43.11

*1 Cor 1:27

*Josh 21:37

committed sins worthy of death and eternal punishment may repent and be converted to God and
flee to them for salvation. How many schisms he
has ended, how many heresies he has put to shame,
how many times he has brought peace to discordant
churches and people! All these things were for the
good of the general public. Who could enumerate all
the good things he has given individually to count-
less people, for special reasons, for personal needs, in
a particular place, in a time of want?

[41] Moreover, even if his holy zeal is blamed for
being excessive, he certainly holds a place of reverence even for that excess among those with devout
mentality, for *all who are led by the spirit of God** have
great esteem for the servant of God and would be
slow to criticize him for it. Among such people he
is easily excused, since *no one would dare to condemn a
person whom God justifies** and has performed through
him and by him so many things, such sublime works.
Happy is he who is reckoned to be at fault over the
things that other men usually presume to glory in.
As a youth he harbored doubts about his own goodness, since *blessed is he who always fears the Lord,** for
he was keen to acquire that full tally of virtue that
he had through grace and to increase the relevance
of his labor.

*Rom 8:14

*Rom 8:33

*Prov 28:14

POWER PERFECTED IN WEAKNESS

If his life was to be a model for everyone to imitate, it should not be lacking in the example of frugal
continence. In this respect, even if the servant of God
sometimes overdid it, he left an ideal of fervor for
other ardent minds to follow rather than excessive
zeal. Why should we try to excuse him in this? After
all, he himself is still quite diffident about all his

works, and right up to the present he is not ashamed
to accuse himself, treating it as sacrilegious that his
body should withhold something from the service
of God and his brothers because he has rendered it
useless and idiotic by his own indiscreet fervor. But
now he has recovered from his sickness, and this
sickness has made him stronger and more effective.
*For power is made more perfect in weakness,** shining out   *2 Cor 12:9
from that time until the present with more dignity
among men and women, bringing with it reverence,
and reverence eliciting authority, and authority eliciting obedience.

[42] Now his preaching is endowed with divine
energy, since, as we said above, it was once foretold
of him *from his mother's womb,** attested by divine   *Luke 1:15
revelation. Not only was this the case, but he was appointed to it by an appropriate heavenly plan, which
equipped him to follow it at every moment of his life
either while he was a subject* or as a superior. He   *e.g., a novice
was made ready to do this work by ignoring what
he wanted to do, not only in things pertaining to
the monastic life but also in those pertaining to the
whole business of the church. Indeed, first of all he
dedicated his youthful enthusiasms to reviving the
fervor of the ancient religion in the monastic order.
To this end he devoted all his effort, by his example
and his words, among the brothers in the community
within the boundaries of the monastery. Afterward,
when he was forced to adopt another way of life
because of his physical sickness, as has already been
said, the demands of his sickness and its necessities
forced him to live sequestered from the common life
of the community in a more solitary manner.

This necessity provided the initial occasion when
he began to make himself available to people; many
of them flocked to him while *he preached the word
of life,** and he made himself known to them more   *2 Tim 4:2

freely and more copiously than before. Later, obedience drew him for a long time from the monastery to deal with general concerns of the church, so that wherever he went he used to speak of God and could not keep silent about him, and he could not stop doing *the things of God.** Thus in a short time he became well known, so that the church of God, finding such an effective member within the Body of Christ, could not but use him for whatever needed to be done. However, although from the first flowering of his childhood he was always replete *with the fruits of the spirit,** from this time onward these fruits were added to him so copiously that, as the apostle says, *To each is given the manifestation of the Spirit for the common good.** This means that he abounded in more fruitful words of *wisdom and knowledge,** performing works of power through the grace of prophecy and various *deeds of healing.**

*2 Cor 2:11; Matt 16:23

*Gal 5:22

*1 Cor 12:7
*Rom 11:33

*1 Cor 11:28

I have learned about these things from the faithful men who have told me of them with confidence, and I now leave them to my readers.

Josbert Is Healed

*John 2:11

*This was the first of his signs** that Christ did by the hand of his servant, making him known to the world. **[43]** When Bernard had been at Clairvaux for some years, it happened that a nobleman called Josbert,[43] who was closely related to him, fell seriously ill in La Ferté, a town near the monastery. Suddenly this sickness took possession of him, and he lost both his mind and his speech. His son, Josbert Junior, and all his friends were so overcome with grief that such a

---

[43] Josbert le Roux, viscount of la Ferté-sur-Aube.

highborn man and one of such eminence should die
without confession or viaticum. A messenger hurried
off to the abbot, who was not in the monastery then.
When the abbot returned, he found that Josbert had
been lying sick for three days. He had compassion on
the man and was moved by the tears of his son and
the others who were likewise lamenting.

Placing his trust in God's mercy, Bernard pro-
nounced this extraordinary statement, saying to them,
"It is well known to you all that this man has harmed
the church in many ways by oppressing the poor and
offending God. If you give credit to me and restore
to the churches and put back the practices he has
usurped to the detriment of the poor, he will then
be able to speak and make confession of his sins and
also devoutly receive the divine sacraments." They
were all amazed; his son cheered up, and all the family
rejoiced. Whatever the man of God had ordered they
resolutely promised they would do, and they carried
it out. Bernard's brother Gerard and his uncle Gaudry,
however, were much disturbed and fearful about this
promise; they got together in private and criticized
him vehemently and strongly upbraided him. But
he curtly and with simplicity replied, "It is easy for
God to do what you can only believe with difficulty."
Then, after a prayer in private, he went and offered
the immortal sacrifice of the Mass.[44]

While he was still offering the sacrifice a messenger came in. This messenger said that Josbert was now
speaking freely and had abjectly requested that the
man of God should come quickly to him. As soon as
the sacrifice was finished, Bernard came along, and
Josbert confessed his sins with tears and sorrow. He
then received the sacraments, and after two or three

[44] *Fragm* I.17 (VP 283; *Notes* 108–11).

days, still living and speaking, he ordered all those things that the holy abbot had specifically demanded to be put into place without reneging on his word. He dealt with the affairs of his household, gave alms, and so finally breathed forth his soul in a Christian fashion, with a sound trust in the mercy of God.[45]

HEALING OF A BOY WITH A WITHERED HAND

[44] Once when the holy father had returned from the meadows, he met a woman carrying in her arms her little son, whom she had brought from a distance. While still in his mother's womb, he had had

*Mark 3:1

a withered hand* and a totally distorted arm. Moved by the mother's tears and prayers, Bernard ordered the child to be set down, and then he prayed for a long time, making the sign of the cross over the arm and the hand. Then he told the woman to call her son. She called the infant, and he ran to his mother and embraced her with both arms, and *he was instantly*

*Matt 9:22

made well.*[46]

[45] The brothers and spiritual sons of this blessed man were always marveling at what they heard and saw about him. They were not uplifted in a merely human fashion, however, nor did they give him glory; rather they were fearful on account of his youth and solicitous because of the novelty in his spiritual methods. His uncle Gaudry and his eldest brother, Guy, forestalled the other brothers in their zeal. They were like a pair of *thorns in the flesh* to him to *keep*

*2 Cor 12:7

him from becoming too elated* by the greatness of the graces that he seemed to have received in a divine

---

[45] Josbert d. 1125; see *Fragm* I.14 (VP 281–82; *Notes* 104–7).
[46] *Fragm* I.16 (VP 282–83; *Notes* 108–9).

way. They did not spare him, even abusing him with harsh words to shake up his tender diffidence, and even making nothing of all these well-attested signs. They opposed this *most gentle man*,* who never answered back, and they frequently brought him to tears with their hasty and reproachful speech.

*Num 12:3;
Vulg *mitissimus*

Geoffrey, the venerable bishop of Langres,[47] a man who was a relative of the holy man and close to him in conversion of life and an inseparable companion in everything, often tells this story. The first miracle he saw Bernard doing was when his brother Guy, mentioned above, was present. He was passing through the town of Nanton[48] in the territory of Sens, and a young man who had a fistula in his foot begged the holy father to touch him and give him a blessing. He made the sign of the cross and healed him at once. After a few days, they went back through the town and found the man healed and healthy. The blessed man's brothers, however, could not restrain themselves even by this miracle but still rebuked him, accusing him of presumption in agreeing to touch the boy, though he did watch over him with bountiful love.

[46] It was at about this time that his uncle Gaudry, who with a like zeal used to upbraid him with harsh reproaches for his meekness, as we have mentioned, suffered from a serious fever. When the sickness grew severe and he was overwhelmed with frightful pain, he was forced to turn to the abbot, humbly entreating him to bear with him, as he had often done with other people. Bernard, who possessed a spirit *sweeter than honey*,* first of all recounted gently in a few words how often Gaudry had rebuked him with

*Sir 24:27

---

[47] Geoffrey de la Roche-Vanneau, a distant cousin of Bernard and nephew of Josbert le Roux.
[48] Château-Landon, between Fontainebleau and Sens.

*Matt 8:3;
Mark 5:23

reproaches and then hinted that he might now just be testing him, but when Gaudry insisted, *he laid his hand on him and ordered the fever to depart.** At once the fever left Gaudry at this command, and he felt within himself the healing he had complained about in other people.[49]

This same Gaudry departed from this light after living at Clairvaux for many years, fervent in spirit and avid for every good thing. He had been a little while disturbed, for almost an hour before his death, and his whole body was trembling terribly, but just before he died he regained his former serenity, and his countenance was calm and peaceful. The Lord did not deprive the abbot's caring soul of knowledge of the meaning of this thing. Indeed, after a few days

*Dan 7:7

Gaudry appeared to him *at night in a vision.** When Bernard asked him how he was, he replied that he was prospering very well, and he thanked God that he was in a place of great happiness. Then he was asked why the dire distress came upon him so unexpectedly just before his death. He replied that at that moment two evil spirits had been preparing to shove him into a pit horribly deep and dark, so that he was all quaking with terror, but then blessed Peter came to snatch him up, and at once he felt not the slightest hurt.

THE HARSH BROTHER SAVED BY PRAYERS

[47] For a long time Bernard spoke of all the things that happened to those who departed from this life, their happiness or their needs, and what heavenly grace had revealed to him from the moment of their entry into bliss. There is one thing I

[49] *Fragm* I.17 (VP 283; *Notes* 108–11).

should say, however, namely, a warning he repeated several times. There was a brother who was well intentioned but quite harsh about the way that other brothers acted and less compassionate than he should have been. He died in the monastery. After a few days he appeared to the man of God looking wretched and miserable, indicating that all was not going for him as he desired. When asked why this was happening to him, he complained that he had been handed over to four savage beasts. As he was saying this, he was suddenly struck and, as it were, kicked out of the presence of the man of God.

Bernard cried out with acute distress after him. "I order you," he said, "in the name of the Lord, that whatever happened to you concerning those who oppose you, you should make known to me." He gave himself to prayer for him and offered the Host of Salvation. He admonished some of the brothers whom he knew to be sincere and holy men to entreat the Lord in the same way for the brother. He persisted in prayer until after a few days he was consoled to learn, since it was made known to him by another revelation, that on account of his command the man had been freed.[50]

[49] It was about this time that famine spread in the kingdom of France and regions close by, but the Lord heaped blessing on the barns of the brothers. Indeed, until that year, the annual produce of their labor had never been sufficient. That year as well, after they had sedulously gathered the harvest and reckoned up everything, they calculated that it would be hardly sufficient to keep them going till Easter. When they wanted to purchase anything, they could not pay, because what was sold was far more costly than usual. But from the time

---

[50] See *Exordium* 2.2 (CCCM 138:99–100; *Beginning*, 130–32).

of Lent a great crowd of poor people came to them. They faithfully gave them what they had from the modest annual produce, since the Lord had blessed them with it, and they also eagerly provided for the poor who crowded around them until harvest time.

There was a poor man living not far from the monastery whose wife, an adulterous woman, tormented him with venomous words. She used to threaten him in her anger and fury and came out with wicked incantations, so that his life was a misery and he became so eaten up that he could neither die nor be allowed to live. Very often he lost his power of speech and even his physical senses, and when he came back to himself he returned not to life but to a cruel drawn-out death. Eventually he was brought to the man of God, who was staying in the monastery, and this wretched tragedy was explained to him. Bernard became terribly angry that the ancient enemy should arrogate to himself a Christian man, so he called two of the brothers, and they carried the man to the holy altar. When they got there, he placed the ciborium containing the Eucharist on the man's head and ordered the demon by the power of the sacrament to put a stop to harming a Christian. So it came about as he commanded, and after so much torment that miserable man was healed, perfect faith restoring him to perfect health.[51]

THE LETTER TO ROBERT

[50] Brother Robert,[52] a monk under the holy man and a close relative of his, was as a young man

---

[51] *Fragm* I.28 (VP 288–89; *Notes* 128–29).

[52] Robert of Châtillon, the son of a sister of Bernard's mother, Aleth (see *Exordium* 3.11, 12 [CCCM 138:168–75; *Beginning*, 240–52]).

deceived by the persuasive talk of certain people and betook himself to Cluny. The venerable father, after hiding the fact for some time, stated in a letter to Robert that he should return. He dictated this letter to the venerable William,[53] later the first abbot of Rievaulx,[54] who recorded it, writing the letter on parchment.[55] They were both sitting outside in the open, having gone out of the confines of the monastery in order to keep the dictation secret. All of a sudden it unexpectedly started to rain. The one who was writing, as we have said above, wanted to put the document away. But the holy father said, "It is the work of God; keep writing, do not fear." He therefore wrote the letter in the pouring rain, without the rain's getting it wet. For while the rain was pouring down, the sheet exposed to it was covered with the power of charity, and what charity wrote in the letter, charity likewise preserved. Because of this glorious miracle, this letter was selected by the brothers, not undeservedly, as the first one in the volume of his letters.[56]

[51] Once there was an important solemnity, and a brother who because of a secret sin had been debarred from receiving communion at the holy altar was afraid of being caught and could not stand the embarrassment. So he had the audacity to approach the abbot with the others. Now although Bernard intuitively knew about the hidden secret, he was not willing to rebuff the man, but *in his inmost heart** he prayed to God that he might arrange a better outcome for such

*RB 7.51

[53] See Marc Debuisson, "La provenance des premiers cisterciens d'après les lettres et les *vitae* de Bernard de Clairvaux," *Cîteaux* 43 (1992): 5–118, here 84.

[54] An English monk of Clairvaux and Bernard's secretary; d. Aug. 2, 1145; Rievaulx was founded in 1132.

[55] See *Exordium* 3.11 (CCCM 138:168–74; *Beginning*, 240–50).

[56] *Fragm* I.21 (VP 285; *Notes* 116–19).

presumption. Now when the man had received the Eucharist he could not swallow it. However much he tried, he just could not do so and became anxious and frightened, and he kept his mouth tightly closed. After Sext, the midday office, he drew the holy man to one side, threw himself at his feet and with profuse tears told him what was disturbing him. He opened up his mouth and showed him the Eucharist. Bernard reproved him and absolved him from the sin he had confessed, after which he received the Lord in the sacrament without any difficulty.[57]

THE FLIES OF FOIGNY

[52] We have known him to have done great things even over very small creatures. Once he came to Foigny.[58] They were getting ready for the dedication of the new oratory, but there was such an incredibly large number of flies in the place that their noise and exasperating buzzing to and fro gave rise to a severe disturbance to everyone who entered. As nothing could be done about it, the saint exclaimed, "I excommunicate them." Next morning they were all found dead, and they covered the whole surface of the place. The workmen got shovels and scooped them up so that the basilica was finally cleaned up. This event soon became so popular and celebrated that the great number of people who had come to the dedication from the vicinity changed it into a slogan: "Those infernal flies of Foigny."[59]

---

[57] *Fragm* I.26 (VP 288; *Notes* 126–27).

[58] Clairvaux's third daughter, founded July 1121, whose first abbot was Clairvaux monk Raynaud; Foigny was one of the first abbeys he built, situated in the region of Laon.

[59] *Fragm* I.19 (VP 284; *Notes* 112–13).

[53] In another monastery called Cherlieu[60] a young boy was incessantly weeping and wailing, and the holy man healed him with a kiss. As he had been weeping for a long time without any letup and could not be calmed, and the doctors were ignorant of that type of sickness, he was gradually declining into misery. The holy father took him aside and urged him to make a confession of his sins. Once he had made his confession, all of a sudden his face became serene, and he asked the blessed father to give him a kiss. After that kiss of peace from the holy man's lips, he immediately quieted down and was at peace. The source of his tears dried up, and he returned home safe and sound.[61]

[54] Once again, when the abbot went out after the other brothers to work, a father brought to him his son, who was lame. He begged the abbot to consent to lay his hand on the boy. But the man of God excused himself, claiming that he himself did not have the gift by which he could perform the favors asked for, since to give the gift of walking to a lame person was for the power of an apostle, not for him. The boy's father stood his ground and won him over, so Bernard made the sign of the cross over the boy and sent him off. From that moment the boy began to recover, and within a few days the father brought him back with immense gratitude, offering him to Bernard fully healed.[62]

The Group of Noble Knights

[55] Once a group of noble knights turned aside to Clairvaux to see the place and its very reverend abbot.

---

[60] Caruslocus, affiliated to Clairvaux in 1131.
[61] *Fragm* I.23 (VP 286; *Notes* 120–23).
[62] *Fragm* I.37 (VP 293; *Notes* 140–41).

The season of Lent was close at hand, and almost all of them were young, committed to military service in the world. They were on the lookout for one of those detestable jousting fairs, commonly called tournaments. There were a few days before Lent, and Bernard began to ask the men not to use their weapons during that period. They refused, being obstinate, and would not listen to him, so he said, "*I trust in the Lord** that he will give me the truce that you refuse." He then called a brother and ordered him to bring some ale, and he blessed it, saying that they should drink to the good health of their souls. They therefore drank with him, but some of them were unwilling to do so, afraid of it because of their love for worldly things, for afterward they experienced the effects of God's power in that draught.

As soon as they were outside the monastery they began to get heated in their conversation with one another, because *their hearts were burning within them.** God was inspiring them, and *his word was moving them swiftly,** so that they turned and were converted from their normal ways and enlisted themselves in the spiritual struggle. Some of them are still *fighting in God's service;** some of them, released from the shackles of the flesh, are now reigning with him in heaven.

[56] Is it not a thing of wonder that older people should honor this man with such great devotion? After all, the power of God stirred him up in infancy with devotion while he was not yet at the age of reason or devout.[63] Many people knew William Alcherum of Montmirail,[64] an illustrious youth. (His

Margin notes:
*Ps 10:2

*Luke 24:32

*Ps 147:15

*2 Tim 2:4

---

[63] *Fragm* I.36 (VP 292–93; *Notes* 140–41).

[64] MSB MS. 1 has William Alcherum (*Guillemus Alcherum*), but the critical edition has *Waltherum de Montemirabili* for the youth and *Waltherus* for his uncle.

father's brother, William, was one of those knights we have mentioned and was professed in the sacred knighthood at Clairvaux.) This was William Alcherum, Junior;[65] when he was still an infant a year old and knew only his mother's breasts, his mother had offered him to the man of God with gratitude and rejoicing to be blessed. She had been privileged to have the holy man as a guest in her house. And when the man of God, as he was always accustomed to do wherever he went, spoke to those around him about spiritual health and growth, the mother sat near his feet holding her child in her lap. While they were talking, he sometimes stretched out his hand, and the baby tried to grasp it. Eventually he noticed these efforts because the little one kept reaching; everybody was quite taken by the fact that the infant had the knack of being able to grasp the hand just as he wished. Then in a lovely and generous way Bernard held out his other hand and brought it up to the mouth of the child, who kissed it. This did not happen only once, but time and again the little one was allowed to hold Bernard's sacred hand.

Bernard's Sickness and Satan's Defeat

[57] There came a time when the man of God was sick, and there flowed from his mouth something like a stream of phlegm. His body became so exhausted that he began to fail, so that after a little while he was drawing close to death.[66] His sons and friends gathered round for the last rites of their dear father, and I myself was present among them, for he considered

[65] VP *Waltherum iuniorem*; MSB MS. 1 (*Guillemus alcherum iuniorem*).
[66] See *Fragm* I.29 (VP 289; *Notes* 128–31).

*Acts 10:10;
Ps 30:23

*Job 1:6

*Matt 7:21

me worthy of being numbered among his friends.
When he seemed to be almost on the point of drawing his last breath, *he fell into an ecstasy of mind** and
saw himself before the tribunal of the Lord. *Satan also
was present** as an enemy smiting him with fraudulent
accusations. But when Satan had attacked him with
all these things and then allowed the man of God
to speak for himself, Bernard, being neither terri-
fied nor even disturbed, replied, "I confess that I am
not worthy, nor can I by my own merits obtain *the
kingdom of heaven.** Nevertheless, I have a lawful right
to claim it for two reasons, for the Lord my God has
obtained it for me by the bequest of the Father and
the reward of his passion, for on the one hand he
has gained it himself and on the other he gives it to
me. I am not ashamed, then, rightly to claim it for
myself by his gift." The enemy was confounded by
these words, the matter was resolved, and the man
*Acts 12:11
of *God came back to himself.**

[58] Because of this vision Bernard expected that
the dissolution of his body was imminent, but a quite
different one followed. He was placed on a certain
seashore, and it seemed to him that he was waiting
for a ship to carry him across. When the ship pulled
in to the shore, he quickly made to board it, but
withdrawing from him, it moved off into the water.
This happened three times, and then the ship sailed
off, leaving him there, and did not return. From this
he understood that his departure from this life was
not yet to be. The pain still increased, however, and it
became so grievous that the hope of imminent death
did not now comfort him. It came about that as the
day drew to a close, when the rest of the brothers
went as was customary to their reading of the *Confer-*
*RB 42.3
*ences,** their abbot was left alone with two brothers
assisting him in the lodging place where he lay. He
was so afflicted with intense pain, which increased

beyond his strength, that he called one of the two brothers and ordered him to go quickly and pray for him. The brother excused himself and said, "I am not prayerful enough," but he enforced him by the authority of obedience.

The brother went to pray at the altars, three of them in the same basilica. The first of these was in honor of the blessed Mother of God, and the second two, placed on either side, honored the martyr Blessed Laurence and the abbot Blessed Benedict. At that moment the Blessed Virgin was present to the man of God accompanied by the two others, namely, Blessed Laurence and Blessed Benedict. They were present in that serenity and calmness that is proper to them, and they were so clearly visible to him that from their very entrance into the cell he distinguished each of them personally. *Laying their hands on him,** they soothed the painful place by their gentle touch, and from that moment they removed all his sickness. Then the river of phlegm *dried up,** and all his pain disappeared.[67]

*Acts 13:3

*Mark 5:29

WILLIAM'S SICKNESS AND THE REMEDY

[59] Once I myself was sick in our own house* and completely drained. The sickness was prolonged and went on and on for a very long time. Hearing about it, Bernard sent to me his brother Gerard,[68] a man of happy memory. He pressed me to come to Clairvaux, and he promised me that I would either be soon cured or die. I set out at once for the place, as if the opportunity was divinely given and accepted.

*the Abbey of Saint-Thierry

[67] *Fragm* I.29 (VP 289; *Notes* 128–31).
[68] Debuisson, "La provenance," 75.

I do not know which I preferred, either dying close
to him or being with him for some time. I made that
journey, even though the task was very burdensome
and I was in great pain.

Once I got there, it was as he had promised me
and, I confess, what I had wanted. My health returned to me from that very alarming sickness, but
my physical strength came back only gradually. O
good God, how good was that sickness for me, that
time of rest, that time of prayer, which was mainly
just what I wanted. For during the time he himself
was confined by his sickness, he helped me with my
needs in my sickness for the whole time that I was
with him. Both of us, sick though we were, discussed
for the whole day the soul's spiritual well-being, that
is, the remedies of the virtues against the flagging of
vices. He then commented on the Song of Songs to
me, explaining the moral meaning to me during the
time of my infirmity, leaving on one side the deeper
mysteries of that part of Scripture, since that is what
I wanted and what I asked of him.

Each day whatever I heard on this subject I used
to put it down in writing so that it might help me
to remember what God had given me through him.
He used to expound it to me kindly and without any
envy, to communicate his understanding of the text
and his own meaning drawn from experience. He
brought light to his teaching in many ways, which
could usually be discerned only through experience.
And even though I could not as yet comprehend
what he put before me, he made me understand what
I had failed to grasp.

But let that be enough about these things I have
talked about.

[60] When the Sunday named Septuagesima came
round, at Vespers of the Saturday before the Sunday, I was now regaining my health and was strong

enough to get up from my bed and move around on my own, so I began to get ready for my return to our own brothers. When he heard of this he simply would not hear of it and put a stop to it, giving me no hope of a return until Quinquagesima Sunday. I easily agreed with what he commanded, because I went along with his desire, and my weakness seemed to require it. But when after Septuagesima Sunday I wanted to abstain from meat, which I had eaten till that day out of necessity and because he had demanded it, he forbade that too. I would not agree to this injunction, however, and would not listen to him when he made this request, nor obey what he demanded, so we disagreed with one another until the Saturday evening. He went off tight-lipped to Compline, I to bed. Now see what happened: my sickness revived and grew much worse, resuming all its former strength.

This attack came upon me with such ferocity and violence that I was tortured all night and devastated with such malice that I believed I would be overcome by it, despairing of life itself since it was beyond my strength and beyond the limit of my endurance that I might not still have a final word with the man of God. But after I had spent the whole night in pain, late in the morning he came at my bidding, offering me not so much the expression of his sympathy that I was used to, but rather a rebuke. Nevertheless he said with a chuckle, "What do you want to eat today?" Now I quickly interpreted the real cause of my affliction to be his silence at yesterday's disobedience, so I said, "Whatever you order." "Be at rest," he said; "you are not going to die yet." Then he went off. What can I say? All the pain went away at once, except that I felt drained after the pain I had had during the night. So for the whole day I hardly had enough energy left to get up from the bed. What about the pain or its severity? I do not remember ever having suffered the like. The next day I felt *healed once more,** and my strength returned. After a few days, with the blessing and kindness of my good host, I returned home.

*John 5:14

BERNARD'S WIDENING MISSION; CLAIRVAUX, THE VALLEY OF LIGHT

*Sir 45:1

[61] Bernard was *beloved by God and mankind.** In that valley of his and in the local towns and regions that he was often obliged to visit for the requirements of the house, he blossomed with his virtuous deeds and miracles. Then he began to be drawn farther afield into distant places either because of the common needs of the church or the love of the brothers, or by obedience to superiors, or else to bring back peace so desperately needed and restore it between churches and secular princes in discord with one another. Also, he was needed to put an end peacefully with God's help to the never-ending disputes defying human reason and counsel and by the power of faith to make possible many things that seemed impossible *to the spirit of the world;** as it were *by moving mountains,** he appeared more and more in everybody's eyes to be highly esteemed and even venerated.

*1 Cor 2:12

*1 Cor 13:2;
Mark 11:23

His powerful preaching began especially to shine out to such an extent that he even softened the hard-hearted among his hearers, so that he hardly ever *returned empty handed.** After a while he became so remarkably proficient in his sermons and in his exemplary way of life that he was like a net for the word of God in the hand of a fisherman, so great was the *quantity of* rational *fish** that he began to catch.

*Isa 55:11
(*revertetur ad me vacuum*,Vulg)

*John 21:6

From each of these captures the boat of the house
of God seemed to be filled.* Briefly, then, it came
about that what this little-known and ailing man, at
death's door and strong only in speech, did in this
life was a greater miracle than all his other miracles.

    *Luke 5:6

  At that time Clairvaux (in name and in reality a
Clear Valley), that valley whose light radiated with
divine brilliance as if from the peaks, was spreading
its vigor down into the sloping plains of the world.
Formerly called a valley of absinth and bitterness, from
then on in that valley *the mountains began to distill their
sweetness.* This was a void, a sterile place totally lacking
in goodness, but now it began to abound in spiritual
fruit, *from the dew of heaven and the blessing of God* the
pastures of the wilderness overflow with richness;* the nation
has been multiplied and increased in joy.* Then there was
fulfilled in that valley what the prophet once said to
the city of Jerusalem: *The children who were barren will
say in your hearing, the place is too narrow, make room for
me to settle, and you will say in your heart, Who has borne
me these? I was sterile and barren, who has reared these?*

    *Joel 3:18;
    Amos 9:13

    *Gen 27:29
    *Ps 64:13
    *Isa 9:3

    *Isa 49:20-21

  [62] From a valley within narrow limits it has grown
exceedingly wide and spacious into a cloistered dwelling, moved now into *an open and spacious plain,** with
those dwelling there having revelations of divine things,
growing rapidly and increasing in numbers, so that now
this place is too cramped for the great number of those
abiding there.[69] Now the houses of the Order, daughters of Bernard's own house, have filled many deserted
places, on this side and beyond the Alps and the seas,
and still they are coming and still they flow in, those
for whom a place must be found. From all sides the
brothers are sought after and sent, since the kings of the

    *Num 33:49

---

[69] Clairvaux moved to a more spacious site in 1135. *Fragm*
I.30 (VP 289; *Notes* 130–31). See book 2.29-31 below.

nations and princes of the church reckon themselves blessed, as do the cities and regions everywhere, if they can merit to increase in renown by having a company from that house and regime of the man of God. What shall I say? Further still, this form of religious life has reached people as far off as the barbarous nations, in which the natural ferocity has shed its human attributes, where through it those fiends of the woodlands have become human again and have grown used to living with men and *sing a new song to the Lord*.*

*Ps 95:1;
Isa 42:10;
Ps 32:3

*Luke 5:4

God's fisherman, then, did not fail *to let down his net for capturing fish** at the Lord's command, and while some turned away and others followed their own path, the full tally of that holy congregation never lessened. To this very day, those catches of his have come and amazingly are still coming from Châlons, from Paris, from Mainz, from Liège, and from many other cities. From other regions too: Flanders, Germany, Italy, Aquitaine. Wherever he goes, for whatever reason, or wherever he is needed, or where still to this day the man of God is required to visit, wherever he goes he comes back full, totally supported by the grace of the Holy Spirit. This fullness accompanies him everywhere.

[63] Nor does he forget those he has sent elsewhere, but wherever they are he himself always preserves fatherly concern over them. Just as rivers *return to the place from which they arise,** so either his sons' glad news or their sorrowful news comes back to him daily. Often what is happening among them is made known to him from his fatherly concern for them, by divine intuition without *any human contact,** though they are far away from him. If anything is provided, if anything is to be corrected among them, their temptations or their extravagances, sicknesses or death, or any intrusion of worldly troubles, he knows. So he often enjoins on those at home prayers for cer-

*Sir 1:7

*Gal 1:16 (Vulg
carnis et sanguinis)

tain needs of absent brothers. Sometimes even those dying in far-off places make known to him through a vision that he should come to them, asking him for his blessing and indeed for permission to die. This is done out of obedience in those being sent and love in the one who sends them.[70]

BERNARD'S PREDICTIONS

Once when I had come to him and while I was speaking to him, I saw and I heard what I cannot be silent about. There was a certain monk from Foigny who was about to go back home. As he had received a favorable reply about the matters he had come for, he was about to go off, but the prophet of God called him back *in the spirit and power of Elijah** and in my hearing mentioned the name of a brother from that house, ordering him to correct those things that he was doing in secret. If not, he said, he might expect the judgment of God to come upon him. Taken aback, the monk asked him who had told him about these things. Bernard replied, "Whoever it is has told me, go off and tell him what I say to you and do not hide anything, lest you also should be involved in a similar penalty for the sin."

*Luke 1:17

I marvel over this thing, but while I am marveling, much greater marvels about him have been told me in a similar case. **[64]** Guy, the most senior among Bernard's brothers, was a serious and truthful man, as everyone who knows him is aware. When we were here in some place talking together, I was inquiring from him about this matter in a jovial way as friends are accustomed to do. "These things," he said, "that

[70] *Fragm* I.55 (VP 301–2; *Notes* 168–69).

*2 Tim 4:4

you have heard are *just fables*."* When he in his usual careful way devalued his brother's powers but was unwilling to disturb me, he said, "What I do not know I cannot tell you, but *one thing I do know*,* and I have experienced it: many things have been revealed to him in prayer."

*John 9:25

Then he recounted to me how, when they began at first to build new houses of the Order and the honey-filled hives of spiritual bees were being asked for everywhere, the Lord Bishop William* asked for and received his request, and they constructed in his Diocese of Châlons-sur-Marne one house called Trois Fontaines. They sent out to that place the abbot with his monks—Dom Roger,[71] a nobleman in the world's opinion but more noble in sanctity, and other men of a similar quality. Bernard, their spiritual father, did not forget those sons whom he had sent but was there with them in his fatherly concern and his devout affection. So it came about that when they were alone together, the abbot and he who was telling me this story, while they were speaking to one another about these brothers, suddenly Bernard the abbot gave a great sigh, and grieving within himself from his heart concerning them, he called out: "Go," he said to his brother, "Pray for them, and whatever God shows you about them relate to me." He replied, "Good heavens! I am not a person who knows how to pray like that and merits to gain my plea!"

*of Champeaux

When Bernard insisted on his bidding, however, Guy went off and prayed. He prayed with all his strength, *pouring out his soul** to God for each one of the new community. While he was praying, he was filled with such a loving gentleness in his heart for

*Ps 41:5

---

[71] Roger of Trois Fontaines, one of the converts of Châlons in 1116.

each one of them and an overwhelming grace of spiritual consolation that he rejoiced in spirit. And he had certain trust that he had been heard for them all, except for two of them for whom his prayer faltered, his devout feelings hesitated, and his trust failed. When he related this fact to Bernard who had sent him, Bernard straightaway delivered his verdict about those two, which in the event proved true.

Bernard Visits Châlons

[65] Abbot Roger and the others who were with him were those whom the man of God used to visit whenever he drew near to the city of Châlons. A similar thing also happened then to them and among them. For when at the request of the bishop Bernard had visited Châlons, he returned bringing with him a great number of noblemen, educated men, clerics, and laymen. While he was still in the guesthouse *refreshing these new plants** with his heavenly discourse, a monk, the porter, came in and announced that Stephen de Vitry,[72] their master, was present. He too had come to renounce the world and desired to live with them. Who other than Bernard would not rejoice in the arrival of such a man, especially since that *valley had not yet thrived much in the fruit** of such corn as he?

But the Holy Spirit revealed to Bernard *the snares of spiritual wickedness;** he groaned for a while silently and then cried out in the hearing of everyone there, "An evil spirit has brought him here.* He comes alone, he shall return alone." As he was still unwilling, however, *to scandalize the little ones,** his sons, he

*Ps 143:12

*Ps 64:14

*Eph 6:11-12

*Luke 8:2

*Matt 18:6

---

[72] Master of a group of scholars from Châlons who joined Clairvaux.

*RB 58.5

received the man and carefully warned him about perseverance and the need to give himself to the other virtues. He admitted him *into the novitiate** for a trial period, where those truly seeking God and going to persevere proved themselves. Yet he knowingly and shrewdly discerned that he would promise to do everything and do nothing. But concerning everything he had *predicted, none fell to the ground.** This man Stephen, as he himself confessed, saw while he was still in the novitiate a little Moorish fellow dragging him out of the oratory. After Stephen had remained there for almost nine months he left, and the prediction came true: he came alone and went away alone. In this way the *wiles of the enemy** were frustrated, and what the devil had instigated for the wreckage of the novitiate was fulfilled instead in his own defeat.[73]

*1 Sam 3:19

*Mark 12:15

[66] Before we leave Châlons aside, when on one occasion the holy father returned there, he and those who were with him were laboring under harsh conditions because of the cold and the winds. Many of those who were then in his company went on ahead and did not wait for him on account of the cold, so that he was left almost alone. It so happened that the horse of one of the two with him, who had dismounted, evaded him and galloped off across the open plain. They could not capture it, and the intemperate weather did not allow them to remain there any longer. "Let us pray," he said, and knelt down in prayer with the brother who was with him. Hardly had he finished the Lord's Prayer when behold, the horse returned as meek as could be, came to a halt before him, and went back to its rider.[74]

---

[73] *Fragm* I.25 (VP 287; *Notes* 124–25).
[74] *Fragm* I.35 (VP 292; *Notes* 138–39).

Bernard at Reims

[67] We now move on from Châlons to the city of Reims. There was an occasion when the man of God was present, trying to reconcile the differences between the archbishop and the people of Reims.* While he was there in the palace of that city staying with Josselin of Soissons, the bishop,[75] a great assembly of clerics and citizens filled the house to sue for peace. A sorrowful woman brought along her son, offering him in front of everyone with a plea for mercy, for the boy was reckoned to be possessed by a demon. Indeed on that very day he had attacked his mother and almost killed her. He had become mute and blind and deaf, and he was not able to see when he opened his eyes. All his faculties were seriously impaired, and he remained without any understanding. Bernard felt deep sympathy for this distraught mother who was so tortured by the agony of her boy. He caressed the pitiful youth, and laying his gentle hands on his head and face he began to speak to him with soothing words; he inquired of him how he could presume to attack his mother. The boy then came back to himself and at once recalled his sin; from then on he promised to reform himself and was restored unharmed to his mother.

*1139

In the monastery that is called Aulps,[76] among other sick persons who needed healing there came to him a woman sick with epilepsy. At that very moment, while she was standing in front of him, she fell down struck with her illness. The man of God immediately *took her*

---

[75] Six of Bernard's collected letters were addressed to Josselin (also Jocelin) de Vierzy, bishop of Soissons 1126–1152: Epp 222, 223, 225, 227, 263, 342 (SBOp 8:86–90, 94, 97, 172, 284–85; James ##298, 299, 301, 303, 336, 387).

[76] In Savoy, founded by Molesmes in 1090 and affiliated to Cîteaux in the Clairvaux filiation in 1136.

*Mark 16:9

*by the hand and lifted her up,** so that she was henceforth perfectly cured from her infirmity, not just for a time.[77]

[68] The duchess of Lorraine[78] was a noblewoman, though no longer living in such a noble way, when she saw in a dream the man of God extracting seven terrible serpents from her womb with his own hands. Afterward, because of his admonition, she converted

*at Tart   her life and became a religious,** and to this day she
*Mark 16:9   takes delight that *he cast out* of her *seven demons.**[79]

I know one cleric, called Nicholas,[80] almost desperately given to worldly matters but freed from this attachment by Bernard. After he had entered Clairvaux and received the habit and the observance of monastic life, he saw those who had fled there from the shipwreck of the world and were redeeming the plight of their shipwreck with the continuous gift of tears; he desired to do the same but was unable to do

*Mark 10:5   so because of *the hardness of his heart.** He asked Bernard with great sorrow in his heart to pray for him to God for the gift of tears. Bernard prayed, and he obtained for him such a great and such continuous

*RB 20.3, 49.4   *compunction of heart** that from then on the expression on his face was completely changed. Even when he was eating his eyes were filled with tears, and this too happened wherever he went or whatever he said.

THE INFLUENCE OF BERNARD ON HIS CONTEMPORARIES

[69] So many and so great are the powerful deeds we have heard about Bernard concerning the various

---

[77] *Fragm* I.33 (VP 291; *Notes* 136–37).
[78] Duchess Adelaide, d. 1158, sister of the Emperor Lothair.
[79] *Fragm* I.34 (VP 291–92; *Notes* 136–39).
[80] See Debuisson, "La provenance," 96–97.

needs of people and the different ways he has helped others that if anyone wanted to make a statement or write about them, that person would arouse either disbelief in those who are disdainful or disdain in those who are incredulous. In all his works his intentions were so pure and enlightened that they pointed clearly *to a body full of light** in whatever he did. He did not arrogantly reject all those high ecclesiastical honors that were always being pressed on him,[81] and indeed he was worthy of them but declined them for religious reasons, and sensibly so. But he made it clear that in everything he did he was always seeking how he might bear himself. He was so worthy that he could have been forced into them (I know not by what judgment of God), for he had gained reverence for his remarkable sanctity among everyone, so that sometimes he may have been forced into something against his will.

*Matt 6:22

Yet while he escaped from the honors of this world, he did not escape the authority that comes with these honors. In the conviction of all who fear and love God he is revered and loved, since wherever he is present, he does not dream of saying or doing anything against righteous living. Whenever he says or does anything to promote good living, he is obeyed. **[70]** Strengthened by this same authority, whenever the needs of obedience or *charity* in the church of God *impels him on*,* he accepts every inconvenience found in the work. Is there anyone among powerful men, either seculars or church dignitaries, who submits himself with such

*2 Cor 5:14

---

[81] The people of Milan wanted to elect him as their archbishop in 1135; in 1139 he was elected archbishop of Reims but refused. See Ep 449 (SBOp 8:426–27; James #210). Bernard also refused the sees of Châlons in 1131 and Langres in 1138. See *Fragm* I.27 (VP 288; *Notes* 126–27). See also bk. 2.26-27 below.

willingness to God's will, to whose counsel he hu-
miliates himself?

Proud kings, princes and tyrants, knights, and ex-
tortioners fear him and reverence him so that he
seems to fulfill what we read in the gospels that the
Lord says to his disciples: *Behold, I have given you authority to tread upon serpents and scorpions, and over all the
power of the enemy, and nothing will hurt you.** Indeed,
where spiritual things are looked at in a spiritual way
and when spiritual persons are being dealt with, quite
another authority is given to him, just as it is said by
the prophet about holy creatures: *For there came a voice
from the firmament that hung over their heads, and they
stood and lowered their wings.** So in these days, wherever spiritual persons are speaking to him or dealing
with him, they are steadfast in yielding precedence
to him and in submitting their thoughts and understanding to his thoughts and understanding.

*Luke 10:19

*Ezek 1:25

His Humility, His Charity, His Patience

So great is the badge of holiness that commends
this man of virtue in the sight of God and of men
to this very day, so evident the witness of sanctity
surrounding him and the charisms of the Holy Spirit
shining forth in him, and—what is greater than all
these and more difficult in human matters—all these
things are evident in him without inspiring the
slightest envy. What drives envy from him is that he
is above any envy. The evil in the human heart often
ceases to envy in a person what it cannot aspire to.
[71] He himself crushes every trace of envy by the
example of his humility or changes it for the better *by
provoking charity,** or if it is too depraved or too hardened he overpowers it by the weight of his authority.
Who is found these days so efficacious or so loving

*Ps 108:24

at fostering charity wherever it is, or at promoting it where it is not? Who is so beneficial to those whom he can help, so benevolent to everyone, so gracious to his friends, so patient with his enemies? Indeed, he could not have any enemies, he who never wishes to be inimical to anyone.

Just as friendship exists between two persons, so it cannot exist except between two friends, and in the same way enmity is perhaps between two enemies. The person who hates or does not love the one who loves him is not so much an enemy as simply a wicked person. But the one who loves everyone never has an enemy because of his virtue. It does happen, however, that a person may suffer enmity against himself by another's uncalled-for wickedness. Charity, when it possesses him completely, *is patient, is kind,** defeating malice by wisdom, impatience by patience, pride by humility.

*1 Cor 13:4

The following is an appendix to the preceding work, which, because the author had died, Burchard, the abbot of Balerne, added.

The particular reason for writing the previous work was friendship for that faithful man, Bernard. It was written by the venerable William, once abbot of Saint-Thierry, on the life of Saint Bernard, abbot of Clairvaux. At that time, William was a monk of the community of Signy, where he went because of his desire for solitude and quiet, and he remained there until the time of the schism against Pope Innocent by Peter Leonis. This work was considered to be an orderly account of the *Fragmenta.* Such was the grace found in it that hardly anything found therein more intimately reveals the hidden secrets of mutual love disclosed in those friendly talks about spiritual mysteries. The gracious familiarity that emanates from this work is still now clearly seen in the letters Bernard wrote to William[82] and makes clear to those who read them what he felt about him. Bernard also wrote to him his *Apologia*[83] and his other work, *On Grace and Free Will*.[84] William, however, had a far stronger and more general reason for writing, namely, the good of the whole church of God, so that this vase filled with such desirable treasures should not be hidden, and likewise that this treasure, the man himself, might not be hidden. It is not then inappropriate that he who desired to write about this should lament and say, *An unseen treasure and hidden wisdom, what profit is there in them both?** He himself sets forth the riches of salvation, the desirable treasure, so that it may not be buried like a dirty clod of soil that is by no means a clod, but rather a most precious jewel.

*Sir 41:17

Nevertheless it happened to him, contrary to his desire, that he was overcome by death, as he had himself feared and had intimated in his preface, and did not complete what he had conceived in his mind and wished to commit to writing. So then anyone who begins to read this work can quite easily understand that this devout and religious boy, Bernard, like another Benedict, was predestined from the first moment of his conversion, since he was seen to have been sanctified *even in the womb of his mother.** From her the future holiness of his life and teaching was realized and accounted for in the former work. What that young man, Bernard, began to do until he arrived at perfect manhood and from then on is

*Luke 1:15

---

[82] Epp 84 *bis*, 85, 86, and 327 (SBOp 7:219–24, 8:263; James ##87, 88, 89, and 236).

[83] *Apologia ad Guillelmum* (SBOp 3:81–108).

[84] *De gratia et libero arbitrio* (SBOp 3:155–203).

portrayed diligently, as has already been said, in the previously narrated work. This was written by that first-rate artist, William, but he was prevented from completing it.

This is the end of the first book of the life of Saint Bernard, abbot of Clairvaux.

BOOK 2

BY ARNOLD OF BONNEVAL[1]

*The preface of Dom Arnold, abbot of Bonneval,
to the second book of his life.*

Those authors who have related the deeds of
illustrious men have often celebrated them
with awe-inspiring words of praise. They
have done this, as far as they were able, with con-
summate art in highly gifted and skillful language.[2]

A FAULTY PAPAL ELECTION

[1] But the delegate and the other agent, who
were collaborating without reason with a brazenly
infamous and violent attempt, resisted the others
and precipitously named and ordained Peter Leonis,[3]
who was aspiring to the high office* by fraud and
plots, and named him Anacletus, while the others
were repudiating it. Those who were of the catholic
party gathered together in the cathedral and solemnly ordained the man Innocent,* whom they had
elected. They conducted him around those places
where according to the ancient customs the Roman

*of the papacy

*Innocent II,
1130–1143

---

[1] Arnold of Bonneval, Benedictine monk of Marmoutier,
then abbot of Bonneval; see Bernard, Ep 310 (SBOp 8:230;
James #469).

[2] At this point MSB MS. 1 omits the rest of Arnold's lengthy
preface and the two sentences that begin his continuation of
Bernard's life.

[3] A former monk of Cluny elected antipope in 1130.

pontiffs had held their sessions, and the honor of apostolic dignity was conferred on him at that time. From then on they lingered for a time near the Lateran Palace, because there was no safety in their own houses, as they were infested with the embittered Peter Leonis's satellites. Even though they were not able to put up much resistance, they had places where they could remain for the time in the castles of some of their confederates among the Roman nobility. But even in those places fidelity was not found. For after a brief period the nobility were unnerved either by force, by fear of the frightened crowds, or by bribes.

The multitude was so attached to Peter, because of either his powerful control or the closeness of those who adhered to him, that almost the whole city followed him or was under an obligation to him financially or by grants. He had collected incalculable wealth both by the exactions of the Curia and by the activities of his legates, money that he kept for handouts. Moreover, he distributed the full collection of ornaments from his father's wealth, and through means both right and wrong he armed the common people whom he bribed. When he had paid out these gifts, from the very altars he plundered the gifts of kings given as ornaments to the church. And when the false Christians either feared or were ashamed to break up the chalices and the gold crucifixes, they sought out Jews who dared to smash the sacred vessels and images dedicated to God. Therefore whoever had in his own way so acted with the agreement of Peter, whether more or less criminally and publicly, sold things taken from the general sacraments; altogether they bloodily took up arms and weapons. They assembled together daily, and with curses and swords they pursued the party that was with Innocent.

[2] The servants of God held a council, and because they could not succumb and save *themselves*

from human force, they made *a choice and secretly procured ships from the mouth of the lion, Peter Leonis, and from the hand of the beast.** They sailed off through the Tiber into the Tyrrhenian Sea, and from there, driven by favorable winds in their sails, they disembarked joyfully in the port at Pisa.

**1 Sam 17:37

BERNARD SUMMONED TO THE COUNCIL AT ÉTAMPES

[3] Before the messengers* arrived in France they intimated the truth of the matter to the Gallican church, and they exhorted the bishops that they might be accepted into unity with them and bind themselves against the presumptuous avenging spirit, so that having condemned the party of the schismatics, the bishops might endorse the unity of the church. The story of what had happened was not yet fully known to the bishops, nor had anyone presumed to give his private opinion until when gathered at a general meeting at Étampes they in common discerned what they should accept and what they should condemn. For France and the other subject regions had not yet come to an agreement about such a division, which might lead to a schism, lest they acquiesce to the errors of evil people, raise up in the church a false idol, or venerate an evil monstrosity in the chair of Peter. For sometimes in such cases important edicts did not frighten them or cause them to prefer personal advantage to the general good, favoring one party and depriving others, but to act for all.

**of Innocent

With a council called near Étampes,* the holy abbot of Clairvaux, Bernard, was personally summoned by the king of France himself* and the principal bishops. Afterward, as he himself confessed, he came with fear and trembling, as he was not ignorant of the pitfalls and

**the Council of Étampes, 1130

**Louis VI, 1108–1137

gravity of the business. On his way there, however, God consoled him, showing him in a vision at night a great church singing the praises of God in harmony; after that he hoped without any doubt for the peace that would prevail. When he came to the place, he first of all celebrated a fast and poured out prayers to God, and then when the king and the bishops with the princes sat down together to decide what they were going to do on this matter, there was total agreement among them all, a single decision that the business of God should be handed over to the servant of God and the whole matter rest on his word. Now, although he was fearful and agitated, he acquiesced with the admonitions of these men of faith and undertook this duty, diligently looking into the way the election had been carried out by the electors and into the life and fame of Innocent, the first one elected. Then he opened his mouth, and the Holy Spirit filled it.

Innocent II Chosen as Pope

Speaking for all, he named Innocent the supreme pontiff, to be accepted by all, and they all at once acclaimed this judgment and ratified it. They all sang the customary praise to God* and then promised obedience to God, in this way verifying Innocent's election. **[4]** Meanwhile the lord pope, giving thanks and bidding farewell to Pisa, was brought by boat to Tuscany and the other provinces that were favorably disposed. Passing through Burgundy, he arrived at Orléans. There, where the bishops were gathered, he was instantly and honorably received by King Louis, the pious king of France. From there he was taken to Chartres by Geoffrey, bishop of Chartres,[4] a man of eminent virtue.

decantatis ex more laudibus Deo

---

[4] Geoffrey de Lèves, bishop 1116–1149.

There, they also met Henry, the glorious king of England,[5] with a huge gathering of bishops and nobles. The venerable abbot came to this king, having sent a message to him. Henry was reluctant to receive Innocent, having been entirely dissuaded from doing so by the English bishops. He backed off in every way possible and drew back. Bernard said, "What are you afraid of? Are you afraid of incurring a sin if you obey Innocent? Just think of all your other sins, for which you are answerable to God. Leave this one to me; let this sin be mine." At this the king was persuaded, and so powerful was he outside his own domains that he accompanied the lord pope as far as Chartres.

[5] Meanwhile the legates of the lord pope came back from Germany bringing the consent of the bishops and the king, so that with these letters of consent and the public approval when he went to them he might express the joy of his presence among them, as they desired. They were easily persuaded to receive him because all the others had already received him. But the love and devotion of the French bishops kept the pope in France, where one and all desired him to make an apostolic visitation. He traveled throughout France and then convoked a council at Reims.[6] After he had done a great many things there to the honor of God, he crowned and anointed Louis as king,* while his father was still living, instead of his brother Philip. In all of these things the lord pope would not allow the abbot to be separated from him but obliged him to sit with the cardinals in public functions. They consulted the man of God secretly on any matters they needed to deal with in private. Bernard, however, referred

*Louis VII, r. 1137–1180

---

[5] Henry I, son of William the Conqueror, r. 1100–1135.
[6] The Council of Reims, October 1131.

whatever he heard back to the Curia and showed himself a patron to the oppressed.

Once the council was over, the lord pope met the king of the Romans at Liège.[7] He was received in a worthy fashion, but very quickly the calm was clouded over. Thinking it an opportune moment, the king took the opportunity to have the investiture of bishops restored to him, since the Roman church had received a legal claim to it from his predecessor Henry,[8] who had gained it through great efforts and many dangers. At this affront the Romans were afraid and blanched, reckoning that a decision to offend the Roman emperor was more dangerous in Liège than what they had experienced in Rome. Nor could the council agree until the holy abbot himself put up a strong bulwark against the proposal. With marvelous freedom he boldly opposed the king and resisted his iniquitous words, putting a stop to his demand with astonishing authority.

POPE INNOCENT VISITS CLAIRVAUX

[6] Returning from Liège, the supreme pontiff visited Clairvaux. These poor men of Christ did not put on *purple and fine linen** to greet him, nor come with gold-plated gospel books, but bearing a rugged cross, not with the thunderous applause of classical cheering or noisy jubilation, but with most heartfelt affection modulating their gentle chanting. The bishops wept, as did the supreme pontiff; they marveled at the gravity of that congregation, which in this moment of such solemn joy had the eyes of all

*Luke 16:19

---

[7] King Lothair II; they met March 22, 1131.
[8] Henry V, Holy Roman Emperor, r. 1086–1125.

cast down to the ground, never darting around with vapid curiosity but with eyelids lowered in prayer, seeing no one yet seen by all. There was nothing in that church that a gypsy* could find to covet. No ornate furniture met the eye to be desired; nothing in the oratory save bare walls could be seen.

Romanus

These monks aspired with longing only for a good moral life; there was no unhealthy plot to harm one's brothers, because their religious life could in no way be diminished or removed. Everyone rejoiced in the Lord and held a solemnity, not of food but of virtues. They placed before themselves plain bread in place of fine wheaten loaves, herbal tea for sweet wine, vegetables for tasty turbots, and cabbages for any delicious food. If there was any fish, it was placed before the lord pope; it was presented in front of them all, to be seen but not to be eaten. The devil saw with envy the glory of these servants of God, for the presence of such a worthy guest gave them the honor that he could not bear, for they sang eagerly and devoutly in choir in the presence of some of the cardinals, who were delighted to hear and see them.

[7] The devil disturbed some of the brothers with dreadful feelings of anxiety. For one who was possessed spoke blasphemous words, saying, "I who am speaking am the Christ." Many of the others were greatly disturbed and were shaken and sought refuge by following the opinion of the blessed father. But turning to the others, he said, "Pray for him," and silently led away those who were disturbed and restrained them. In this way that wicked man who was trying to transform the community of the pious into a theater and the school of innocence into a mockery, as he thought, should not be able to corrupt the thoughts of the religious men but should himself go elsewhere and bring his sick attempts to an end. Then all were quickly seated, including those

who had been standing on account of those persons, and the place was altogether at peace over what had happened. The evil enemy had been energetically rebuked and was no longer a scandal to them. He could no longer do what he had prepared or bring to their notice any such thing.

After that it came about that the brothers guarded themselves with greater care, and their merits and numbers increased; from then on the possessions of Clairvaux grew, as did the many houses, so that the monastic way of life in that place spread very nearly throughout the whole of the Western church. From that moment the holy abbot became even further renowned than before because of his miracles and other signs.

INNOCENT RETURNS TO ROME

[8] The lord pope could no longer delay in France, but with King Lothair he made his way to Rome. There, they took him to the Lateran Palace, where

*spring 1132

they forced an entry.* Many of the Roman nobility who were faithful to the church received him honorably. Peter Leonis, however, *did not make God his*

*Ps 51:9

*helper,** but maliciously bringing together his confederates and placing himself in his designated safe towers, he derided Lothair's power. He ordered his forces not to have a public encounter that might bring his own security into danger and gave his enemies no excuse for conflict, but he did impede their free discussions by his superior forces and powerful obstacles. He obstinately refused to meet the emperor, nor would he bow to threats or flattery. He would also not listen to the counsel of any person concerning his status. Innocent then left Rome while the emperor went off elsewhere. But after Innocent had gone away, Peter sallied out through the town, thirsting after the ruin of the faithful.

Innocent, therefore, realizing that during that period any delay in Rome would be fruitless for himself, returned to Pisa so that his presence might not infuriate the raging of that beast. At Pisa he gathered together all the bishops of the West and other religious men and celebrated a synod with great glory.* The holy abbot was present during all that went on there, at the counsels, judgments, and definitions, and everyone showed him great reverence. The doors of the house had to be guarded by priests, not out of disdain but because the great multitude of people hindered his movements, for some were entering while others were going out. So this humble man was seen to arrogate none of these honors to himself, but they were shown him because of his loving solicitude, and even more because of the impressive sway of his presence.

It would take too long to follow through all the acts of the council. Nevertheless their chief purpose was the excommunication of Peter Leonis and the definitive rejection of his actions; this decree persists to this day.

*the Council of Pisa, 1134

BERNARD IS SENT TO MILAN, WHERE HE IS ACCLAIMED

[9] After the council had ended, the lord pope sent the abbot of Clairvaux to reconcile the Milanese,[9] since they had made many requests to see him and longed to do so, and with him Cardinal Guy of Pisa and Cardinal Matthew, bishop of Albano, as legates

---

[9] *Exordium* 2.16 (CCCM 138:88–89; *Beginning*, 148–49).

a latere.[10] They were to quench the schism started by Anselm[11] in that city and recall to the unity of the church those who had strayed. The abbot added the venerable Geoffrey, bishop of Chartres, as company and counselor to those men whom he had accepted from the lord pope as colleagues. Geoffrey's sincerity and probity in many matters was certain, and the cardinals saw him as a good man. In matters of such importance he would strengthen the case with vigorous backing.

The party crossed the Apennines, and when the Milanese heard that the celebrated abbot was in their territory and approaching the city, about seven miles away, the whole populace went out to greet him: the aristocracy, the gentry, the knights, those on foot, the middlemen, the poor. They all left their own homes and went out from the city, and in their distinct ranks they received the man of God with incredible reverence. They were all delighted to see him and counted themselves fortunate if they were able to hear him. The whole world kissed his feet, and although he accepted this unwillingly, since he could not reasonably agree to these prostrations and devotions, yet he could not restrain them with a reprimand. They plucked bits from his clothing when they could, and they extracted remedies for sickness from the edges of his garments, reckoning everything that he had on him to be holy and expecting to be sanctified by the touch or use of such things.

Those going before the abbot and those following cheered him with mighty acclamations of joy, and

---

[10] Matthew of Albano, monk of Cluny and prior of St-Martin-des-Champs, Paris, became cardinal in 1125, d. 1134. See Bernard, Ep 131 (SBOp 7:326–28; James #140).

[11] Anselm V Pusterla, archbishop of Milan and supporter of Anacletus.

though he was for a long time delayed by the dense crowd, they finally made a lodging available for this august guest. And when the business that the man of God and the cardinals had come for had been dealt with, the city forgot about its strong resentments and put aside all its ferocity; they all then prostrated themselves in submission before the abbot. Their obedience was such that the verse of the poet Lucan might match it well: "I must be as able as I am willing to follow where you lead."[12] **[10]** Once peace had been established, the church reconciled, and harmony secured among the people, other affairs began to be brought up. The standard of Christ was set up in opposition to the devil's madness, and the man of God rebuked the ravings of those possessed, so that the evil demons, fearful and trembling, fled from their dwellings, driven away by his much more powerful force of virtue.

See, a new form of legate, no longer under the law of the Roman Court but relying on the pages of the divine law of God, sets forth in front of everyone letters written in the blood of Christ and the bull of the cross, to whose authority both earthly and infernal idols must bow down and subdue themselves. Such confidence among the populace, such virtue in a man, is unheard of in our times. A holy strife existed among the people when the abbot ascribed these glorious signs to their faith but they to the abbot's sanctity. They certainly felt this about him: whatever he asks from the Lord he obtains.

---

[12] Lucan, *De Bello Civili*, 1.372: *Iussa sequi tam posse mihi quam velle necesse est*, the words of the Caesarian Labienus expressing his commitment to Caesar's cause (Lucan, *The Civil War*, ed. A. E. Housman, trans. J. D. Duff, Loeb Classical Library 220 [Cambridge, MA: Harvard University Press, 1928], 2).

At Milan Bernard Heals Possessed Women

Counting on him, they brought to him a woman known by everyone to have been troubled for seven years by an unclean spirit. They earnestly begged him in the name of the Lord to command the devil to depart and to restore the woman to her right mind. The people's faith would not allow the least hesitation in the man of God, and because of his impressive humility, he did not presume to put to the test these unaccustomed requests or to be embarrassed when the people made them. If he obstinately resisted the loving-charity of those asking for this, he would seem to offend God, and if his own faith might dissent from the faith of the people, he would be seen by his diffidence to cast a shadow over God's omnipotence. He burned within himself over this matter, and although he thought it necessary to do these signs not so much for the faithful as for the unbelievers, he committed his bold efforts to the Holy Spirit and, relying on prayer, putting his trust in the power coming from heaven, with the spirit of fortitude he rebuked Satan, who fled from him, and restored the woman to health and tranquility. All those who were present rejoiced, and lifting their hands high to the stars, they gave thanks to *God who had visited them from on high.* *

**Luke 1:68, 78;
Isa 32:15*

This thing became known, and his fame quickly spread out through the churches of the whole city, through the ruling classes, through all the places where the populace gathered, everywhere where the man of God was preaching, so that they all said, "Nothing is impossible to him that he asks the Lord for." They say and they believe, they affirm, they talk openly about it: "To his prayers the ears of God are always open." Nor could anything dampen their enthusiasm at the sight of him or when they listened to him; some of them rushed eagerly into his presence, and others stood readily outside waiting for him to appear. The whole city ceased its business and its works, remaining in suspense at this spectacular event. They gathered together, they asked for a blessing and begged to touch him, and each of them was seen to be healed.

[11] On the third day the servant of God went in procession to celebrate the mystery of the Mass at the church of Saint Ambrose. There, a huge number of the populace were waiting for the solemn Mass while the clergy were chanting. He was sitting near the altar when a little girl was brought to him, one whom the devil had disturbed with a violent blow. They prayed that the poor little thing might receive healing and he might throw out the devil raging about within her. When those standing around heard their urgent request and saw the girl grinding her teeth and hissing so that even those who saw it were filled with horror, he had compassion on her age and the painful distress that he felt for her. As he was going to celebrate the divine mysteries, he took the paten of the chalice, and praying within himself, he dipped his fingers into the liquid. Trusting in the power of the Lord, he let the sacred drink flow into the girl's mouth and poured into her body a healing drop.

At once Satan was not able to stand the power of this infusion, which shriveled him up, and when this antidote, the cross of Christ, was applied, he burst out of her with a tremendous flow of filthy vomit. Thus the girl was purged, the devil took flight and was shamed, and the church sang out fitting praises to God. After these heartfelt cheers of approval, the people stood eagerly attentive until the divine mysteries were completed. In the sight of everyone the girl returned home safe and sound, and hardly had she been sent back than the man of God went off to his lodgings.

[12] It was by the judgment of God that a violent storm of trouble infested many people in Milan

*Isa 34:14

with its furious clamor, according to the words of Isaiah: *Hairy beasts shall cry out one to another, and the demons shall meet with monsters.** There was no one who could stand up against their arrogance, since for a long time they were under the schism started by Bishop Anselm, who favored Peter Leonis and occupied the cathedral of Milan. The priests were in tears, the nuns were besmirched, holy things accursed, the altar desecrated. These things provoked God's wrath against the populace.

But when the man of God came, Bishop Anselm's trickery was overthrown and the church was brought back into obedience to the Apostolic See under Innocent II. The freedom given to the demons, which was still in place, was stopped, and the devil was driven off at the prayers of the man of God. And even when he tried to resist he was gloriously overcome, submitting in the combat.

A Possessed Woman at Milan

[13] Among those who were troubled was a noble woman, a citizen of Milan and an honorable matron. Some people brought her to the church of Blessed Ambrose after the blessed man. The devil had afflicted her for many years with pains in her chest and had so smothered her that she was deprived of sight, hearing, and speech, and she gnashed her teeth and shoved out her tongue like an elephant's trunk so that she seemed to be like a monster rather than a woman. Her face was hideous, her countenance awful, and her breath disgusting, witnessing to the foul dregs of Satan, who dwelt within her. When the man of God saw her, he knew that the devil was alive in her and had invaded her, and that he would not easily be thrown out of the abode that he had

possessed for such a long time. Therefore he turned to the great number of people who were present and ordered them to pray fervently; he also directed the clergy and monks who were sitting with him near the altar to restrain her and hold her fast. Resisting and kicking with diabolical strength rather than any natural power; she kicked the abbot himself with her foot and hurt some of the others.

But he in his meekness looked with contempt at the devil's challenge. He appealed to God as his helper with humble and peaceful pleas and proceeded with the offering of the sacred host. As often as he made the sign over the sacred host he turned toward the woman with the same sign of the cross, like a strong athlete threatening the evil spirit. Now as often as the wicked spirit saw the sign of the cross made against him, indicating that he had been struck, he raged savagely and, *kicking against the goad,** showed himself unwilling to take what was thrown at him.

*Acts 9:5

[14] When the blessed man had said the Lord's Prayer, he tackled the enemy more efficaciously. Placing the sacred Body of the Lord on the paten and raising it over the head of the woman, he spoke these words: "Evil spirit, your judge is present here, the Supreme Power is here, now resist him if you can. The One who suffered for our salvation is here. Now," he said, "*the prince of this world is cast out.** Here is the body taken from the body of the Virgin, which *was stretched on the wood of the cross,*[13] which *lay in the tomb,** which *is risen from the dead,*† which *ascended into heaven while the disciples looked on.*‡ In the power of this dread Majesty, I command you, loathsome spirit, to go out of this, his handmaid, and never again presume from now on to come near her." When the

*John 12:31

*Matt 27:60
†Matt 28:7
‡Matt 28:7

---

[13] The hymn *Crux fidelis*, liturgy for Good Friday.

devil reluctantly let go of her and could not any longer remain in her, he afflicted her atrociously with redoubled fury because he had little time left.

The holy father returned to the altar and completed the fraction of the saving host; at the same time that he gave the kiss of peace to the minister to be handed on to the people, peace and full health were restored to the woman. In this way the evil spirit showed that he was forced to flee, not by confessing his wickedness, but through the efficacy and power of the divine mysteries. After the devil had fled from the woman whom this vicious carnivore had *Lev 6:21 roasted in the furnace of such torments,* her health of mind and the use of her senses were restored, and she gave thanks to God with her tongue, which had rolled back into her mouth. She then perceived that Bernard was her deliverer and fell at his feet. A tremendous noise was made throughout the church: everyone was jubilant with rejoicing, the brass band resounded to God, and God was blessed by all. Yes, their veneration for the servant of God even went beyond what was due to a mortal man, if one might say so. The city was liquefied with love.

[15] The things that had happened in Milan were heard about, and the reputation of the man of God was diffused throughout the whole of Italy. Everywhere people were saying that *a great prophet has arisen* *Luke 7:16; *who is mighty in deed and in word,* one who by *invoking* 24:19 *the name of Christ*† *cures the sick and frees those possessed* †Acts 4:10 *by demons.*‡ Indeed his greatest grace lay in the curing ‡Matt 10:8 of those who were sick, but his more frequent actions were those of getting rid of demons, because a greater number were troubled in that way and came up to him on account of his proven help, so the effect of his acts of greater power overshadowed those of the lesser.

Now, as the crowds outside thronged about him from morning till evening, he was almost smothered

on account of his physical weakness, so he went up
to the windows of the house where he could be
seen by them, and *lifting up his hand he blessed them.** *Luke 24:50
They carried bread and water away with them to
remind them of his blessings and for the sacramental
benefits conferred on them. From the castles nearby,
from the villages and cities, the multitudes flocked
to Milan to follow the holy man, both strangers and
citizens. They sought his blessings, they listened to his
words, they watched his wonderful works, and they
delighted beyond belief in his teaching and miracles.

Healing a Boy with Epilepsy

[16] Among those who were present from the
suburbs, one person brought with him a boy possessed by the devil. Whenever the man of God made
the sign of the cross, this boy constantly rushed forward holding his staff in his hands in front of them all.
He then fell on the ground as if dead and appeared to
be motionless and without his faculties, having neither speech nor breath in him; such was the pressure
on his chest that his feeble breathing overcame him.
The rest of those around gave the man of God some
space so that he could move forward and admit the
man carrying this boy, who was almost dead, to him.
Those thronging about were amazed at this pitiable
case and stood waiting to see what would happen.
The man therefore made his way to the man of God
and laid the half-witted boy at his feet and said,

> This boy, O lord father, whom I have laid at
> your feet, has been grievously afflicted by the
> devil for three years. And as often as he goes
> into church or is sprinkled with the salt water
> of exorcism and the sign of the cross is made

over him, or else he is forced to listen to the
gospel or indeed take part in the divine sacraments, the devil within him makes a commotion and torments him in an atrocious fashion.
While I with the others was waiting outside
for you to form the sign of the cross and to
extend your hand over the populace with the
power of the sacred signs, the troublesome
devil began very strongly, as usual, to agitate
the boy entirely with his afflictions. As you
see, he has occupied his whole body, and he
has almost shut off the life-giving spirit
within him.

But this boy, when he gratefully heard
among our group about the fame that you
have received from God, he, hoping to be
healed because of the healing others have received, begged me to bring him to you. So I
beg you through the mercy of God that you
may help us with your kind and customary
love in my duty, which I have taken upon
myself in guarding him through this burden
and this dangerous work, and help us too in
this misery, which is so great, as you can prove
with your own eyes. And may you pacify
these continuous diabolical ravings.

The man wept profusely with tears, moving those
who were present so much that they all likewise
entreated Bernard.

[17] Then the man of God ordered them to trust
in the mercy of God, and he touched the boy's neck
lightly with the staff he was carrying. But his brother
Gerard, wanting to experience what had been said by
the man, secretly impressed the sign of the cross on the
boy's back. And because at first the boy lay there flat
on the floor at the feet of the abbot for a long time
without moving or feeling, neither seeing nor hearing,
crying out at the touch of the staff and the sign of the

cross, groaning in a disturbed state, the abbot instructed him to be placed on his own bed. But he, as if feeling he had been injured, reacted from the ground, gnashing his teeth, biting the one who was caring for him, and starting with all his force to get hold of the hair of those who were present and tear himself away from their hands. They were hardly able to hold him. "Aha," said the abbot, "bring him to my bed."

And so while the abbot was praying and the brothers prostrated themselves in prayer, the devil flared up as if on burning straw contained in the bed, and by the pain of his torments the boy witnessed that the power of God was at hand. The holy man then called for some blessed water to be poured into the boy's mouth. But he, compressing his lips and teeth, would not allow it. They tried with a sharp wedge and were hardly able to force his mouth open, but whether he liked it or not they got the water into his jaws and down his throat. As soon as this holy substance penetrated him and went down inside, it was as if a great force had erupted: he vomited up a filthy mess like a surging torrent, and suddenly the demon was flung about and whirled around and went out with a mighty curse.

Immediately the boy who had appeared dead came back to life. He rose up from the abbot's bed, quieted and unharmed, and embraced his healer. "Thank God," he said, "I am healed." All present gave thanks to God together. Where there had been weeping, now there was rejoicing. Their shouting spilled over outside; *they shouted from the rooftop** what they had felt within. The whole city gathered together at this wonderful scene. They blessed God, the people rejoiced over the abbot, and the affection of the whole populace rested on the one who had achieved such a deed.

*Matt 10:27

[18] The holy man placed his hands on many people who were sick with fever, and he gave them

*Luke 6:6
*Matt 4:4

blessed water to drink and healed them. By touching, he restored to health those *with withered hands** and *paralyzed limbs.** In the same city he made the sign of the cross over those who were blind so that they might see, as many of them testify, and he powerfully obtained healing for them from the Father of lights.

A Boy with a Withered Hand

*Cardinal
Matthew of
Albano

At about the same time he went as a guest of the bishop of Albano,* whom the lord pope had given to him as a partner to function as a legate, in order to deal with the business that had to be done. After they had carried out the things that were enjoined on them, a young man with a withered hand twisted up toward his shoulder came running up and fell down at Bernard's feet, humbly begging to be healed. Bernard, who was otherwise occupied, blessed him and ordered him to go away and no longer trouble him, debarring him with words more off-putting than usual. The youth went off, though he had not received what he desired, when the venerable bishop quickly ordered him to come back and presented him to the abbot. He said, "This man obeyed you when he did not gain from you the favor he asked for. You should not stop up your heart of mercy. Rather you should obey it, and by the virtue of obedience, obliged by my request do what he asked, give him what he asked for. Have trust in the power of him through whom he waits for healing; ask him and beseech him that from God's goodness both he and we may glory in the healing taken away from him."

[19] At the bishop's insistence the abbot took hold of the boy's hand, invoking the Lord who heard him and making the sign of the cross; the tendons that had become contracted were then stretched out freely.

The flesh, which the sickness had set and made rigid, had now become warm, movable, and flexible and returned to normal. His arm, for a long time useless, was healthy again. The bishop was stupefied at the effect of such an unexpected strength of goodness, and from then on the man of God was honored with even greater respect. Having witnessed those miracles, the bishop related them to others. He compelled Bernard to remain there for the night and have a meal, though obtaining his consent with great difficulty, for Bernard was persuaded that the people everywhere were waiting for him unreasonably, nor could he be seen to depart without danger. When the meal was finished, the bishop gave the servant the dish from which the abbot was eating, to be preserved, and ordered him to hide it carefully. Within a few days this same bishop was stricken by a fever, with an intense burning pain. Remembering the man of God's servant, he ordered him to be summoned. "The abbot's plate," he said, "that I gave you to conceal—bring it, and hurry." When the bishop had accepted what the servant brought, he said, "Fill it with water and cut up some small pieces of bread." When this had been done, the bishop—trusting in the Lord and commending himself to the prayers of the abbot—ate and drank, and without any delay he was healed.

[20] The number of those coming increased, and these marvelous deeds attracted the people to the man of God so that he could not get any rest, while from his weariness others found rest for themselves. Those who came met those going away, and those begging replaced those who had received benefits. Among them, a knight brought in his arms to the man of God a little girl who had such a dread of light that she kept her arms over her eyelids with her eyes always closed, afraid that the slightest ray of light should get into them. When a ray of light

struck her eyes she cried out, wept, and sometimes threw her arms violently against it. Brightness was for her a terrible cross, and seeing light was like an arrow piercing her brain. The man of God blessed the infant, and when he had made the sign of the cross over her she went away more tranquil. While she was being carried home she opened her eyes and got to her feet without any support.

Bernard Confronts the Devil

In the same place, in the sight of many who were there, the holy man obtained healing from the Father of mercies for a woman troubled by the demon. **[21]** Then he approached Pavia, and the fame of his powerful works so went before him that the city was enraptured with delight, as was to be expected, and received him with a magnificent preparation. The people did not have to wait too long in suspense. They had heard of the miracles he had done in Milan; they now saw a sign done by him. A peasant who had followed him from Milan came up to him bringing a woman who was possessed by a demon. He laid her at Bernard's feet, and with a voice choked with tears he gave vent to his personal agitation.

Straightaway the devil spoke through the mouth of this wretched woman, insulting the abbot and poking fun at the servant of God. The devil said, "This leek-eater, this cabbage-glutton, will not throw me out from this, my little terrier." In this manner he hurled many violent insults at the man of God, who was thus impatiently provoked by these blasphemous words, and putting up with the reproaches, he was humiliated in the presence of the populace when he heard himself attacked by these angry words. But the man of God understood the devil's cunning, and he countered his mocker with mockery. He did not give way to anger, but leaving it to God he ordered the devil to be led off to the church of Saint Syrus.* He wanted to give the glory due to this healing to the saint and the first fruits of the works to be ascribed to Syrus's holiness. But Saint Syrus sent the business back to his guest, for he wished to return the complete work to the abbot, preferring that anything done in the church should be referred to him.

*first bishop of Pavia

So the woman was brought back into the abbot's company, while the devil was cackling through her mouth and saying, "Syrus won't cast me out, nor will Bernard."

Bernard replied, "Neither Saint Syrus nor Bernard will cast you out, but the Lord Jesus Christ." And he turned to prayer for the woman's healing and besought the Lord.

The evil spirit then changed his tune from his former impudence and freely admitted, "I will go out of this little wretch, for I have been badly tormented in her, though I do not want to go out." When asked what he meant by this, he retorted, "Because the great Lord does not yet want it."

> Our saint then said to him, "Who is this great Lord?"
> The devil replied, "*Jesus the Nazarene.*"*
> Again the man of God: "How do you know Jesus? Have you ever seen him?"
> "Yes, I have seen him," came the reply.
> "Where have you seen him?"
> "In glory."
> "You. Were you in glory?"
> "Yes, I was indeed."
> "Well, how did you get out?"
> "With Lucifer," he retorted, "many fell."

*Mark 10:47

He said all these things in a lugubrious voice through the mouth of the medium while everyone was listening. And then the abbot asked him, "Do you not want to return to that glory and be restored to your pristine position?" He once more changed his voice and cackled in a stupid way, "It is too late!" And he would say nothing further. So the man of God prayed more intently. The evil spirit was overcome and went out of her, and the woman returned to herself, now healed, and was able to give abundant thanks.

[22] The man went back with his wife, rejoicing all the way at her healing. When he returned to his house where all his friends were waiting for them, all those who had heard what had happened were very glad about it, but very soon their happiness turned into distress, because when the woman arrived near her house, the devil once more entered the poor creature and tore her about atrociously, as he does. What the miserable man, her husband, could do to resolve this state he did not know. To live with this demoniac would be terrible, but it seemed improper to abandon her. So he rose up and took the woman with him and returned to Pavia. When he got there he could not find the man of God, so he followed him to Cremona, where he had gone. He told him what had happened and begged him with tears of sorrow that he might find grace in his eyes. The abbot could not resist this holy petition. He insisted on entering the church of that city and prayed there, waiting for what would come about. Then, mindful of his promise, alone by himself, he spent the whole night in prayer until morning while everyone had gone to bed, until finally he obtained from the Lord what he asked for. And when he had gained his request that she should regain her health, he ordered her to go back to her own place safe and sound. He feared that the devil would go back with her as he had already expected, so he commanded that a notice should be tied to her neck containing

the words, "In the name of our Lord Jesus Christ I order you, demon, never again to presume to contact this woman." This command made the devil so afraid that once the woman arrived back home, he never again presumed to come near her from that time on.

Healing a Man Possessed

[23] In the same city there was a demoniac whose antics moved many people to laughter, but others with a more sincere mentality treated him with affection and much more humanely. He used to bark, so if you heard him but did not see him, you would think he was a dog. When he was shown to Bernard, the man of God heard him barking at him and groaned, for he barked in the way that dogs do, those that are often beaten and, snarling with anger, bare their teeth at their tormentors. In the presence of the man of God he growled, panting and barking more fiercely than ever. When the devil, making a lot of noise, was cast out in the power of Christ, the man of God ordered the man to speak. Now purged of the devil, the man went into the church and took part in the service. Strengthened by the sign of the cross, he listened to the gospel, made his confession, and began to pray. Afterward he took part in the other offices and became sound in mind and devout.

Healing a Demoniac Woman

[24] When for a second time in that same year* the holy father passed through Milan, a demoniac woman was presented to him. It was at that time that the man of God had made his illustrious presence felt in that city. The demon had possessed the woman,

*1134

sometimes talking in Italian, sometimes in Iberian, and it was not certain whether her bilingual speech was one or two, because she used both languages idiomatically. But when she spoke in her own way it sounded, you might say, as if she spoke now in Ligurian, now in Spanish. She was troubled with knee problems and a trembling hamstring.

When she was brought to the man of God she tried to jump out of the wheelchair she was sitting in, leaping up with inopportune haste. When she was put back, they asked her why she wanted to fling herself out and run away, and where, as someone so sick, she got the power and agility to be able to jump out of such a vehicle. She replied that this agility happened to her because of the devil's presence within her, so that those who were running alongside could understand themselves to be like horses and she might mount on their back without any assistance. On the following day when the abbot was in the church and taking part in the divine offices that he was celebrating, she was most cruelly and persistently agitated in front of everyone. He had compassion on the woman, who had been in such trouble for a long time, and, as an approved follower of God's kindness, he ordered the devil to depart. He, shaking with fear, vanished out of sight, and the woman was not only freed from this distress but also in a moment healed from the problem in her knee.

IN ITALY

These and many other things the man of God performed while he was beyond the Alps. Moving through different places, he brought healing and assistance to those who were sick: he returned sight to the blind, made cripples walk, and cured those with fever. Above all, with special diligence he cleansed those possessed by the devil, and those whom an evil spirit had sullied, he consecrated as temples acceptable to God.*[25] A great number of people gathered around showering him with the praises he had merited. Some marveled at his teaching, others at his holy way of life, and others at his miracles. I myself pay deference to all these honors, but more than that, insofar as is in me, I profess the following to be more wonderful: I predict that since he is *a chosen vessel to carry the name of Christ before the Gentiles and kings,** he will be an intrepid champion.

*see 2 Cor 2:16

*Acts 9:15

Since the Roman church has bestowed on him its special privileges, has subjected both nations and kings to him, and has made him as it were a universal legate, the princes of this world will obey him, and the bishops in every country will acknowledge his every wish. All this is indicated in a more glorious fashion by the fact that his deeds and words are confirmed by miracles, though he never goes beyond his limitations, never *has he walked in marvels beyond him*;* he always humbly believes himself to be not the person who performs these holy works but simply a minister of them. Moreover, since the Most High is his judge, in his own opinion he considers himself the lowest of all. Whatever he does he ascribes to God alone, or rather he feels and says that he neither wants to do nor can do anything good except under the inspiration and working of God. God's power is present *at the acceptable time, and on the day of salvation** he set his servant apart for his gospel and looked upon his humility** when the Holy Spirit adorned his soul. Because no double-dealing cast its shadow over his sincerity and no suggestion of deceit touched his good works, this same Spirit remained firm and fast within him.

*Ps 130:1

*2 Cor 6:2
*Rom 1:1

[26] He was daily put to the test in the furnace of trials, testing that made him more splendid and

more pure. Further, to keep him from becoming stale and rusty, he was struck as with fierce hammer blows on the anvil, beaten and criticized not as a penalty for wrongdoing but for the grandeur gained from virtue. He was never free from the barb of sickness. He knew that *virtue must be made perfect in weakness*,* and he experienced in himself adequate grace from this knowledge to see all his own weaknesses and to understand that as far as possible they should be gradually shaved off with the file of daily affliction. Of course *the flesh was weak but the spirit was willing*,* but rather than taking delight in his bodily needs, he delighted in the Lord.

*2 Cor 12:9

*Matt 26:41

He was never even tapped by any ambition for this world's doings, for every breath he drew was for the things of heaven alone. Whenever churches were in need of pastors they chose him for themselves to be their bishop. The church of Langres elected him; so did the church of Châlons-sur-Marne. In Italy, the city of Genoa and the Ligurians in the metropolis of Milan opted to have him as their pastor and teacher. Reims, the most noble city of France, the second capital, tried to gain his domination.[14] The honors offered to Bernard did not gain much favor with him, since he had put all these vocations aside, nor was he influenced by the prestige he would acquire. Much less was he likely to relish the tiara and the ring over the hoe and the mattock.

[27] He did not assent to those who sometimes sought him,* but he did not deny their request in an uncivil or improper manner; instead he said that this position was not for him, because he was deputed to

*i.e., to become their bishop

---

[14] It is unlikely that Bernard was offered the see of Genoa, in spite of the claim made by Arnold; see Elphège Vacandard, *Vie de saint Bernard abbé de Clairvaux*, 2 vols., 4th ed. (Paris: Librairie Victor LeCoffre, 1910), 1:336.

the service of others. When this matter was referred to the brothers, they replied, "*We have sold all that we possess and have bought the precious pearl that we have found*,* so we cannot return to the inheritance we have left behind. If the things we prize and value should perish and we were to be deprived of that precious pearl, what we are looking forward to with hope and joy would come to nothing, and we would go begging like *the foolish virgins, and our oil would be poured out after the doors are closed*."* These holy brothers took counsel and looked to their future, and with the authority of the lord pope they were protected so that no one should be able to take away from them their joy and that what was comfortable for others should be hardship for them. Their state of need became changed for them like wealth for other people.

**Matt 13:46

**Matt 25:1-13

For these and other reasons the servants of God fought off those who sought them, and now the abbot has been proclaimed everywhere as a statute from God in the church, just as Moses was to the Hebrew people. Moses was not a priest himself, but nevertheless *he anointed Aaron and consecrated him as a priest*,* and from that time onward the whole Levitical succession was disposed according to his ordinances.

**Exod 30:30

BERNARD RETURNS TO CLAIRVAUX

[28] After this he crossed the Alps and descended from the heights along his itinerary, where the shepherds and herdsmen and country folk gathered to greet him from all around, seeking his blessing. They came slowly through the mountainous defiles and then went back to their own pastures, gossiping to one another and rejoicing that they had seen the holy one of the Lord. He extended his hand over them, and they received the grace of his blessing they had

so desired. Finally, he came to Besançon and was
solemnly taken to Langres, around whose borders his
brothers at Clairvaux met him. They surged round
him, kneeling to kiss him, and while he was talking
to each one of them they brought him quickly to
Clairvaux. There, the brothers *gathered as one** and
welcomed their beloved father with amazing devotion. This was done *without any commotion** but *with
joyful dignity.**

    They were not able to hide the clear happiness in
their welcome, but by restraining their actions and
their cheerful words they kept everything within
bounds. They moderated their show of affection so
that they might not decrease the maturity of their
religious attitude with a semblance of disorder. Such
was the life of the abbot that there was nothing at
Clairvaux that the devil might weave into evil. He
could afflict nothing of his shameful deceits on their
pure minds, nor in any way did *the house of God
founded on the rock** fall. The servant of God, who was
*absent in the body but present in spirit,** strengthened
and promoted his work with the urgent application
of his prayers so that no cleft in the construction
could be found to bring it down.

    No deceits were brought forward at his coming,
no stored-up hatred emitted in the presence of the
judge. In no way did the junior members complain
to their seniors about the austerities or the harshness
of the life, nor the seniors to the juniors* about their
weaknesses or relaxations. They all lived together in
free rapport, a harmonious society, a genuine unity,
all of one mind in the house of God. You would
find them *climbing Jacob's ladder** in peaceful holiness,
hastening to the deep knowledge of God, who shone
out for them from on high in his delightful presence.

    The abbot, then, recalled Jesus' word, *I saw Satan
fall like lightning from heaven,** all the more humble, all

*Ps 47:5

*2 Macc 11:23
*see RB 22.6

*Matt 7:25;
RB Prol. 33
*1 Cor 5:3

*RB 63.10-12,
15-17

*Gen 28:12

*Matt 25:1-13

the more obedient to God insofar as in his deepest
desires he understood God to be present in his gracious kindness. Yet from this he did not take glory
to himself that the demons were subjected to him;
rather he rejoiced all the more in the Lord, because
he saw the *names of his brothers written in heaven,** for   *Luke 10:20
their unity *kept them unstained from this world.**   *Jas 1:27

THE NEED TO CONSTRUCT
A PERMANENT MONASTERY

[29] Bernard's venerable brethren were present
with him in their council. So too was Geoffrey,[15]
the prior of the place, close to Bernard in the flesh
and also in spirit, a man true and constant, who
later became bishop of the church at Langres, a man
distinguished for his prudence and religious spirit,
who retained his holy religious way of life and his
dignity without lessening his integrity. To this day
he perseveres in this way, going about* his duties   *Deut 28:6
in a praiseworthy manner. For this and many other   (Vulg: *ingrediens*
reasons the men who took care of the common   *et egrediens*)
good and were solicitous about it forced the man
of God, *whose way of life was heavenly,** sometimes   *Phil 3:20
to bring himself down to earth, pointing out to
him that the domestic requirements demanded his
attention.

They then suggested to him that the place had
become too confined,* for the place where they   *Isa 49:20
lived had no room for such numbers.[16] Since the

---

[15] Geoffrey de la Roche-Vanneau, bishop of Langres, 1138–
1163, Bernard's cousin. See Marc Debuisson, "La provenance
des premiers cisterciens d'après les lettres et les *vitae* de Bernard
de Clairvaux," *Cîteaux* 43 (1992): 5–118, here 79–80.

[16] *Fragm* I.30 (VP 289; *Notes* 130–31).

daily numbers of those coming there had increased in number, it was no longer possible to receive them within the buildings so far constructed, and the oratory was hardly sufficient for the monks alone. They added that there was a place farther down, more advantageous for the river that flowed below, and a place fine for the necessities of the monastery, for fields, for farms, for shrubberies, for vineyards. Even if there were no woods to serve as an enclosure, it would be easy to build walls from the stone that was there in abundance.

At first the man of God did not agree to the proposal.

> "You see," he said, "with what great effort and sweat the stones of the house have already been completed, and the aqueduct has at such an immense cost brought water through all the workplaces. If we now abandoned all these, the men of the world would be able to think evil of us either because we are fickle and changeable or because we have so much wealth, which in fact we do not have, that it makes us act foolishly. Since, as you most certainly realize, we do not have much money, I say to you in the words of the gospel that it is necessary to calculate the expenses of the work to be undertaken before beginning to build a tower. Otherwise when he begins to build and *fails to finish it, they will say to him: This foolish man began to build, and was not able to finish.*"*

*Luke 14:30

[30] To this the brothers replied, "Your opinion would be right if, after we completed all that was needed for the monastery, God ceased sending people to dwell here and stopped all the works for a reasonable cause. But now, since God has day by day multiplied his flock, either we must send away those whom he has sent or we must build a suitable residence to receive them. There can be no doubt that he who sends dwellers prepares dwelling places for them. God forbid that on account of our lack of confidence in him about the expenses we should incur his displeasure." When the abbot heard this, he was charmed at their faith and charity and finally agreed with their verdict. Before going ahead, however, he poured out his prayers to God that he might make clear his will in this matter. *The brothers were glad** when his decision was made public.

*John 20:20

[31] When the noble prince Theobald[17] of holy memory heard the news he gave many things generously and sponsored the new construction with his princely munificence. The bishops of the region, other eminent persons, and local councilors also heard about it and without hesitation got together cheerfully to assist in this work of God with copious gifts. A huge supply of donations was quickly given to the workers, and the brothers themselves took on much of the work: some of them felled trees, others squared the stones, others built up the walls, and others constructed canals to confine the flow of the rivers and steer the swirling waters toward the mills. The fullers, the fishermen, the tanners, the carpenters, and other workmen got on with their own works, rushing around and producing whatever was needed in every part of the monastery, constructing subterranean ducts to guide the fast-flowing waters through all the buildings and with them conveying all the sewage from every part where they flowed, then to return through their principal channel to their source. The walls were soon built with incredible speed, embracing the whole area of the monastery within a spacious

---

[17] Theobald II, count of Champagne 1102–1152.

boundary. The house rose up, and like a living and mobile soul, in a short time the new-born church had grown and was completed.[18]

THE SCHISM AT BORDEAUX

[32] The whole province of Bordeaux was in turmoil under the oppressive regime of schismatics. No one in Aquitaine could stand up against the prince, William,[19] who had hardened his heart against God. As Gerard, the bishop of Angoulême,[20] instilled into his heart the seeds of dissension, the prince became the defender and promoter of the schism. Whoever refused to acknowledge the authority of Peter Leonis was exposed to persecution: some were condemned, others were punished by banishment, and others were compelled to flee into exile from their own sees. Like the ancient serpent, Gerard murmured in the ear of his count all sorts of evil suggestions. Having for a long time been a legate of the Apostolic See but now rejected from such a magisterial position, he could not suffer himself to be the bishop of his church alone but saw himself as prince and master in the whole of Aquitaine. He was embarrassed to return to his first household, he who had had dominion over provinces subject to Tours, Bordeaux, and Auch, extending from the mountains of Iberia as far as the Loire and the ocean. Accustomed as he was to prey on the provinces that were under him, he thought up a ruse, under the pretext of justice and for other reasons that emerged,

---

[18] The second monastery was built in 1135 under the supervision of Geoffrey de la Roche-Vanneau.

[19] William, count of Poitiers.

[20] Bishop 1106–1136 and archbishop of Bordeaux 1131–1135.

and collected their wealth, which was for him an idol
and a likeness of apostasy.

When Gerard saw that the authority for making exactions was taken from him and that he had
only his own property, growing impatient that his
hands were not filled with gifts, with the cunning
of a serpent he hurriedly sent to Peter Leonis, asking that he grant him the position of legate, saying
that then he would swear fidelity and obedience to
Peter. Moreover he would persuade the prince of
the region to side with him and do whatever he
possibly could. Peter Leonis, that man of perdition,
rejoiced at this, because he thought he had found a
collaborator in his evil in the place in which he had
extended his malice and quickly agreed. He at once
delegated Giles the cardinal bishop of Tusculum,* he
who alone, with Peter the bishop of Porto* among
the Romans, stood by him.

[33] Now indeed Gerard, who had previously
regretted that his authority had been damaged, resumed his power, and from that moment he began to
appear more unassailable and audacious. He started
to go about with a mitre, as he had not done before,
and claimed the insignia of sacred offices and greater
reverence among the people. He furnished the count
with a great deal of money and introduced into his
heart baneful ideas. He seduced this easygoing man
with his talk and easily corrupted him.

In the first place he violently expelled William the
bishop of Poitiers,[21] a good honest man, a Catholic
who firmly defended the universal church and was
condemned by Gerard and the cardinal, his abettor,
because he had rejected Peter Leonis. The infuriated
count had quite dishonestly persecuted William and

*bishop of
Tusculum
1122–1138

*bishop of Porto
1116–ca. 1130

---

[21] Bishop 1124–1140; deposed and then reinstated 1135.

disclaimed him for other well-known reasons when the occasion arose. It also seems that, to confirm their position, Gerard and the count had promptly created a new bishop in Poitiers. They had discovered an ambitious man, of noble birth but ignoble in the faith, whom they chose from among certain willing clerics, and they laid their sacrilegious hands on his despicable head, not so much to anoint it as rather to pollute it and thus with him to impose their species of evil on the church. So they intruded a monster into the church of Limoges, one Ranulph, once the abbot of Le Dorat, who not long afterward, pursued by divine wrath, fell headlong from his horse onto the smooth ground and as a punishment struck his head against a great stone that was lying there; twitching all over, he died.

Bernard Comes to Help Geoffrey, Bishop of Chartres

[34] Hearing of these things and the like, Geoffrey, bishop of Chartres, a revered and elderly man, who as a legate had been sent by Pope Innocent to Aquitaine, was in grievous distress about them. He determined that without any delay, postponing all other business, he should come to the help of this church that was in such danger. Beseeching the abbot of Clairvaux, Geoffrey begged him to help in the task of eliminating this great evil. The man of God, agreeing, came to the nearby congregation of monks in Brittany, into a place that Countess Ermengarde[22] had prepared close to Nantes. She

---

[22] Countess of Brittany; see Bernard, Epp 116 and 117 (SBOp 7:296–97; James ##119–20).

promised that when he had established a house there according to his own order, she would go with him into Aquitaine. They went together and, to cut a long story short, came to Nantes.

Woman with an Impudent Devil

There was in that region a pitiable woman who was troubled with an impudent devil. She had a husband to whom the devil's disgusting habits were altogether unknown. This devil, an invisible and very impure adulterer, abused her even when she was in the same bed with her husband and troubled her with his unbelievable sexual advances. **[35]** For six years the misused woman concealed this evil, nor did she describe the lewd conduct of this offense. During the seventh year she was confused within herself and sorely afraid both because of the filth and the continuous wickedness and, more to the point, because of her fear that God, whose judgment she at every moment feared, would intervene and damn her. She betook herself to priests and piously confessed. She made pilgrimages to holy places and implored the help of saints, but neither confession nor prayers nor the giving of alms gave her any satisfaction. Every day like the one before she was troubled and harassed by the demon. Finally she publicly poured out her awful offense. When her husband heard about it and understood, he was so appalled that he found their cohabitation abhorrent.

Meanwhile the man of God had come to the place with his company. When the unhappy woman heard of his arrival she threw herself at his feet, trembling all over. With weeping she poured out the dreadful suffering and the demon's undesirable mocking, explaining that when she was ordered to go to the

priests they could do nothing for her. She added
that Bernard's coming had been predicted to her
by her oppressor, who had threatened her with dire
consequences if she came into his presence, because
she would get nothing out of it, and he declared that
when the abbot had gone away, he who had formerly
loved her would become a cruel persecutor.

Hearing all this, the man of God comforted her
with gentle words and promised her *help from heaven*.*
He ordered her to wait till the morrow when, as
night was drawing on, he would return, trusting in
the Lord. She came back the next day to the man
of God and told him of the blasphemies and threats
that she had listened to that same night from her evil
incubus. "Take no notice of those threats," said the
man of God, "but go back taking this staff of mine;
lay it on your bed, and if anything happens, use it."
The woman did what she was told. She lay on her
bed and, strengthening herself with the sign of the
cross, placed the staff beside her. Immediately the
devil came to her, but not in his usual way, nor did
he presume to approach the bed. He threatened her
terribly, however, saying that when the man of God
had gone away he would return to torment her.

When Sunday came, the man of God wanted to
summon the people to the church at the command
of the bishop. When on that day a tremendous throng
crowded into the church, with the accompanying bishops, Geoffrey of Chartres and Bristus of Nantes,[23] for
the solemn Mass, Bernard ascended to the lectern, and
when all in the church were holding lighted candles in
their hands, he began to speak. With the bishops and
clergy listening, he spoke out publicly of the devil's
incredible audacity and his fiery evil and his fornicat-

*2 Macc 8:20

---

[23] Brictius, bishop of Nantes 1112–1140.

ing spirit that had blazed up in such a horrendous
fashion, quite contrary to the woman's natural feelings.
With the consent of all the faithful who were present
and with the authority of Christ he condemned the
devil and put a stop from then on to his access to
the woman and all other women. So when the sacramental lights had been extinguished, the whole of
the devil's power was also destroyed; never afterward
did the enemy appear to the woman who had made
her confession, but he fled away expelled.

Bernard Confronts Count William

[36] When all these things had been accomplished,
both the abbot and the legate went to Aquitaine.
Meanwhile Gerard, with the consent of the count,
had taken possession of the archbishopric of Bordeaux
and at the same time occupied the church of Bordeaux
and Angoulême. But when the money he had given
into the hands of his flatterers had run out and he had
finally realized the truth of the matter, the wealth given
by the princes vanished, and his treacherous defenders were afraid to emerge openly. He settled in those
places where he felt more secure and would not easily
present himself at public assemblies.

We need to go back a little to what had happened
before, when what Gerard had cunningly contrived
against the church of God was first heard of. Our
abbot of Clairvaux and Josselin, the venerable bishop
of Soissons, had been sent by Pope Innocent while
he remained in France to go to Poitiers and confer
with Gerard and William, that prince.*24 But Gerard,   *1134–1135
under the influence of that prince, insolently began

---

24 See Vacandard, *Vie de saint Bernard*, 1:319–29.

to emit violent insults at the Catholic church, from which he had been cut off, and he rejected his former obedience to Innocent. He also began to proclaim that Anacletus, his preferred choice, was more worthy and that anyone who did not obey him was in error and a schismatic. So he stirred up the clerics and armed them, and from then on they started publicly persecuting the Catholics.

Before their infidelity had been made public and confirmed, the holy abbot had offered the sacrifice to God in their church. A misguided deacon of the same church in which the divine mysteries had been celebrated impiously broke down the altar but was punished for it. Shortly afterward he was struck by God, and, when at death's door, he saw the house where he was dying filled with demons and himself asking from one of those standing around for a knife to thrust into his own throat so that when the devil was extracted he might live. But while he was speaking, the devil who had been assigned to him snuffed him out and thrust his pestilent soul down into hell.

The archpriest too, who had taken over the church of Poitiers,[25] denounced the synod of Peter. This Peter had been corrupted by the devil in the presence of those whom he welcomed to his faithless assembly. But the hand of God exerted open anger against many others who were fomenting that schism. Because of this event and others like it, Gerard began to be avoided by everyone, and fearing the opposition to himself that he could not contradict, he kept away from public meetings.

[37] Meanwhile it was made known to Count William, through various important officials who dared to

---

[25] Peter de Châtellerauld, schismatic bishop of Poitiers 1134–1135.

approach him safely, that the abbot of Clairvaux and
the bishop of Chartres and other bishops and religious
were seeking an audience with him, that they were
making it their concern to secure the peace of the
church with him and to try to remove the present
evils. He was persuaded not to steer clear of a meeting
with such men, because it would become apparent
that when he had expressed his mind to them, what
he had so far considered difficult might become easier,
and what had seemed to be impossible could become
possible and have a happy outcome. Therefore they
came together from all parts at Partenay, where they
considered the vision of the church and the obstinacy
that had on this side of the Alps settled like a dark
corrupting fog in Aquitaine alone. It was pointed out
to the count that since the church is one, whatever is
outside the church is outside Noah's ark and by God's
judgment must necessarily perish and be drowned.
They brought forward the example of *Dathan and
Abiron, whom, as they were* guilty of schism, *the earth
swallowed up alive.** He was reminded that for such an
evil God's punishment would never be left unseen.

*Num 26:9;
Deut 11:6

When he heard these arguments, the count listened to the sound reasons of his counselors and
replied that he himself would consent to obedience
to Pope Innocent, but in no way would he be induced to the restitution of the bishops whom he
had driven out of their sees, for they had implacably
angered him, and he had sworn that from that time
onward he would never receive them back in peace.

BERNARD WIELDS A DECISIVE
SPIRITUAL WEAPON

For a long time this dispute dragged on among
the parties, and while they were wrangling with one

another among themselves, the man of God took up the more effective weapons of God and approached the holy altar to offer Mass and supplication. Those who were allowed entered the church to take part in the divine mysteries, but the count stayed outside. **[38]** After the consecration had taken place and the kiss of peace had been given among the people, the man of God, no longer acting as a mere man, placed the Body of the Lord upon the paten and took it with him, his face flaming and his eyes ablaze; not now with pleading but with a menacing visage he went out and confronted Duke William:

> "We have pleaded with you," he asserted, "and you have scorned us. All the servants of God have joined with us in beseeching you, and the whole multitude has united before you, and you have treated them with contempt. Behold! The Son of the Virgin comes now before you, he who is the Head and Lord of the church that you have persecuted. Your judge is present here, and in his name *all bow the knee—in heavenly places, on the earth, and under the earth.** Your judge is present here, and in his power this soul of yours will come for judgment. Do you spurn him? Do you despise him just as you despise his servants?"

*Isa 45:23;
Rom 14:11;
Phil 2:10

The whole assembly of those present dissolved in tears and with ardent prayers keenly looked forward to the outcome of the matter. They were all in total awe and suspense, waiting for I know not what the God of heaven might do. The count, when he saw the abbot *proceeding with a fierce spirit,** carrying the most holy Body of the Lord in his hands, was over-come and petrified. Trembling in his limbs he sank down and fell on his face as if senseless. His soldiers lifted him up, but again he fell on his face, nor could

*Ps 47:8

he speak or understand anything; his saliva dribbled over his beard, and he gave out deep groans like an epileptic. Then the man of God came up to him and, leaning forward, touched him with his foot and ordered him to get up.

So the count stood up on his feet to hear the sentence of God: "The bishop of Poitiers is here present, whom you expelled from his church. Go and be reconciled to him, and with a kiss of peace join with him in a treaty and restore him to his see. Render satisfaction and glory to God for the wrong you have done and recall to the unity of charity the divisions and discords in the whole of your principality. Submit to Pope Innocent; just as the whole church obeys him, so you too must obey the chosen one of God, the supreme pontiff." When the count had heard all this, he did not dare to contradict the man of God, nor could he, for he was overcome by the authority of the Holy Spirit and the presence of the holy sacraments. He immediately went up to the bishop and received him with the kiss of peace. And with the same power with which he had rejected him he restored him to his own see amid the rejoicing of the city. From then on the abbot spoke familiarly and kindly with the count and admonished him in a fatherly way. He urged him not to indulge in such ungodly and brash ways any longer, for with such shameful things he would test the patience of God to the limit; nor should he violate the peace he had made in any respect.

[39] Now that peace had been restored to Aquitaine, it was only Gerard who persisted in his evil way, but not for long: after a little while the anger of God came upon him, and he died a miserable death in his house. As Scripture says, *there is a sin that leads to death; I do not say that one is to pray for that.** Impenitent, Gerard died suddenly; his spirit departed from his

*1 John 5:16

body without confession or *viaticum*. He had shown himself a servant of the devil, and he remained so up to the end. His nephews, to whom he had given honors in that church, found his body in his bed covered with worms and enormously swollen. They endowed it with honor in that church, burying him in a basilica. But afterward Geoffrey, bishop of Chartres and legate of the Apostolic See, had it exhumed and discarded elsewhere. These same nephews of his were also ejected from their office in that church, and all their progeny and property* were rooted out from the whole territory and, bearing the disgrace of that verdict, were exiled.

plantatio

MEDITATIONS ON THE SONG OF SONGS*

*begun toward the end of 1135

When Gerard's evil had been overthrown and his schism reduced to ashes, the man of God returned to Clairvaux with immense joy. His brethren were there around him and gave thanks to God, who had granted such a happy outcome to these good initiatives. Everywhere God was glorified and rejoiced in *the humility of his servant.** **[40]** The man of God rested for a little quiet time and then occupied himself with another business. He secluded himself in a tiny hut, and encircled with spiritual garlands and divine pomegranates, he gave himself up alone to the restful vacation of divine meditation. He was soon occupied in that humble abode as though at the manger of the Lord, dwelling on the canticle of love and the banquet of the bride's wedding feast.

*Luke 1:48

He pondered and was awestruck that *he who was the fairest in form of the children of men,** upon whom *even the angels long to gaze,*† deeply loved the swarthy bride, extolled her *who was darkened by the sun,*‡ for she was totally fair and *had in her no stain.*§ He

*Ps 44:2
†1 Pet 1:12
‡Song 1:5
§Song 4:7

marveled at that bride *who languished with love** and
diligently inquired about the love whose *kisses are
sweeter than wine,** the one in whom the soul delights
and for whom she longs so impatiently and with such
love. But when the Spouse greets the bride with so
many praises, he does not offer her the fullness of
himself; nor does he grant her the full satisfaction
that she so desires. *Sought after, he is not found;** after
seeking him *about the city with long pursuits, she finds
him and will not let him go.**

*Song 5:8

*Song 1:3

*Song 5:7

*Song 3:2

The holy man poured out his soul in this meditation at length, and he often expounded these things
through which he himself had profited. He daily
feasted on those delights and gave us what he had
gained; he served up for us in the Scriptures what
remained from this blessing, as is clear to those who
read it.

BERNARD AGAIN CALLED TO ITALY

[41] Meanwhile the man of God received apostolic letters from the cardinals, who begged him to be
present for the defense of the church. He had to inter-
rupt his work on the Song in order to carry out what
was now of immediate concern; then after an interval
he resumed work on his commentary. No period of
rest came to him. The servant of God was always either
at prayer or meditating or reading or preaching. But
seeing that all excuses would be in vain, he called his
brethren together from many places, and after a long
time, sighing deeply with grief, he said,

> Do you see, my brothers, how great are the
> problems that afflict the church? The follow-
> ers of Peter Leonis in Italy and in Aquitaine
> have sidled away from the authority of God;

now they do not bring forth but abort. The defenders of the schism have sprung up in those regions. The greater part of the nobles in Rome follow Innocent, and many of the faithful favor him, but being deterred by the strength of their opponents, they do not dare to agree openly with those who have supported him. Peter Leonis has conspirators, men who are lost and corrupted with gifts of money and weapons, and he displays not the faith of Simon Peter but the trickery of Simon the magician.*

*Acts 8:18-19

Against the one people of God, while the West is at peace, the game still goes on. *May Jericho yet fall** while you are praying and rejoicing, and *while you stretch out your hands with Moses to the Lord, Amalech will be overcome and flee.** Joshua fought, and that the day might be sufficiently long for his victory, he did not so much pray but command the sun to stay where it was. And his faith merited to obtain the obedience of the sun and, moreover, victory over the fallen enemy.* While we are fighting, you yourselves must bear us assistance and implore the help of heaven with your beseeching. Do what you must do, *stand firm where you stand,** and although you may not be conscious of any judgment against you, do not reckon yourselves to be just, because *only God can make righteous** those whom he makes righteous.

*Heb 11:30

*Exod 17:16

*Josh 10:12-14

*Dan 10:11

*Rom 8:33

However perfect a person is, let him not neglect the strict trial of God's judgment. Do not worry about *being judged by human opinion** but *stand firm under the fear of God,*† giving approval neither to your own nor to any other judgment, so that you do not feel elated when judging someone else or be depressed at the opinions of others made in jest, but giving due consideration to each, *reckon your-*

*1 Cor 4:3
†Luke 17:10

selves to be unworthy servants.* We must go
where obedience calls us. We give over and
commend to God the paternity of this house
and the watchful care of you for whose sake
we have taken on this work, confident in his
loving mercy.

*Luke 17:10

[42] *After he had said this and blessed them he departed
from them,** *while they all wept.*

*Luke 24:51

BERNARD'S ROLE IN THE DEFEAT OF ANACLETUS

After that Bernard was received everywhere with
great respect, until at last he came to Rome.[26] When
he arrived there both the pope and the brothers
rejoiced, and they conferred with him in council
about the way things had turned out and the state of
affairs, but he approached the matter in another way,
not putting his trust in chariots or horses;* entering into
talks with some of them, he examined what was the
drift of their thinking, whether they were influenced
by error or by malice to protract and defend such an
evil. In a private meeting, a cleric who was with Peter
Leonis talked of his own state of mind as he worried
about his sin but did not dare to return, lest when
his mind was known he might be held as a reprobate
among the others, who preferred to remain as they
were under the veil of loyalty rather than be expelled
from their sees and publicly exposed for lying.

*Ps 19:8

This was the response of those who were among
Peter Leonis's relatives: that no one would give them
credence if they carved up their own family and relinquished him, the head and lord of his relatives. Others
under the oath of fidelity excused the treachery, nor

---

[26] Bernard's third journey to Italy, 1137–1138.

would anyone of sound conscience help that party. The abbot denounced these disgraceful oaths of allegiance as sacrilegious and worldly. He said that such contemptuous conspiracies could not be defended by law or canon law, nor could the sacraments of the truth be supported by deceit. Those who held to such oaths, he went on, were idiots, who reckoned that an illicit matter could be protected by a sacrament, since such extraordinary agreements, without the sanctity of any religious standing, should be revoked as useless and dissolved by divine authority.

Those who heard these words of the man of God drifted away from Peter Leonis, and day by day the chains binding the ranks of that party to him were broken. Peter Leonis himself was losing heart because his party was gradually drifting away; no one could doubt that Innocent was gaining support. Peter Leonis's wealth ran out, a great number of his courtiers faded away, the ministers of his household withered, the guests who frequented his table became scarce, and the rich food was changed to an ordinary diet. The cult of those who of old had surrounded him faded because of the lack of funds, and the whole appearance of his household grew so pallid that it pointed to approaching extinction.

THE PRIDE OF ROGER, KING OF SICILY

[43] Meanwhile Roger, the king of Sicily, who was the only one of the princes to refuse to obey Pope Innocent, asked him to send the chancellor Haimeric[27] and the abbot of Clairvaux to him. He

---

[27] Cardinal deacon and chancellor of the Apostolic See (d. 1141), to whom Bernard wrote numerous letters and dedicated *De diligendo Deo*.

also asked, however, that Peter of Pisa[28] be delegated as his legate. He said that he wanted to ascertain the origin of this schism, which had been going on for such a long time, and that when he had learned the truth of the matter he would either correct his error or confirm his view. But this statement was in fact deceitful. He had heard that Peter of Pisa was a very eloquent person, well up in law and second to none in canon law. He thought that he would furnish proofs by the force of his rhetoric for the benefit of those who heard his eloquent words in public debate and overwhelm the simplicity of the abbot, thus silencing him with the brilliance of his words and his reasoning.

To delay no longer, both parties came to Salerno, but wrath fought and overcame the stratagems of this crime. Having prepared himself for war with an innumerable army against Duke Ramnulf,[29] the king arrayed the battle line of his forces on the field. But when he saw the duke moving in intrepid manner to meet him, he fled in terror, exposing his scattered forces to plunder and slaughter, so that many of his knights were captured or killed. Thus he enriched the duke with gifts and exalted him with glory. Indeed, all these things happened to him in conformity to the words of the man of God. Since the abbot was the first of those the king had called, the abbot came to him and found him positioned in his camp. For a long time he implored him not to commit his forces to battle, warning him that if he began the conflict he would be defeated and depart in disorder. In the end, when the king's army had greatly increased, forgetting *that the outcome of war does not consist in*

---

[28] Cardinal and canonist; see Bernard, Ep 213 (SBOp 8:73–74; James #283).

[29] Ranulf of Alife, adversary of King Roger II.

*Jdt 9:16; see
2 Sam 11:25

†Rom 14:19

*great forces,** the king dared to despise the man of God, who was *seeking the things that make for peace.*†

[44] But Bernard exhorted Ramnulf and the Catholic army with powerful encouragement, so promising them victory and triumph. He then went into a little village close at hand and settled down and gave himself to prayer. Then suddenly he heard a deafening uproar outside from those running away and being pursued. One of the brothers who was among those with the abbot went out and met one of the knights and asked him what was happening. This knight, an erudite fellow, replied, *I have seen the wicked high and mighty and towering like a cedar of Lebanon. Again I passed by and behold they were no more.**

*Ps 36:35–36

The monk saw the duke himself following; armed as he was, he jumped down from his horse and, falling on his knees, said, "I give thanks to God and to his faithful servant that it is not by our strength but by his faith that this victory has been gained." Then, jumping back on his horse, he went in pursuit of the enemy.

BERNARD'S REPLY TO PETER OF PISA

[45] This setback, however inflicted from heaven on the king, did not alter his mind or lessen within him the storm that the pride of his depraved mind had aroused. After his followers had returned from their flight and rejoined him, he hastily took up his regal pomp. Supporting his court with his knights, he stirred up both parties, and, having already instructed Peter of Pisa, he incited him with his authority and many promises, ordering him to speak in favor of his cause. First, Peter zealously attempted to prove the canonical election of his lord, furnishing many strong proofs from canon law. But the man of God, understanding the matter to be not one of words but of the power of the kingdom of God, spoke:

> I know, Peter, that you are a man wise and learned. Would to God that your talents had occupied you in a more reasonable and honest business. Would to God that your patron had obtained you in a more favorable cause. Then no doubt nothing could have impeded the fluency of the words you employ in your allegations. But we ourselves are more accustomed to using mattocks than fine speech, and if it were not for the cause of the faith, we should surely have to keep to our rule of silence. Now charity forces us to speak, because the tunic of the Lord, which during the time of the passion even the Gentiles did not presume to rend, nor did the Jews,* is being torn and rent apart by the promotion of this lord Peter Leonis.
>
> *There is one faith, one Lord, one baptism.** We know neither two lords nor two faiths nor two baptisms. I read of old that at the time of the flood there was one ark.* In it there were eight souls who were saved;* all the rest perished, and whatever was outside the ark was destroyed. No one will deny that this ark is held to be a type of the church. Another ark has been recently built, and since there are now two, it must be that one of them is a sham and must be swallowed up in the sea. If the ark that Peter Leonis rules is from God, then the ark that Innocent rules must go under.
>
> In that case the Eastern church will perish, the whole of the West will perish, France will perish, Germany will perish, Spain will perish, and so will England; the barbarian kingdoms will sink into the depths. The religious of the Camaldolese and the Carthusians, the Cistercians and the Premonstratensians, and all the other innumerable congregations of God's

**John 19:24

*Eph 4:5

*Gen 6:15
*1 Pet 3:20

servants and his handmaids must go down into
the abyss in that great hurricane. The bishops
and the abbots and all the other princes of the
church, all of them *with a millstone tied to their
necks, will be swallowed up in the greedy jaws of
the depths.** Among all the princes of the world
this Roger alone will have entered the ark of
Peter, and while all the rest are done away
with, he alone will be saved. God forbid that
the religion of the whole world should perish
and that the ambitious Peter Leonis, whose
life is too well-known (and what a life!),
should gain the Kingdom of heaven.

*Matt 18:6

[46] Hearing these words, those who were present
could not contain themselves any longer but recoiled
from the life of Peter Leonis and his cause. Taking Peter
by the hand, the abbot then stood up and lifted him
up, saying, "If you now believe my advice, let us enter
together into the safer ark." Cardinal Peter was mentally convinced by this. He acknowledged the salutary
implication of these words and, cooperating with God's
grace, was at once persuaded. So he went back into the
city and was reconciled to Pope Innocent.[30]

But the king was not willing to accept the results of
this meeting, because the papal estates of Saint Peter in
the provinces of Cassino and Benevento, on which he
had his eye, were widespread, and he considered that
by keeping the Romans in suspense about this matter
he could extort a legal right to the privileges he had
established for himself. Like Herod, who mocked the
Savior when he saw him, he desired to see him when
he was absent but mocked him when he was present.
But Almighty God *gives to men the glory that he received
from the Father** and makes despicable those who mock
him while lifting the humble up to the heights.

*John 17:22

---

[30] *Fragm* I.38 (VP 293–95; *Notes* 142–47).

Now we come to the cure of a nobleman in Salerno. Although he had been under very well-known doctors practicing their skills and remedies on him, he despaired of being helped by these doctors. But in the night a person appeared to him and told him to go to Salerno, meet a holy man, and obtain a cure. This person ordered the nobleman to make inquiries and to drink the water from the lavabo where Bernard washed his hands. The nobleman sought, he found, he asked for the water, he drank it, and he was cured. This event was spread abroad through the whole city until it reached the ears of the king and his company. All the people acclaimed the abbot, but the king remained obdurate in his malice, so the abbot returned to Rome, where he reconciled Peter of Pisa and others to the church and restored harmony between Peter and Pope Innocent.

THE DEATH OF PETER LEONIS

[47] There came a time when the malice of the Amorites[31] was at its full, and the avenging *angel now brandishing his sword* passed over the houses whose lintels were sprinkled with the blood of the Lamb.†* Yet when he came to the house of Peter Leonis, he found it unmarked with the sign of salvation.* He struck that wretched man, but he did not discharge his threat there, giving him three days' time for repentance. Peter Leonis abused God's patience, however, so despairing and dying in his sin. His body was given little or no ceremony, and his corpse was buried in a hidden, unknown place. To this day his grave is unknown to Catholics.

*Exod 13:23;
2 Sam 24:16
†Exod 12:23

*Dan 10:11

---

[31] Semitic nomads from two millennia BC.

*Victor IV, 1138

Nonetheless, his party elected another pope for themselves in his place.* They did this not so much because they persisted in the schism but to create a delay during which they could be reconciled to Pope Innocent. But with no delay at all, through the efforts of the man of God, Christ became triumphant. For this foolish pontiff, the heir to Peter Leonis, went to the man of God in secret, and he, Bernard, took him to the feet of the lord Innocent after he had rid himself of insignia that he had usurped. When this happened the city of Rome thankfully rejoiced, for the church was brought back to Innocent and the Roman people could again honor Innocent as their lord and pastor. The abbot of Clairvaux was held in wondrous reverence, and everyone proclaimed him the author of peace and *pater patriae*. The noblemen went where he went, the people acclaimed him, the women followed him, and they all submitted to him with lively minds. But for how long could he tolerate all this glory? For how long could he enjoy such peace after so much labor every day?

He could not agree to receive it for a day, let alone a year. When everything was settled and sorted out, he could not be held in Rome for more than five days. He had exerted himself for seven years* or more to heal the schism. As he left, the whole of Rome followed him, the clergy led the way, the people went to meet him, the whole of the nobility met with him. He could not get away without everyone's grieving, for they idolized him with unbounded love. **[48]** But when he had received permission from Innocent, with peace firmly established, the man of God took his leave, and with the exultation of the whole world he accepted a double portion of their joy.[32]

*1130–1137

---

[32] *Fragm* I.39 (VP 295–96; *Notes* 146–49); *Fragm* I.40 (VP 296; *Notes* 150–51).

Peace Restored*

Meanwhile at Rome, Innocent started to exercise his authority. Visitors came from all parts to meet him. Some came on business, and others came to rejoice with him in thanksgiving. The churches celebrated with solemn processions, and the ordinary people laid down their weapons to listen to the word of the Lord. After so much scarcity and need, the city regained its opulence once more. Discord had disturbed them for a long time, but now genuine peace had returned to them. The wilderness overflows, the deserted places come to life. All people rested *safely under their vine and fig tree*;* at night they rested in security and feared not at all when their doors were open wide.

Given time, Innocent soon restored the ruined church, brought back those who had been exiled, restored the ancient services to the churches that had been banished and had their colonies depopulated. What is more, he gave them gifts suited to their needs. He built a monastery in honor of the martyr Saint Anastasius near Aquae Salviae,[33] which was the first built there. At that time, however, it had a church but no one living there. After the cloisters and buildings had been built and the church reconstructed, the lord pope granted fields and vineyards as an alms for the house and then asked the abbot of Clairvaux to send him a company of brothers, obtaining this request. Bernard, vice-regent of the church of Pisa, was sent,[34] along with religious brothers who served the Lord in that place according to the Rule of Saint Benedict. This foundation grew quickly, and the number of the servants of God multiplied, drawing many local

---

[33] Tre Fontane, founded 625, became Benedictine in 795; in 1140 it was handed to Bernard.

[34] Bernard Paganelli, the future Pope Eugenius III.

men to join them. Their fields were filled with food, and in a short time they had many other properties.

[49] The holy abbot returned home to his exposition of the wedding song, the Song of Songs, which he loved so much. His work was soon distributed in many regions, perfuming them with the sweet odor of its deep meaning, so that the brothers were invited to found other monasteries. These also were subject to his authority. Once founded and established, they placed themselves under the rules of that more strict discipline.

The cities of the different regions also merited to have bishops from this society, beginning with Rome, which was honored by the supreme pontiff. Palestrina had Stephen,[35] a man of full glory. Ostia had Hugh,[36] another notable man. In the Roman Curia itself there were Henry[37] and Bernard,[38] the former a priest and the latter a deacon, both ordained cardinals. In Tuscany, Baldwin,[39] born at Pisa, shone out like the glory of the sun and a great light for the church.

On this side of the Alps, Amadeus was made bishop of Lausanne.[40] At Sion, Garinus,[41] and at Langres, Geoffrey.[42] At Auxerre, Alan of Auxerre.[43] At Nantes, Ber-

---

[35] Cardinal bishop of Palestrina 1141–1144.

[36] Abbot of Tre Fontane, cardinal bishop of Ostia 1150–1158; see Bernard, Ep 290 (SBOp 8:207; James #355).

[37] Henry of Pisa, cardinal priest; see Bernard, Ep 295 (SBOp 8:262; James #360).

[38] Bernard, cardinal deacon of Saint Clement in 1145, bishop of Porto 1158–1176; see Bernard, Ep 302 (SBOp 8:207; James #368).

[39] Baldwin, first Cistercian cardinal, archbishop of Pisa 1137; see Bernard, Ep 144 (SBOp 7:344–46; James #146).

[40] Abbot of Hautcombe 1139, bishop of Lausanne 1145–1159.

[41] Garinus, abbot of Aulps, bishop of Sion 1138–1150; see Bernard, Ep 142 (SBOp 7:340–41; James #151).

[42] Geoffrey de la Roche-Vanneau, abbot of Fontenay 1118, prior of Clairvaux 1128–1138, bishop of Langres 1138–1163.

[43] Monk of Clairvaux 1131, abbot of Larrivour 1140, bishop of Auxerre 1152–1167.

nard.[44] At Beauvais, Henry.[45] At Tournai, Gerard.[46] At
York, Henry Murdac.[47] In Ireland, two bishops, both
named Christian.[48] In Germany, in the city of Coire,
Algotus the wise,*[49] revered in both age and grace.   *bishop

These luminaries taken from Clairvaux made the
above cities shine out by their presence, like a pure
lightning flash, and made their pastoral office strik-
ingly glorious, giving the other bishops an example,
and being humble men, they were set on high.

[50] After Pope Innocent had died, followed by
both his successors, Celestine II and Lucius II, who
died abruptly, Bernard,[50] whom we have formerly
mentioned as the abbot of Saint Anastasius, became
the ordained pope of the city of Rome. Here, because a sedition had arisen among the people who
were making trouble, he shook the dust off his feet
and went to France. And since at Rome they had
devoured and consumed one another with their
fighting, he waited there in France until they had
become tired of their conflicts and oppressed by the
damage and at last desired his presence and opted
for it. Meanwhile he humbly visited Clairvaux after
celebrating a council at Reims, and his pontificate
displayed its glory in the sight of the poor in France.

---

[44] Monk of Clairvaux, bishop of Nantes 1147–1169.

[45] Henry of France, brother of Louis VII; monk of Clairvaux, bishop of Beauvais 1149–1162, archbishop of Reims
1162–1175.

[46] Monk of Clairvaux, abbot of Villers, bishop of Tournai
1149–1166.

[47] Abbot of Vauclair 1134–1143, abbot of Fountains 1143–1147,
archbishop of York 1147–1153.

[48] Monks of Clairvaux, bishops in Ireland. See Debuisson, *La
provenance*, 63.

[49] See Debuisson, *La provenance*, 48.

[50] Bernard Paganelli, abbot of Tre Fontane, Pope Eugenius III
(VP 223, note to 1303).

Everyone marveled at the unchangeable humility shown by such a high-ranking person, for his goodness remained untarnished after such an excellent culmination to the holy enterprise, and he in no way lost his interior balance because of this power. He wore a linen tunic as an undergarment, and day and night he wore his cowl wherever he went or lay down to rest. He retained the habit of a monk interiorly, even when he had to put on his pontifical robes and standard of living, having the difficult task of expressing in one person the functions of several persons. Splendidly embroidered cushions were spread all around him. His bed, covered with a pallium, was enclosed behind a purple curtain, but if one turned back the covering one would find it made up with linen coverlets and a straw-filled mattress.

*Prov 3:4

He was seen as a man, but God was in his heart. He showed himself to be pleasing *before God and men.** With eyes full of tears he spoke to his brothers, mingling his words with sighs drawn from his heart; he exhorted them, consoled them, and showed himself among them not as a lord and teacher but as a brother and companion. When he could not delay there any longer, with a great number of people accompanying him, he bade farewell to his brothers and took his leave, taking the road to Italy, arriving at Rome.

BERNARD'S BOOK ON CONSIDERATION

[51] The holy man wrote a book to this pope,[51] expressing his thoughts and with very perceptive observations putting forth those matters that concerned him and those below him, but also the things above

---

[51] Csi (SBOp 3:379–493).

him rising up to the nature of God, so that he seemed
*to be assumed into the third heaven,** where *he heard*   *2 Cor 12:2
*things that cannot be told, that no man may utter,** and   *2 Cor 12:4
*looked on the king in his beauty.** The things below him   *Isa 33:1
and concerning him are those about the customs in
society, the equality of nature, the diversity of offices,
the distinction of merits, the discerning of the very
subtle judgments having to do with promotion to
high offices, and the recognition given to all persons
in their state of life.

In those things that are above human thoughts, he
gave his attention to heavenly matters, not in the way
that the angels contemplate, those who always adhere
to God, but in the way that a man with a pure heart
and mind may conform the temporal priesthood to
the celestial hierarchy. Since in the heavenly army
it is enacted that some have dominion over others
and ministering spirits are delegated to different offices at the bidding of the higher powers, any who
closely assist them receive from them what they wish
to be done or understood by others. And since a
man in the office of superior is shown reverence, it
is only right that all things should be referred to the
Supreme Power, since because a person is subject
to another person and a spirit is subject to another
spirit, each one should in the first place be subject
to God. Leadership is a gift from God. It is clear that
knowledge of the Lord himself is made manifest by
faith and by hope, and favorable access to divine
contemplation is given as God's gift.

The man of God dictated these things and sometimes wrote them on writing tablets, giving sweetness
to the wax and indeed more grace to the tablets. He
settled the strife between churches, imparting calm and
kindness with a breath of fresh air to those importunate
appeals that raised discord among clerics. Sometimes,
even with a sharp rebuke, he restored tranquility. When

the angry crowds came in a turbulent spirit and with an angry flow of words poured out their complaints before him, they returned home pacified.

Count Theobald's Humility and Generosity

[52] Count Theobald[52] was more devoted to Bernard than were the other princes, and his love was enhanced with good works. He gave Clairvaux offerings both of himself and from what he possessed, and he placed his very soul in the hands of the abbot. He put aside his princely importance, showing himself among the servants of God as a fellow servant, not as a lord, so that in all things he heard and responded to whatever the house needed, however small. He bought farmlands, constructed houses, and offered large donations to new abbacies; wherever the servants of God extended their properties, he gave them gifts of money. These deeds applied not to one house alone, as when King Solomon built his house at Jerusalem,* but wherever the monks settled in this fashion, he made an effort to provide for them and made a dwelling place for them as if Christ was present in that site. He also placed this in the free hand of the man of God so that he paid the expenses for whatever they needed for the *Opus Dei*.

*1 Kgs 5–8

When the abbot saw the responsive mind of the prince, he fired his devotion with devotion and asked him to be especially *submissive to those who were of the*

---

[52] Fourth count of Blois and second count of Champagne; son of Stephen of Blois and Adela, daughter of William the Conqueror. See Jean A. Truax, "*Miles Christi:* Count Theobald IV of Blois and Saint Bernard of Clairvaux," CSQ 44, no. 3 (2009): 299–320.

*household of the faith** and to agree to support these
immortal temples, so disposing his alms wisely that
they might always bear good fruit and continually bear
new fruit for the additional houses that were springing
up. Thus for those in need, whose grinding poverty
here and there had agitated them as if stung by wasps,
the count learned to have compassion in many ways,
giving clothing to some and food to others. Bernard
advised and suggested to him that he should by himself
visit hostelries* and not flinch from the face of the
sick, because in such acts lies a twofold clemency, in
seeing and caring, but also in consoling and refreshing. He indicated to the count that his principal office as a prince, required as a duty, was that he should
incline to the praise of goodness and the punishment
of evil. He instructed him that this office included
humbling those who oppressed the poor, defending
orphans, showing compassion to widows with words
of consolation, dispensing words of right judgment,
providing for the peace and quiet of the church, and
understanding the rudiments of the use of the sword.

[53] These and other salutary cautions the man
received in a reasonable and reverent way and changed
the excesses of his court and his own arrogant pride
into humility and honesty. From then on no one dared
to do or say anything unbecoming in his presence.
But those who were making an effort to please him,
either by guile or with good intentions, often put into
practice what they saw their lord liked. So those who
were close to him made known to him the poor who
suffered calumny; they told him about those lying sick
in the streets and anyone who was weighed down
with bitterness or misery. He was happy to be given
the opportunity of offering indulgence, and he willingly embraced this very high grace. He saw that the
man of God would not allow any person of his own
to hold back, either in his court or in his cause, from

*Gal 6:10

*xenodochia

being solicitous for those in need. He assigned two religious of the Premonstratensian Order to give alms on his behalf; to their care he assigned the castles and towns of the district in which he dwelled to bring to his table the sick and the lepers to be fed and clothed abundantly as long as they lived there. For other poor people, however, he insisted that the ministry of these two religious should provide ample alms proportionate to their needs both in food and clothing.

Only with those in his own house did he wish to live as the lord. So he gave to the manservants and cooks and other ministers the power to order what they wanted and take what pleased them, nor was anyone to prohibit anything or refer it to the count if the ministers seemed to be generous. These two previously mentioned men, who feared God and desired to please him and the count also, did not diminish the magnificence of the prince, who ordered the fullness of charity to be fulfilled toward his own people. These ministers did not wish to be ungrateful to God. Both the will of God and the eminent goodness of the prince prevented their being idle or greedy where they should be eager, zealous, and lavish dispensers.

Moreover, these men, as monks and religious, who were sent on many business affairs to the court, were responsible for providing hospitality from the count's stores and barns. Even in the coldest days of winter they took with them prepared bundles of clothing for the poor, sheepskins and weatherproof coats, and footwear properly greased, with which they provided for the needs of those in the villages. No work of mercy was lacking in that county; at the seaport all the boats had safe harbor.

In time of famine, unlike Pharaoh, *who sold grain to* *Gen 42:6* *the people** and subjected Egypt to slavery when they asked for provisions, but like the holy abbot, like another Joseph, the count became as a divinely inspired

counselor and *freely opened the barns** for the needy; he
did not impoverish the people or oppress the afflicted
with cunning or transfer to himself public funds for
private use or bury them as personal treasures in the
ground. Rather, *laying up his treasures in heaven,** as a
tireless distributor he distributed his money and his
wealth with the greatest dispatch.

THE KING AND THE PRINCES ATTACK THE COUNT

[54] The temptation to despise this man who so
sighed* for heavenly things was becoming enormous.
The king as well as the princes attacked him; *the earth
was moved and trembled,** and it seemed that *God was
angry.** Almost everything that he had was exposed
to rapine and fire and plunder, and the army of the
king *covered the face of the earth.** Everything was devastated throughout. Nor was he safe to resist or meet
his persecutors, because his own people deserted him
without scruple and invaded his properties, and those
who insidiously remained were of no help. Everywhere there was serious want, because neither could
anyone shelter him at home nor could anyone provide
what was needed outside, since not one of his own
people welcomed him, on account of both the perfidy
of those fleeing and the duplicity of his people.

In the thick of all these troubles the count turned to
the Lord of heaven, seeking help; he relied heavily on
the counsel of the man of God, whom he summoned
for advice, and he did not despair of God's mercy.* He
accepted Bernard's answer to these troubles. It then
dawned on him that God often chastises the child
whom he loves* and by these reproofs tests the soul
and proves its sincerity. Thus the soul becomes like Job,
more splendid *when he was seated on his dunghill** than
the one who sat unharmed on his throne surrounded

*Gen 41:56

*Matt 6:20

*inhianti

*Ps 17:8
*Ps 17:8

*Num 22:5

*Luke 10:20

*Heb 12:6;
Prov 3:12

*Job 2:8

by his army. The holy man showed the count that
Solomon sinned while in idleness and abused the gifts
of peace, letting them drift down into vice.* And when
his father David was fleeing from his son Absalom and
the whole of Israel was incensed against him, David
remained in gracious peace.* Bernard also pointed out
*how Satan had harrassed the apostle,** but in his trouble
he remained steadfast, meriting to be heard, *for virtue
is made perfect in weakness.** In the present life we who
are sluggish become prosperous, and those who are
circumspect become impoverished.

[55] When he heard these things the worthy count
livened up considerably and quickly ordered that two
huge gold vessels of splendid workmanship, with precious stones worked into them, be brought out. His
uncle Henry, the king of England,* for the solemnity
of his crowning had had them fashioned to show off
his riches and his glory, and he was accustomed to
have them placed on his banqueting table. The count
ordered that the gems be extracted from their settings
and the gold broken up and sold, so that from their
value tabernacles should be founded *worth more than
gold and green topaz.** Though Amalech did not cease
from troubling Israel, Moses by lifting up his hands
to heaven gained the victory,* and so, withdrawing
himself from hostilities, as a solicitous mediator the
holy abbot went out to fight for those crying to God
and weeping for the brothers at home, so that *reconciliation was made in a time of wrath.** When the storms
had died down among those sent to intercede on
behalf of God, tranquility and the desired serenity of
peace returned between the king and the prince.[53]

*1 Kgs 11:1-11

*2 Sam 15:1-13
*2 Cor 12:7

*2 Cor 12:9

*Henry I,
r. 1100–1135

*Sir 44:17

*Deut 25:17-19

*Sir 44:17

---

[53] The MSB manuscript lacks the closing rubric found in another manuscript of Recension B (Copenhagen Royal Library,
MS Gl. Kgl. Samling 181, fol. 63v), which reads, "The end of
the second book. The beginning of the third."

Book 3

BY GEOFFREY OF AUXERRE
(CALLED BOOK 1 BY GEOFFREY)

*Here begins the prologue to the final three small
books on the life of Saint Bernard, abbot.*[1]

Distinguished men commend the memory of
the renowned abbot of Clairvaux, Bernard
our father, for his writings in the praise of
Christ and the edification of many people. The truth
of his actions are more certainly made known, insofar
as anyone can do so, after discovering the deep meaning in his words. It must seem to many that one of
his children, one of his sons, and one of his students
should be silent rather than write about such sanctity,
such dignity, and such goodness. After about thirteen
years, during which I could not speak without tears,
I can no longer remember, nor can I offer anything;
he alone, he alone could do this, but death took him
away. Would that what I write could please you now,
holy father, as it seemed to do when once I pleased
you. Who am I other than a debtor to you? Who am
I but a wretch? Who am I but yours?

Death took him, I confess; an improvident death
swallowed him up but did not devour him totally.
Cut off, not destroyed; mercy accepted the portion
that was his. Death took him from sight, took away

---

[1] Geoffrey added this prologue in his revision (Recension B)
of the first version of the *Vita*. Sections 11 and 31 of Recension
A do not appear in Recension B.

his words, even took his bodily allegiance, but it did not snatch away the trust of his presence, or his goodness; it did not consume forever the hope of a future vision or take with it the love of filial devotion, deeply rooted as it is in the memory of his past.

I have neither the knowledge nor the eloquence, as I know too well, to supply a word worthy of this task. But neither the genius of Origen nor the tongue of Cicero would suffice to portray your praises or your great deeds. Prudent readers should be able to gather the fruit from your works rather than despairing of the unworthy foliage of my words, so that when they have tasted the sweetness of those works, rather than blaming the sterile appearance of my foliage, they may enjoy the taste of those before cracking their teeth on the harmful effects of mine. What is seen is usually more securely and more sincerely remembered than what is heard; again, the cup gulped down too easily sours the stomach. Water is drunk more sweetly when it is drawn from the narrow channel at its source than when collected from scattered pipes or from a very long river or copious stream.* So I do not want to appear to have built on a different foundation than did those who wrote about the early days of our most blessed father or even about his middle years. Yet when it comes to those things that I have written about (for I was present among almost all of them), perhaps I may be allowed to insert a few things from the reports of those brothers who were present at the time.

With this goal in mind, the reader will find this book divided into three parts. The first part chiefly follows what pertains to the way of life and the teaching of this blessed father. The second speaks of the many powerful things he did. The third completes his life in good faith, with the warning that in telling these things, I have desired to stick to like

*See Jerome, *Against Helvidius* 8

matters rather than to a time sequence. Indeed I have written neither the signs nor the works in the order in which they took place but sometimes inserted them at opportune places. It seems stronger and more acceptable to shape the work as a building supported on suitable columns and to illustrate it with examples. Also I have transposed some things to join similar matters and to make them concur with things of the same kind. But these things apply to the two former books, for in the third the events are nearly always in the order of time sequence.

The Prologue ends; the first book begins.

[1] With innumerable signs and miracles the whole world, as everyone knows, glorifies Bernard, the abbot of Clairvaux, faithful servant of God, for just as God is glorious in his saints,* so he is   *Ps 67:36
marvelous in his majesty. Besides, just as he himself commended Saint Malachy,* his first and greatest   *V Mal
miracle, he showed himself to be the same: serene in face, modest in habit, circumspect in words, fearing God in deed, assiduous in meditation, and devout in prayer. And just as he warned others, so he himself was only too aware from his own experience that in everything fidelity to prayer is more important than one's own efforts or work. He was high-minded in faith, untiring in hope, overflowing in charity, unbeaten in humility, foremost in piety. In counsel he was provident, efficacious in business, and yet never less idle than in leisure for God. He was cheerful when under pressure yet bashful when praised. His way of life was gentle, his holiness was well merited, and his miracles were glorious; so too he was *rich in wisdom and virtue and grace before God and men.**   *Luke 2:52

His Physical Appearance

*Gen 2:18
*Ps 20:4

God makes for himself a helper of this holy soul *like unto himself,** and he fashions a body with a special foreseen blessing.** There shone out in his flesh a certain grace that was more spiritual than fleshly, and in his face there was a radiance that was bright not in an earthly but in a spiritual way. His eyes shone with purity like an angel's and the simplicity of a dove. Such beauty pertained to the interior man, and the indications clearly emerged as evidence. The whole man seemed to be externally pervaded with the store of internal purity and overflowing grace. His body was very thin, indeed almost without flesh, yet on his cheeks there was the slightest touch of redness.

He had a natural warmth within him, however, induced by prolonged meditation and the pursuit of holy compunction. His hair was a reddish yellow, and his beard a little redder, toward the end of his life mingled with grey. He was not very tall, though his lean body made him look taller. *This treasure in an* *2 Cor 4:7 *earthen vessel** was utterly broken and shaken up. His flesh labored under many sicknesses and weaknesses, so that because of them *the power of his soul was made* *2 Cor 12:9 *perfect.** Of all these weaknesses the most troublesome was the narrowness of his throat, which hardly allowed him to eat any dry or solid food. The problem with his stomach was more serious, and also that of his diseased entrails. These problems were continuous, apart from other ailments that occurred more often.

This servant of God took great care to avoid any special show, making himself just one among the others. Glory followed him while he ran from it, however, just as it is accustomed to flee from those trying to capture it. He had a proverb frequently on his lips and always in his heart: "The one who does what no one else does makes everyone wonder."

With this thought in mind he was the more eager to follow the regular common life, preferring in his actions not to be singular in his observance. For this reason he preferred to remove the hair shirt that he had worn secretly for many years when it became known that he wore it, holding that a person who does not follow the common rules of his profession demonstrates no desire for hiddenness. There was, however, a singular purity in the things he did in common with others, and his devotion was not at all commonplace. Neglecting nothing, he did even the smallest things with care and attention, and from his own experience he often defined the sage as one who savors things just as they are.[2]

BERNARD'S TABLE HABITS

[2] From his earliest years he avoided things pleasant to the taste, so that for the most part he lost his ability to discern their taste. Very often a pious fraud of those serving him deceived him, so that he forgetfully took one thing instead of another. By mistake he once drank oil that had been offered to him and was completely unaware of it.[3] Nor did he notice what he had done even when another person, who was looking on, marveled that his lips were closed. His bread was no more than a morsel completely softened in warm water, taken with a few drops. Indeed he was moderate in eating, but his stomach rejected even the smallest part of uncooked food, and though his will forced him to take food, with some peril, when he took any food at all pain made him reject it.

---

[2] SC 50.6 (SBOp 2:81; CF 31:35).
[3] See also bk. 1.33 (VP 1:59).

Thus a kind of dispensation from above provided for this faithful servant according to the desire of his heart, so that he gained the benefits of remarkable abstinence, and hiding it under the cover of necessity, he always managed to avoid any taint of ostentation. With regard to wine, he often said to us, "It becomes a monk to be so careful as to taste the drink without emptying the cup." He dealt with himself this way: as often as he allowed wine to be brought to him, it was seen after the meal that the vessel from which he had drunk seemed to be hardly tasted and indeed almost as full afterward as before.

HIS LOVE OF MEDITATION

He was not able to stand for long but was almost always seated, and he rarely fidgeted. As often as he could, he escaped matters of business to pray, read, or write. Sometimes he engaged in teaching for the instruction of the brothers or else gave himself *to holy meditation.** In this spiritual occupation he obtained the singular grace of undergoing no boredom or any difficulty, dwelling freely within himself and walking *in the broadness of his heart,** where he offered Christ *a large dining room furnished** and bade others to do the same. Every moment given to meditation was too brief; every place was suitable for it.

Despite this love for meditation, however, his reverence for God often took hold of him, or rather the Spirit did so, and he put off this comfort in order to pursue more fruitful gains, *having learned to seek what was useful not for himself but for the many.** Apart from this, whatever company of people or noisy crowd he was in, as long as the matter did not call for his attention, he recollected his mind with total interior facility and tasted the delights of inward solitude, which he

*Ps 18:15

*1 Kgs 4:29
*Mark 14:15

*1 Cor 10:33

carried around within him, heedless of what was going on around him or what he saw outside of himself.

BERNARD VISITS HUGH OF GRENOBLE AND THE CARTHUSIANS

[3] When the servant of God had stayed at Clairvaux a few years, it came to his mind that he should visit Hugh, the holy bishop of Grenoble,[4] and the Carthusian brothers for the sake of devotion.[5] This bishop received him gladly and with such reverence that, perceiving the divine presence in his guest, he prostrated himself on the ground. When the servant of Christ saw this, that an elderly man, so distinguished and renowned for his holiness, was falling down before him, he was extremely shocked and likewise threw himself on the ground before him. So Hugh finally received Bernard with the kiss of peace and complained with sighs of protest about his humility, confused by such a man's veneration. From that time on Bernard obtained a special place in Hugh's heart, so that these two children of splendor became *of one heart and one soul,** enjoying one another in Christ.   *Acts 4:32
Like the queen of Sheba testifying about Solomon, they found in one another something *far surpassing the report that had been spread abroad.**   *1 Kgs 10:4-7

[4] The servant of Christ was also received at Chartreuse by that very reverend man Guigo the prior[6] and by the rest of the brethren with the same love and the same reverence, and they *welcomed him with great joy.** They found in his actual presence what   *Luke 1:44

---

[4] Hugh of Châteauneuf, bishop of Grenoble (1080–1132).

[5] VP 224, note to 3.88.

[6] Guigo I (1084–1136) became fifth prior of Grand Chartreuse in 1109.

*2 Cor 10:11   they had formerly discovered in his letter to Guigo.[7] Though they were uplifted by everything else, however, the Carthusian prior was disturbed about one thing, the fine trappings of the horse on which the venerable man rode, which did not point to poverty or hardship. This prior, a man who loved virtue, could

*Jer 50:45   not keep silent about *what he had in his mind** but mentioned it to one of the brothers and confessed that he was concerned and wondered about it.

When the brother told the holy man what Guigo had said, he himself was surprised about the harness, because he had come from Clairvaux to Chartreuse without ever noticing the harness, had never even considered it, and had no idea what it was like until this very moment. Nor was the horse his own but borrowed from a monk of Cluny who was his uncle, where he had stayed for a while in the district; he had taken it just as his uncle had it usually fitted out. When the prior heard these words he was all the more astonished that the servant of God had circumcised his eyes outwardly and occupied his mind inwardly to such an extent that what he himself had noticed at once Bernard had not seen during the whole journey. Again, trotting beside the lake of Lausanne the whole day, he did not even see the lake, or if he saw it he did not see it. That evening when his companions were chatting about the lake, he asked them where the lake was, and they were all amazed to hear the question.

BERNARD'S WAY OF LIFE

[5] Right from the start he desired to keep himself away from business affairs and never went outside

---

[7] Bernard, Ep 11 (SBOp 7:52–60; James #12) or Ep 12 (SBOp 7:61–62; James #13).

but stayed in the monastery. Afterward, because of his failing health, he kept to it until the occasion arose when he was forced to go out because of the needs of the church of God and the demand of the supreme pontiff and of all the abbots of the Order, to which he deferred in all things as to the fathers, though he was himself the father of all. At their injunction in his later years, besides his cowl and robe, he wore a woolen cape, cut short like a shawl, and a skullcap, but in spite of his ailments and fatigue he never agreed to use woolen fleeces. Poverty always pleased him in regard to his clothing, but never things that were soiled or dirty. For he said that they were indications of a mind that was either negligent or foolishly dwelling on glory for oneself or on external attachment to human approval.*   *Matt 6:16

His gait and bearing were modest and well disciplined, with a preference for humility, suggesting recollection while showing grace and exacting reverence. The very sight of his happy and uplifting ways affected those who saw him. Regarding laughter, we may quote what we have frequently heard him say; when he observed religious people cackling with mirth, he was baffled, because he could not remember at any time laughing like that from the very moment of his conversion, so he had to make more effort to laugh than to suppress it. Laughter for him needed a spur rather than a bridle.

[6] His voice, though coming from an invalid, was both forceful and intelligible, since God *had chosen him out from the womb of his mother** for the work of   *Gal 1:15
preaching.* He found his words to be an opportune   *see bk. 1.2
way to build up the souls of the listeners, so he knew how to adapt them to the lives and the understanding of each individual and to the benefit of every one of his hearers. Thus he spoke to the country folk as if he had always been brought up as a local, but to

other folk of a different class he made every effort to
respond to their occupations. To the learned he was a
literary person, to those who were simple he was very
simple, and to those who were spiritual he was flu-
ent in the teachings of perfection and wisdom. He
adapted himself to all, *seeking to gain all to Christ.**

*1 Cor 9:19

He was skillful in following what he had written
to Pope Eugenius, coming from the fullness of his
heart: "If idle words are sometimes brought up, tolerate
them, but never let them be repeated. To prevent these
idle words handle them cautiously and prudently. You
should break into them with some serious subject,
which though not so useful, may be heard willingly
so that they take the place of the silly ones."[8] **[7]** God
gave him a tongue that was pleasing and persuasive
and also cultured so that he knew to whom he should
speak and when to speak it, so that some needed consolation or appeal, some he was able to exhort or
rebuke.* Sometimes those who had read his writings
often heard his words even though far away from him.

*see RB 2.31-35

Indeed *grace poured out from his lips;** *his words were
a fire burning strongly,** so that no pen, however skillful, could match all that sweetness or recount all that
fervor. *Honey and milk were under his tongue,** and still
the law was like a flame in his mouth, as we read
in the Song of Songs: *His lips were as a scarlet head-
band, and sweet his speech.** When he was speaking to
the Germanic people, he was listened to with great
love, and even though they could not understand
his words, however expertly the interpreter spoke
after him, rendering his meaning, it seemed that the
warmth of his words edified them more, and they felt
instead the power of his words. The proof of this lay
in their thumping their breasts and shedding tears.

*Ps 44:3

*Ps 118:140

*Song 4:10

*Song 4:3

---

[8] Csi 2.13.22 (SBOp 3:429–30; CF 37:76).

He used the Scriptures so freely, so relevantly, that instead of following them, he paved the way for them as he liked, taking their author, the Holy Spirit, as his lead. *In the midst of the church God opened his mouth* and filled him with the spirit of wisdom and understanding,** and according to what we read in the book of Job, *the depth of the rivers he has searched, and hidden things he has brought to light.** As he himself confessed, sometimes when he was meditating and praying, the whole of the Sacred Scripture appeared to him as if it were placed open before him. **[8]** Besides, who could preach so worthily as he who so freely evangelized? Who was so worthy of admiration? It meant little to him to strive for accolades, nor would he agree to receive marks of distinction. He believed that there was little to be gained in seeking transitory advantages for himself; rather, he often refused the ecclesiastical dignities offered to him.

Like another David when going out to war, he argued strongly against *weapons of war,** by which during his lifetime he saw many seriously injured, and his own victory was to be found more gloriously in his simplicity. God's power gave such grace to him that *he chose to be as a cast-off in the house of God,** where he bore more fruit than others who chose to be in high places. He shone out and lit up the church more beautifully like one *under the bushel basket* of humility than others *set up on a lampstand.** The more humble he was in himself, however, the more useful he was for the people of God because of his salutary teaching, but in his teaching he never wanted to hold the place of a master. Clearly blessed, as he used to say of one of the saints, "*he loved the law,** yet he did not have his eye on the seat of authority." Although he would gladly have merited to sit on the high chair of virtue, he would have nothing to do with presiding in the chair of dignity.

*Heb 2:12

*Isa 11:2;
Sir 15:5

*Job 28:11

*2 Sam 1:27

*Ps 83:11

*Matt 5:15

*Ps 118:163

Finally, just as he was upright and strong when he undertook the preaching of the gospel, in the same way he was prudent and cautious always to avoid any prelacy in the church. He never showed the slightest arrogance in his refusals, but although he was frequently elected to the most important and the most honorable functions, he acted prudently, and with the cooperation of divine grace he managed to avoid being constrained to accept them. The holy man Moses ceded the priestly office to his brother Aaron, for he had an impediment in his speech.* No ordinary requirement could turn our Bernard away from preaching the gospel, but his humility kept him away from accepting honors. Quite rightly, then, did he obtain a special grace in the sight of God and people. He placed the gospel first, without gaining anything of worldly influence, without climbing any step of ecclesiastical dignity, but not without the fruit of fraternal salvation: he always took care to be of profit to the people of God, but never did he attempt to rule over them.*

*Exod 4:10

*see RB 64.8

BERNARD'S RELUCTANCE TO PREACH

Rarely did he go out to preach, and then only to local places, but sometimes when some necessity drew him out, *he sowed the word of God over all the streams** publicly and privately. He did so at the command of the supreme pontiff or at the request of another patron whenever something was happening where he should be present. In effect, so great was his humility in these matters that he preferred to leave them to priests, who, he understood, were more fully entitled to the reverence due to ministers of Christ.

*Isa 32:20

[9] But we cannot be silent about the complaints made against him from certain people who through

either simplicity or malice took offense at his preaching the crusade to Jerusalem, since the outcome was so dreadfully sad. Still, we need to say that this event did not originate with him. For when the bold enterprise moved a great number of people, including the king of France, to implore him again and again about this matter, and he even received letters about it from the pope, he did not agree to become involved or to give his opinion on it until a general edict from the supreme pontiff ordered him to expound the matter in the manner of the Roman church to the people and the princes. The whole tenor of this edict was that they should actively take up the route of the crusade for penance and the remission of sins, either to free their brothers or to lay down their own lives for them. They were able to announce these things and the like truthfully, but what was to be related was more easily said than done.

PREACHING THE CRUSADE

He obviously preached this crusade[9] *while the Lord worked with him and confirmed the message by the signs that attended it.** But how great and how many were these miraculous signs? It would be difficult to give the numbers or relate them all. For at the time they began to be noted, the number of the things was too much for the writer to write down, and the details were too much for the author to record. Indeed, on one day alone more than twenty people were healed of various complaints, nor did a single day go by without something of this sort happening. So, at that time Christ, through the touch and prayer of his servant,

*Mark 16:20

---

[9] The Second Crusade, at Vézelay, March 31, 1146.

caused *those blind from their mother's womb to see, cripples to walk, the maimed to be healed, the deaf to hear, and the dumb to speak.** Thus in an astonishing way grace restored what could not be attained from nature.

*Matt 15:30-31

[10] Had they not set out on this mission, the Eastern church would not have been liberated, nor would the heavenly church be completed and filled with exultation. But if it should please God to use such an occasion to free so many from the Western church of their sins, and if the body of the Eastern church should not have been freed from the pagan hordes, who would dare to say to him, *Why have you done this?** Or who is there thinking with discernment about their misfortune who would not sorrow at those who had returned to their former evil habits or even worse ones, or who had returned their souls to Christ purged with the fruit of repentance and yet fallen into various tribulations? Otherwise, like the Egyptians who complained, so these children of darkness complain who could not see the truth or profit: *Craftily he brought them out that he might kill them in the desert.** But the Savior bears insults patiently when the salvation of so many souls is the price to be paid.

*Rom 9:20

*Exod 32:12

The venerable father himself remembered these words when he said, among other things, "If we must choose between one thing and another, I would prefer that men grumble about us than about God. I am happy if God deigns to use me as a shield, and I would willingly accept the detraction of evil tongues and the painful thorns of blasphemy rather than that they be directed against him. I do not refuse to become dishonored if I can prevent dishonor being attributed to the glory of God." He wrote these things in the second book of *On Consideration.*[10]

---

[10] Csi 2.1.4 (SBOp 3:413; CF 37:51).

It happened that when the first rumor of the lamentable destruction of their army reached France, a father offered his blind son to the servant of God with many prayers that he might receive his sight and overcome his lack of faith. The holy man placed his hand on the boy and prayed to the Lord, so that if the word of his preaching should go out from him, if his spirit should be with the preacher, God would deign to show his light. So when after this prayer the answer was given to the prayer, the boy said, "*What shall I do?** I can see." All those who were present started cheering, for there were many people there, apart from the brothers who, delighted that the boy could see, were greatly encouraged and gave thanks to God. So much for that.

*Jer 33:9

[12] For the sake of posterity it should be remembered that the teaching of Bernard was a great benefit for the holy church in correcting the conduct of Catholics, in suppressing the fury of the schismatics, and in refuting the errors of the heretics. Indeed, apart from this he taught them *to live sober, upright, and godly lives in the world** and persuaded many to bid farewell to the world for the more perfect way. Or he made it clear that as long as they did not leave the desert of the world, they should live the life of those who had deserted the world. In this way the prophetic word was to be fulfilled bodily: *He has turned a desert into pools of water and a parched land into springs of water. And there he lets the hungry live, and they establish a town to live in, and they sow fields and plant vineyards and yield a fruitful birth. By his blessing they multiply.** But during the time of the General Schism, the servant of the Lord *stood in the breach before him to turn away his wrath from destroying them,** since obviously *in the time of wrath he was made reconciliation,* and a disaster no longer ensued.

*Titus 2:12

*Ps 106:35-38

*Ps 105:23

Meanwhile it should be enough just to quote the words of Pope Innocent himself, writing to Bernard about this matter:

> How firmly and constantly did you labor in
> the cause of Blessed Peter and the Roman
> church, your mother, when by the schism of
> Peter Leonis, the fervor and discretion of your
> Catholic religion needed to be defended.
> Placing yourself as an unyielding defense in
> the cause of the house of God, you changed
> the minds of kings and princes and many oth-
> ers, both ecclesiastical and secular persons, into
> supporting the unity of the church and obedi-
> ence to ourselves and that of Blessed Peter
> with frequent arguments strengthened by
> reason, which showed itself for the great ad-
> vantage of the church of God and ourself.[11]

BERNARD AND PETER ABELARD

*Matt 24:45

How *the faithful and prudent servant** acted magnificently for the faith is now briefly added. **[13]** There
was at that time a famous and celebrated teacher,
Peter Abelard by name, learned and astute, though
dogmatic in his perfidious faith.[12] His writings took
wings and flew around everywhere, though full of se-

---

[11] Innocent II, *Privilegium Sancto Bernardo concessum* (PL 183:
554–56).

[12] Watkin Williams, *Saint Bernard of Clairvaux* (Manchester,
UK: Manchester University Press, 1935), 289–313; see also Sister
Edmée [Kingsmill], "Bernard and Abelard," in *The Influence of St
Bernard*, ed. Benedicta Ward, Fairacres Publications 60 (Oxford:
Fairacres, 1976), 89–134; Sister Edmée here clarifies with depth
and insight the forces that underpinned the movements in the
eleventh and twelfth centuries that ultimately led to the conflict
between Abelard and Bernard, their strengths and weaknesses, and
their influence on their own and subsequent generations. For a
more critical study of Bernard's role in this debate, see A. Victor
Murray, *Abelard and St Bernard; A Study in Twelfth Century "Modernism"* (Manchester, UK: Manchester University Press, 1967).

rious blasphemies. Certain well-informed and faithful men recounted the profane novelties contained
in the words and their meanings to the man of God.
Bernard had a private meeting with Abelard where
he admonished him, only out of his goodness and
kindness, not wishing to rebuke him or condemn
him. In this meeting Bernard was both modest and
rational, so Peter was sufficiently contrite and promised to make all the corrections that Bernard had suggested. When Peter had gone away from this meeting,
however, he was persuaded by the malign counsel of
friends and his own subtle skill with words. Confident in his own unfortunate ability in disputes, he
reneged on those sounder proposals.

He then went to the metropolitan of Sens and
asked that a great council should soon be proclaimed
in his church, complaining that the abbot of Clairvaux had secretly denounced his books. He added
that he was prepared to defend his works in public
and asked that the abbot, if he had anything to say,
should be called to the council.[13] This was done as
he desired, but when the abbot was called, he refused to come, saying that it was not his business.
Nevertheless, bowing to the strong feelings of many
important men that a great scandal would be given
to the people from his absence and the power of
his antagonist, he finally sadly agreed to go, but not
without sincere regret, as he wrote to Pope Innocent
in a letter,[14] in which he more fully and more clearly
explained the whole affair.

[14] The moment arrived, and the whole church
was packed. The servant of God set forth the writings
of Peter in full view and pointed out the chief errors

---

[13] The Council of Sens, June 1140.
[14] Ep 190 (SBOp 8:17–40; omitted from James).

therein. Then he gave him these options: either to deny them, humbly to correct them, or to give his reply if he could, basing his response on the objections put to him on the authority of the holy fathers of the church. But Peter was unwilling to come to his senses; nor was he able *to resist the wisdom and spirit of him who spoke to him,** so to gain time he appealed to the Apostolic See. Then a well-respected member of the Catholic faith made it clear to him that he could reply, knowing that nothing would be done against him personally, and he would be listened to freely and securely with complete patience and without any threat of a judgment against him, but he absolutely refused.

*Acts 6:10

Afterward he confessed to his friends, as they admit, that at that moment his memory was confused, his mind went blank, and his wits forsook him. The council he had convened dismissed him, however, and punished him as an abomination, condemning his teaching as perverse but not going so far as his person. But when Peter looked for refuge in the see of Peter, how long could he dissent from the faith of Peter? The apostolic visitor enclosed the author* in the same sentence as the council had, condemning his errors, burning his writings, and condemning him to silence.

*i.e., Abelard

Gilbert de la Porrée

[15] The bishop of Poitiers was known as Gilbert de la Porrée,*[15] a man very learned in sacred studies. But what was considered as sublime teaching was really *as folly to him.** Speaking on the unity of the Blessed

*bishop 1141–1154

*Ps 21:3

---

[15] Williams, *Saint Bernard of Clairvaux*, 313–19.

Trinity and the Divine Simplicity, he did not think in a simple manner or write according to the faith, but he *propounded hidden bread and offered stolen waters;** nor was it easy to know what he meant, or rather what he did not mean, when he spoke of the Real Persons. He feared what Peter Abelard is supposed to have said to him at Sens:"When your neighbor's house is burning, fear for your own walls that day."[16]

*Prov 9:17

Finally, since scandal was rapidly worsening about this among the faithful and the rumors were increasing, Gilbert was called to appear and ordered to bring his book, in which there were certain serious errors, though the words were veiled in camouflage. And so in the council in the city of Reims, which Pope Eugenius attended, there was a conflict between Bernard, that notable wrestler, and Gilbert de la Porée for the holy church. After Bernard clearly revealed all the mockery that obscured the errors, he then with indisputable logic and the testimony of the holy fathers demolished them in a disputation that went on for two days. Allowing for the fact that those who presided were already aware of the blasphemy in the teaching but nevertheless avoiding any personal injury, he was inflamed with zeal and additionally convoked on his side the local Gallican church.

Thus in the common council of the fathers from ten provinces, along with other bishops and many abbots, with the man of God dictating, a new creed was written opposing the new teachings. The names of each one were added to it, so that the zeal of all of them might be made known to all the rest in a clear and compelling manner. Finally, then, the error

---

[16] Horace, Ep 1.18.84: *Nam tua res agitur, paries cum proximus ardet* (Horace, *Epistles*, in *Satires, Epistles, and Ars Poetica*, trans. H. Rushton Fairclough, Loeb Classical Library 194 [1926; Cambridge, MA: Harvard University Press, 1929], 248–441, here 374–75).

was condemned by the judgment and apostolic authority of the universal church. Bishop Gilbert was questioned about it and gave his consent to the condemnation of the teachings, agreeing and publicly rejecting what he had previously written and affirmed, and he received a pardon from the council. Since from the beginning he had been legally cautioned about entering this dispute, without any obstinacy he himself promised to correct his opinion, because this was the will of the holy church.

BERNARD IN TOULOUSE PREACHES AGAINST HENRY, THE HERETIC

[16] In the district of Toulouse there was a man, Henry, who was once a monk but afterward a vicious apostate, living a disgraceful life. He occupied his time with trickery, with pleasing words persuading the people there to adopt his pernicious teaching and acting like an apostle to some of them; he spoke lies in his hypocrisy: *he exploited them with false words.** He was openly an enemy of the church, deriding the church's sacraments and ministries. He proceeded with impunity in that wickedness. The venerable father wrote about him to the prince of Toulouse, saying among other things, "Everywhere the churches are found without their congregations, the people without priests, the priests without proper reverence, Christians without Christ. To the children of Christians the life of Christ is forbidden, while the grace of baptism is denied them.[17] Prayers and offerings for the dead are ridiculed. Prayers of the

*2 Pet 2:3

---

[17] Only these two sentences appear in Bernard's letter as published.

saints, excommunication by priests, pilgrimages of the faithful, the building of churches, holidays on solemn feast days, the consecration of chrism and holy oils, and all ecclesiastical institutions: all are rejected."[18]

[17] Because of this crisis the holy man interrupted his journey around the churches of the region, which the very reverend Alberic, bishop of Ostia and legate of the Apostolic See,[19] had many times asked him to make. While he was coming there, however, he was received by the people with great devotion, just as if *an angel from heaven** had visited them. Nobody could suppress the crowds who rushed to see him, nor did he delay in doing what he could, but he was besieged day and night by those coming to him, waiting for his blessing, while he did whatever they asked of him. He preached in the city of Toulouse for a long time, and also in other places where that wretched man Henry had been most frequently and gravely infecting the district.

*Luke 22:43

Bernard instructed many simple folk in the faith, strengthening the waverers, encouraging those who had strayed, and by his authority checking those who were obstinate, so that I would not say that he stopped them completely, but at least they did not presume to appear in public. Even if that heretic Henry hid himself and fled away, however, his movements were hampered, and when he was surrounded and was hardly safe anywhere, finally he was captured, brought in chains, and handed over to the bishop. *God was glorified** in his servant, who performed many signs on his journey, recalling the hearts of many from their erroneous lives and healing the bodies of others of their various sicknesses.

*John 12:16

---

[18] Bernard, Ep 241.1 to Alphonsus, count of St. Gilles (SBOp 8:125; James #317).

[19] Monk of Cluny, then abbot of Vézelay, then cardinal bishop of Ostia (1138–1148).

*in the
Dordogne

[18] In that area was a place called Sarlat,* where after the sermon the people offered the servant of God loaves to be blessed, as was customary. He raised his hand, made the sign of the cross, and blessed the loaves in the name of God, saying, "You know that what we have been telling you is true, and what the heretics are persuading you is false. If those among you who are sick taste these loaves, they will be healed." The venerable bishop of Chartres, that great man Geoffrey,[20] who was present and close to the man of God, felt that this promise was a bit much, so he said, "If anyone eats in good faith, that person will be healed." But the holy father did not hesitate, knowing the power of God. "That is not what I said," he declared, "but 'anyone who tastes these loaves will be healed,' for such a one will know that we are true and that the messengers of God are true." Such a great number of those who were sick were healed after tasting the bread that throughout the province this episode soon became known everywhere, and the holy man, traveling about the vicinity, was deterred by the overwhelming crowd of people and hesitant about going there.

A Paralytic Cleric Healed at Toulouse

[19] The most important miracle that Christ revealed in the city of Toulouse through his servant was the cure of a paralytic cleric in the house of Regular Clerics of Saint Sernin, where the cleric was a member. Bernard found the man so close to death that he seemed to be drawing his last breath. The faithful servant consoled the unhappy man, gave

---

[20] Geoffrey de Lèves, 1116–1149.

him a blessing, and (as he afterward confessed) spoke to the Lord in his heart:"O Lord God, why do you wait? *This generation seeks a sign.** But among them *Luke 11:29 we have gained little by our preaching, unless you strengthen them with the signs that follow."* At that *see Mark 16:17 very *moment the paralytic leapt up from his pallet** and *John 5:9 made his way to Bernard, followed him, and embraced his feet with the devotion that was his due. When one of the other canons met him by chance, he was shocked and shouted out, "Good Heavens! *It looks like a ghost.*"* For who would have believed *Matt 14:26 that he could rise from his bed?

The canon who thought he had seen a soul going out of the sick man's body like a ghost ran away, but in the end the truth of the matter became clear to him and everyone. When the event was told among the brothers, they took it lightheartedly, but the bishop and the legate were among the first to acknowledge it for what it was. So the healed cleric was taken to the church in front of everyone, songs of praise to God filled the air, and the people gathered round. Christ was blessed, the people's confidence triumphed, unbelievers were outfaced, the loyal rejoiced, and those who were wrong were put to shame. The man of God took to his cell, however, where he remained, carefully blocking the entrance to observers. He ordered the doors to be bolted so that the entrance should not be open to the people who gathered there.

[20] But when in the same province at the return of the holy man more and more miracles increased and grew in number day after day, what he had done concerning these things could no longer be avoided, whatever he thought about them, for he had consecrated the humility of his heart and his meekness by the power of Christ. Arguing within himself about all this, he finally spoke out from the fullness of his heart and said to some of his religious brothers,

"I am amazed that anyone should want these miracles to be ascribed to oneself, since what comes about in such things is done by God. I do not recall reading anything in the sacred pages about this kind of miracle. Indeed, while sometimes miracles were done by holy men who were perfect, they were also done by frauds. But I am not conscious of being perfect or of being a fraud. I know that the merits of saints have not been given to me, merits that are shown by miracles. I am confident that this kind of thing does not pertain to me, for they did many powerful things in the name of the Lord, and they were recognized by the Lord. He confers often and secretly with spiritual men on these things and the like.

"I am well aware," he said, "that signs like these are not done for the sake of the holiness of one individual, but for the salvation of many, and God does not consider so much the perfection of the person by whom he has done these things but rather the opinion people have of that person. Nor are these things done for the sake of those through whom they are done, but rather for the sake of those who see them and recount them. Neither does the Lord do these things so that he may prove those who do them to be holier than others, but so that he may make them lovers of and seekers after holiness. There is nothing that pertains to me in any way from those signs, except so that I may show others how to live. They come about less to commend me than to admonish others."

Unless we are mistaken, those who weigh up carefully in their minds the spirit of this man and his wise words should think not about the excellence of the faithful person, but rather about those excellent signs and prodigies and should interpret them in a way that honors God. Should they not come to the conclusion within themselves that Bernard's love for others should be imitated rather than his actions held in admiration and the outward signs of his way of life be made known rather than the miracles he has done? But who is worthy to do these things?

[21] In the heart of the man of God purity and gentleness dwelled together in harmony, embracing one another in a marvelous fashion. Indeed the dream of the whole world came together eminently in this one man, so that his gentleness made his purity something lovable, and his purity made his gentleness most acceptable, so that it is hard to discern which is the stronger: grace or reverence. Who is there who does not revere the abbot of Clairvaux exaltedly for his firm model of life? Who is so empty-headed as to lack kindly affection for him? His own breast abounded with the most exceedingly warm love. How freely he embraced those whose causes he so often took up, in a manner full of love rather than unbending in conviction.

Bernard Mourns for Gerard, His Brother

We want to offer a good example of this love, as he himself bore witness in Sermon 26 on the Song of Songs when he celebrated dry-eyed the obsequies of his brother Gerard, who was so close to him, so necessary to him.[21] He buried him in the grave without showing his emotion lest his love for him might seem to have weakened his faith. For he hardly ever, or indeed never, buried anyone else without tears.

---

[21] SC 26.3 (SBOp 1:171; CF 7:60–61); *Fragm* I.40 (VP 296; *Notes* 151); *Exordium*, 3.1 (CCCM 138:138–43); *Beginning*, 209–14).

God had formed Gerard in such a way that Bernard became all the more dependent on him, so that his kindly life modified Bernard's austerities and his holiness preserved Bernard's authority. For to whom should such gentleness be a burden, such goodness be without honor? We read of Solomon that *all the world desired to see his face.** Great praise indeed!

Yet perchance *a greater than Solomon is here.** Is it not astonishing that *Solomon in all his glory** should have received the favor of the whole world while this man received the same for his humility? On the contrary! It appears difficult to find in history one man so renowned and so lovable yet still going about everywhere and meeting everyone and at the same time retaining such a reputation, *from the rising of the sun to its setting, from the north to the sea.**

Bernard Acclaimed in Many Countries

[22] We have in mind those provinces where even today the intensity of his memory is overwhelming, both in the Eastern church and in the sunset of Iberia, in the sunlight of remote parts of Spain and westward in those isles far away in Denmark and Sweden, where he is yet more widely renowned. From all these places he receives letters and replies to them. From everywhere gifts are sent to him; everywhere they seek his blessing. He sends out his branches in all directions *like a very fruitful vine,** except of course in the land of Jerusalem, since that was the place of the incursion of pagans, and the welcome his branches would receive would not be pleasant. He never agreed to send his brothers there, though the king of that country had prepared a place to receive them. But the bishop there did not take his refusal as a rebuke, for after Bernard's death, wishing

*1 Kgs 10:24

*Matt 12:42

*Matt 6:29

*Ps 106:3

*Sir 24:23

to console the brothers, the king was loud in praise of Bernard, because *his voice went forth into all the earth and his words unto the ends of the world.**

*Ps 18:5; Rom 10:18

The humility of his heart was greater than the renown of his name. When the whole world was keen to lift him up on high, he alone preferred to be treated as nothing. Reckoned as the greatest by everyone, he thought of himself as the least, and he who put everyone before himself thought himself to be less than anyone else. Then again, just as he had often confessed, when he was among the great men of honor and favorites of the people or great dignitaries, he seemed to be changed into another man and thought he himself should be elsewhere, mistrusting it all as a dream. But when simple brothers spoke to him with confidence, as they usually did, and he allowed himself to enjoy himself with friendly humility, then he was happy to have found himself again, and he became himself once more.

The shyness[22] that had been innate in him since his childhood remained with him until his last day. So although he was *so great and lifted up in words of glory,** we often heard him protesting that when he preached in however a humble gathering, as he often did, he could not do so without fear and awe. He preferred to remain silent unless stimulated by the fear of God and fraternal charity, when his own conscience forced him to speak.

*Sir 47:9

BERNARD'S PATIENCE

[23] Turning to his patience, we are aware just how much it was painfully exercised and put to the proof

---

[22] *Fragm* II.4 (VP 275; *Notes* 87–88).

by the troubles that the Lord sent him. In fact, from the first moments of his conversion right up to the present, when this holy man renounced his fleshly way of life, he had to endure such afflictions that for those who knew him his life appeared to be a prolonged death. Although on rare occasions he could show himself toward certain men with expressions of slightly less patience, it needs to be said that this happened very briefly, and he was never lacking in this virtue. Because patience of this type is usually divided into three kinds, namely, injurious words, damage to things, and bodily harm, we propose to list at least a few examples of each of these that at the moment occur to us.

On one occasion the servant of God wrote to one of the bishops of the court and council of the king, admonishing this bishop with a few words to persuade and advise the king to act in a better fashion. But the bishop was intensely annoyed and replied to him with a biting letter, saying in the first part of his greeting, *spiritum blasphemiae* "Good health to you, but not with an odious spirit"*— as if the holy man, horrible though it might appear, would write such things with an odious spirit! In reply to this message, the most meek servant of Christ gave this answer, mindful of the response of the Lord: *I do not have a demon*,* as the letter extant today shows: "No way do I believe myself to have an odious spirit, and I know too that I have never wished to curse anyone or say anything evil, especially to a prince of my people."[23] Nor did he afterward show less kindness toward this bishop, who was familiar to him, but he treated what he had said to him as if it had not been said.

[24] The abbot of Farfa,[24] who was going to build a monastery, asked for a group of brothers from

spiritum blasphemiae

*John 8:49

---

[23] Bernard, Ep 223 (SBOp 8:89; James #299).
[24] Altenulfe, abbot of the Benedictine Abbey of Farfa.

Clairvaux, but the bishop of Rome* prevented it,
taking them for himself and choosing another place
for them. The great man just mentioned, the abbot,
was quite upset about this. He was a devout person
who had collected money to the value of almost six
hundred marks of silver with a bond,* which he offered to the man of God when he* came to see him,
asking him to build a new house on this side of the
Alps since he had not been given the happiness of
having one in his own domain. But when the abbot
sent for the silver, it had totally disappeared. When
the man of God heard about this loss, he only replied,
"*How blessed is God,** who has spared us this burden.
Those who took it are Romany people," he said,
"and they should be kindly pardoned, for there was
an immense amount of money, and the temptation
was too much for them." He gave thanks for the
gift but thought that the amount fraudulently and
violently taken away was enough to build about ten
monasteries or to acquire sufficient land to build the
monasteries. He was unwilling to contest the case,
however, for he preferred to be vanquished rather
than to delight in vanquishing others.

[25] A certain cleric once came to Clairvaux from
those who are called Regular Canons, foolishly insisting on being received as a monk. The holy father tried
to persuade him to return to his own church and
would not agree to receive him. But the cleric said,
"How is it that you recommend in your books such
perfection of life if you refuse to show it to a person
who desires it?" Breaking into a bad temper, with an
evil humor, as afterward became evident, the cleric
said, "If I get hold of those books, I will tear them to
pieces." The man of God replied, "I am sure you have
never read in any of them that you cannot become
perfect in your own monastery. If I am not mistaken,
in all those books I have recommended a change in

*Innocent II

sub chirographo
*Altenulfe

*Ps 65:20

a way of life, not a change of place." Then the man became furious, throwing himself like a madman on Bernard and striking his cheek; he did it so violently that the blow at once caused a red mark to appear on Bernard's face. Those who were present grabbed hold of this sacrilegious fellow, but the servant of God restrained them, calling out and swearing in the name of Christ that they should not touch him, but rather lead him away and take care that he not be harmed by anyone in any way. He ordered this so severely that the wretched chap was led away in fear and trembling without any injury and departed.

[26] Indeed, the servant of God was so lambent with freedom of spirit, and his humility and gentleness shone out so clearly, that everyone respected him and all revered him. He rarely rebuked anyone, preferring rather to admonish and entreat. Although unwilling, he might have used harsh words occasionally, though not from any heartfelt severity; as soon as he became aware of his harshness he stopped the flow at once. He was astonished, in fact, at the impropriety of men who when violently disturbed were unwilling to admit any reasonable excuse or make any humble apology, but when the passion of fury pleased these wretched men, they took a dismal pleasure in their uncontrolled anger and hated any remedy. Closing their ears, shutting their eyes, and clenching their fists, in every way they could they strove against being calmed or healed once their violent behavior had arisen.

Bernard's reprimand sometimes provoked a sullen and stormy response rather than a humble and seemly reply, so some people said that he was firm with those who agreed with him but lenient to those who resisted him. He used to say that where harmony made music and was reciprocal, talk was kind and warm; where there was cordiality, it could at least be useful, but where there was no agreement on either side, it was just pernicious. Where harshness resounded, there was conflict, and no good would come of it, no discipline but only anger, so that it was better to play safe for a time than to hold forth. Or, to be sure, if the matter demanded it, it was wise to observe the counsel of the wise man: *the fool is not brought to his senses with fine words.** He himself spoke of rebukes received impatiently in his sermon 42 on the Song of Songs:

*RB 2.28; see Prov 18:2

> If only we never had to reproach anyone, that would be a lot better. But since *we all make many mistakes,** I cannot keep silent. My official position makes it incumbent on me *to reproach those who do wrong,** or rather *charity obliges me.** But if in doing my duties I do correct someone only to find that my reprimand fails entirely to achieve its purpose, echoing its futility back to me like a javelin that strikes and recoils, what do you think, brothers, are my feelings then? Am I not troubled? Do I not feel thwarted? Let me take to myself the words of the master, because I cannot use my own wisdom: *I am hard pressed between the two, yet which I should choose I cannot tell.** Should I be happy because I have done what I should, or should I regret and do penance over my words because what I desired I have not obtained?[25]

*Jas 3:2

*1 Tim 5:20
*2 Cor 5:14

*Phil 1:22-23

Further on he says,

> You will perhaps say to me that my good has returned to me, and because *I have saved my soul,** I am innocent of the blood of this man[†] to

*Job 33:28
[†]Acts 20:26

[25] SC 42.2 (SBOp 2:34; CF 7:211).

*Ezek 3:18

whom I have spoken and *turned him away from his evil ways so that he may live.** But even if you add many other things of this sort, they do not console me, for I am grieving over the death of my son. I am not looking for my own freedom from guilt by this reprimand, but rather his. What mother is there who, after she has done all in her care to heal her sick child and has applied every remedy, knows in the end that it has all been in vain and that all her toil has been utterly ineffective and, in spite of all, her child is dying—will that stem her tears?[26]

That is enough on that subject.

BERNARD'S KINDNESS

[27] Bernard was such a lover of meekness and peace that if perchance any persistent petitioner tried his hardest to extract a reply after being denied, he did not easily dismiss him with a refusal or in vain. As he himself confessed, he naturally hated to give offense, and it was impossible for him not to feel the burdens of everyone and to carry them, however difficult they were. And so he scorned no one and gave little thought to the offenses done by others, putting the truth of God and his justice before all else. Sometimes when it was necessary for him to reprimand individuals for the harm in their actions or to put a stop to their efforts, he did so with such consideration that they who seemed to be in the wrong found themselves made happy in their thoughts and went away satisfied with him. Further, we have often

---

[26] SC 42.5 (SBOp 2:36; CF 7:213).

seen some of them, from whom less could be hoped, to be afterward moved with greater devotion to him through his guidance, or even to become closer to him, with all the marks of sincere attachment.

Nevertheless, some disliked him, but he used their dislike to gain merit from them. Moreover, *the glory of his reputation** shone out so remarkably that their hatred was more akin to desperation than evil intent and arose from fear of letting itself be known. He overcame them by his humility and meekness, suffocated them with his gifts, overthrew them with his appeals. Indeed, he had learned how *to overcome evil with good*,* as he wrote to some of the brothers, saying among other things, "I will stick by you even if *you* do not want it; I will stick by you even if *I* do not want to. I will show myself to those who are reluctant, I will attach myself to those who are ungrateful, I will honor those who despise me."[27]

[28] He certainly embraced all men with a similar love, so that, as he used to confess, he so used their rebuffs as to offer no occasion for those rebuffs. Endowed with a kind heart, more tender toward others than himself, he tended to soften the other person's annoyance rather than show his own feelings. Indeed, he so hoped to be able to heal that he did not see where the anger came from; on the contrary, it was a great solace. Thus he was able to remain undisturbed when he could find no cause for the complaint, but he had the great consolation of finding the means to satisfy either the person who was angry with him or God who was angry with this person.

Toward everyone he showed great affection whether they liked it or not, and for him the greatest desire was the fertile conversion of sinful souls.

*Ps 78:9

*Rom 12:21

[27] Bernard, Ep 253.10 (SBOp 8:149–55; James #328).

He sympathized with the bodily needs of others, showing a most tender love. In fact, such was his humane approach that he was compassionate not only to humans but also to irrational animals, to birds and wild beasts. Nor was his compassion without effect. Very often it happened that when he was on a journey and saw a little hare being pursued by a dog and, as it seemed, on the point of being caught, or a small bird by a hawk, he freed them in a miraculous fashion with the sign of the cross. And he would say to the hunters that their efforts were in vain, nor should they when he was present succeed in satisfying their bloodlust.

BERNARD'S WRITINGS

[29] These things we have briefly put together to the best of our ability concerning the holy customs of our father. Besides, this is much more clearly seen in his books and can also be gathered from his letters.[28] In them he is seen to express himself with his own image, holding up a mirror to himself from the writing of Saint Ambrose, which he can correctly be seen to apply to himself: "He sings of himself by the praises he gives, and adorned by the Spirit he is crowned in his writings."[29]

If anyone wants to know how solicitous he was from the beginning as a judge and observer, let him look first of all at his book *On the Steps of Humility*.[30] Then, if you are looking for the religious devotion of his devout mind, go on to his *Homilies in Praise*

---

[28] Bernard, Epp (SBOp 7–8).
[29] Ambroise de Milan, *Hymnes*, ed. and trans. Jacques Fontaine, et al. (Paris: Les Éditions du Cerf, 1992), ## 6, 22.
[30] *De gradibus humilitatis et superbiae* (SBOp 3:1–59).

of the Virgin Mother.[31] After that he wrote the book *On the Love of God.*[32] If then you want his fervent zeal against his own and other people's vices, listen to his treatise *On Precept and Dispensation.*[33] If you want to see how he was a faithful approver and helper to anyone leading a holy life, he shows it in his exhortation *To the Knights Templars.*[34] How he was thankful for the grace of God becomes clear in his *Grace and Free Will,*[35] in which he writes in a faithful and in a subtle manner. How freely he speaks and discourses in a deep and lofty manner and also on everyday matters, the careful thinker will recognize in his work to Pope Eugenius, *On Consideration.*[36] How he as a devout preacher tells us of the sanctity of someone else, he diligently shows in *The Life of Saint Malachy.*[37] Then, in the sermons on the Song of Songs he is a researcher into profound mysteries and a wonderful builder of holy lives.[38] In the letters[39] Bernard dictated and sent to different people on various matters, the prudent reader will discover with what fervor of spirit he loved all righteousness and hated all injustice.

[30] How many wrongdoers he rebuked, how much hatred he eradicated, how many scandals he checked, and how many schisms he denounced, how many heresies he refuted! His life itself brightened his times, and in whatever country he went to there was

---

[31] *Homiliae in Laudibus Virginis Matris* (SBOp 4:3–58).

[32] *De diligendo Deo* (SBOp 3:109–54).

[33] *De praecepto et dispensatione* (SBOp 3:241–94).

[34] *De laude novae militiae* (SBOp 3:205–39).

[35] *De gratia et libero arbitrio* (SBOp 3:155–203).

[36] Csi (SBOp 3:379–493).

[37] *Vita Sancti Malachiae* (SBOp 3:295–378).

[38] SC (SBOp 1–2). Geoffrey does not mention *Apologia ad Guillelmum Abbatem* (SBOp 3:61–108).

[39] *Epistolae* (SBOp 8–9).

nothing of holiness, nothing of honesty, nothing that was decent, nothing that was lovable or gave proof of good renown or of a virtuous life that his authority did not strengthen, that his own love did not set on fire, or that his diligence did not promote. Was there any good work that he did not desire to encourage, or anything that had come to nothing that he did not try to repair with all his strength according to the place or time? Was there any wicked plotter who did not fear his zeal and authority? Was there anyone who promoted good things who did not feel consoled by his holiness, who did not desire his good favor, who did not solicit his help? Were there any who, finding themselves in good faith in any trouble, did not approach this holy temple with cries for help without being convinced that the divinity was hidden in the breast of this holy man and who did so in vain? Was there anyone depressed who did not find solace in him, anyone afflicted who was not helped, anyone anxious who did not receive counsel, anyone unwell who did not receive a remedy, any poor person who did not find help?

A Beautiful Olive; A Chosen Vessel

*Sir 24:19-23

†Ps 91:13

‡Sir 25:19

§Acts 9:15

¶2 Tim 2:21

*Sir 50:10

†1 Kgs 10:10

[32]⁴⁰ He was *a beautiful olive, a fruitful vine, a flourishing palm tree,* * *a majestic cedar,*† *a plane tree exalted,*‡ *a chosen vessel,*§ *a vessel of noble use*¶ in the house of God, *a solid vessel adorned with gold and every precious gem.** Firm in his faith and sanctity, he was enhanced with charismatic gifts as *with precious stones.*† When he was present every holy person rejoiced and every evil

---

⁴⁰ In Recension B this concluding paragraph replaces section 31 in the critical edition.

person blushed with shame, according to the saying, *The just shall see and shall rejoice, and all iniquity shall shut its mouth.** When he was present every religious house shone out like the sun, but when he was absent it was in darkness and somehow became mute. Like medicine, his hands and his speech cured every sickness, sometimes physical, sometimes moral.

Now then, over and above all these things, which consisted of his wonderful exterior signs and displays of his manifold virtues, we will next tell other things in a second little book, as mentioned in the preface.

*Ps 106:42

BOOK 4

BY GEOFFREY OF AUXERRE
(CALLED BOOK 2 BY GEOFFREY)

The end of book 1. The beginning of book 2.[1]

In the twenty-fourth sermon on the Song of Songs, Bernard of Clairvaux, the servant of the Lord, celebrates and gives thanks to the Lord: "On this third return from the city* a more merciful eye has looked down from heaven, and a more serene countenance has smiled on us. The rage of the lion[2] has cooled, wickedness has ceased, the church has found peace."[3] Such was the rejoicing in the Gallican church on receiving him back that it seemed to show no less joy on his return than at the joyful report that peace had been restored. So it is that he himself was astonished at this joy; he had often complained that while he had to attend so many somber meetings and such quarrels, from the beginning he had wanted to bid farewell to these worldly affairs, to take up again his previous holy way of life, experience once more its more fruitful joys, and honor its allegiances.

*from Rome in 1138

When he returned from the city he brought with him precious relics from the bodies of the holy apostles and martyrs, esteeming them as no small fruit

---

[1] MS. MSB 1 omits §§ 4, 6, 11, 13, and 18 as numbered in the critical edition of Recension A.

[2] I.e., Peter Leonis, Anacletus II.

[3] Bernard, SC 24.1 (SBOp 1:151; CF 7:42).

of his labors. Among them ever to be remembered, he received a tooth of Blessed Caesar. Since the whole head of this martyr was being exhibited and he could take what he wanted, he requested one of the teeth. The brothers who were with him strove in vain to extract this concession but were utterly unable to do so. They broke two or three knives that they were using, but the tooth remained fast. Then he said to us, "We must pray about it. We cannot have it unless the martyr gives it to us." In the end he reverently made a prayer; coming near, he took hold of it with two fingers and with unbelievable ease did what the iron instruments had been unable to move before.

Bernard, Absent yet Present, Raises a Priest Who Was Dying

[2] The brothers of the Temple of Jerusalem, who had taken vows in the faithful army, were at that time beginning to build a new house at Rome, and the holy father was their special patron, so when he returned to France they kept his tunic as a special blessing. In that year a priest among them was taken ill with a grave fever and was desperately sick. He became so weak that he seemed to be at death's door, so they carried him into the oratory, placed the above-mentioned tunic of the blessed father on him, and laid him there, waiting for his departure in death. Then suddenly, snatched up in an ecstasy of mind and as it were released from the flesh, his body seemed to him in the lifeless position in which he lay to be surrounded by a great number of priests holding open books and celebrating the solemn prayers for the dead, as was customary.

Then all at once a certain person, with the appearance and habit of the holy father just mentioned, coming from the altar, lifted his hand and called for silence, and in his own voice he forbade them to reckon him dead whose life God had given to the abbot of Clairvaux. Immediately the priest revived. Discovering that he was restored to health in himself, he recounted to the brothers what he had seen. We were told about this recently by those trustworthy men, and this man, who is still alive and living in the province of Aquitaine, sedulously affirms that he received this gift and praises the person through whom he is alive. If anyone doubts this story, let him recollect Blessed Nicholas and the innumerable miracles with which he is honored and distinguished on the annual commemoration of his birthday into heaven, he who appeared in a vision to the emperor Constantine and turned him from destroying some men.[4]

Nor was this unlike the miracle that we now recount. **[3]** Gerard, the abbot of Mores,[5] which is a monastery near Clairvaux, testified to us that he himself had seen Bernard going round the choir while the brothers were singing the psalms, frequently rousing the sleepy so that they might sing what was left of Vigils more fervently and more firmly. When on the following day he complained to him in a friendly way that he was later than he should be in visiting those singing the psalms that night, he said, "At the night hour I was afflicted with serious physical problems, but even though I was not present in my body, I was there in spirit." Hearing that he had not been present physically, Gerard was seized with awe, because he had himself for quite a time seen him going round both sides of the choir and, as was his custom, laying his hand on each one of the monks.

---

[4] The fourth-century Saint Nicholas of Bari, who in a famous vision ordered Constantine to pardon three innocent men.

[5] Founded by Clairvaux in 1151.

At Auch in Gascony a Sick Knight Is Healed

[5] We believe that the renown of that venerable man William, once the lord of Montpellier but now a true monk and one of the humble poor of Christ, who lives in the monastery that is called Grandselve,[6] has come to the ears of many people. We relate a story from his own lips, which we are going to speak about just as he to whom it happened spoke of it and accepted it:

> In the city of Auch, which is the capital of Gascony, there was a certain sick knight. Because the lower parts of his body, from his loins downward, were afflicted with severe and intense pains, he had been lying on his bed for a good many days, for most of the time half dead. Touched with compunction and confident in God's mercy, he ordered that however difficult it might be, he should be carried to the servant of God, Bernard, whose well-known reputation for virtuous power had spread everywhere. So he proceeded for some days and progressed on the journey with the trust and devotion that the route demanded.
>
> God in his compassion deigned in a wonderful fashion to help the desperately sick man and to release him from his fatigue. Someone who met him on the way asked him who he was and where he was going. When that person had ascertained the purpose of the journey, he said, "I am here standing in the place of that holy man, and I charge you to return home, knowing that when you arrive there you will be healed." God, by

---

[6] Founded in 1114 by Gerald of Sales; became Cistercian in 1145.

whose controlling power all things come into being, persuaded the knight to trust in the man. He retraced his steps, and when he got back he gradually felt in himself the favor that had been promised to him, so that he had hardly arrived home than he received his complete recovery. As often as he heard what had happened, however, he used to say in a humble fashion and as a joke, "This must be imputed to me just as much as to Bernard, who was completely unaware of it."

ABBOT PONS OF BEAUVEAU

[7] In the monastery called Beauveau near the city of Besançon there was a man troubled by a demon, doing and saying very strange things. Even after many prayers said by the brothers, that evil spirit persisted in this man, but then the venerable abbot of the place, Pons,[7] who is still alive, remembered that he had a stole that the holy father used to use when offering the holy sacrifice. Without a moment's hesitation he took up this powerful weapon for God and with confidence approached the enemy. Hardly had he got to the cell in which the wretched man lay than suddenly the evil spirit with horrendous words declared himself vanquished: "See now, I am going away, I will depart instantly, I can remain here no longer." The abbot replied, "In the name of the Lord and through the merits of the blessed man whose stole this is, I order you to clear off quickly and not to delay." Immediately the demon fled away from the man, and he was freed from the demon.

[7] First abbot of Beauveau, founded from Morimond in 1119.

Who else would not exult, perhaps dangerously, when the spirits who are so subject to him give way to him, even when he is absent? But when this event was related to Bernard by the abbot, he was unmoved; instead he made fun of those whom he saw to be moved with astonishment at the event. He replied like this: "Why should we who are two not prevail over one enemy? God can quite easily throw him out, especially since I myself, as you say, have been given a companion and helper." He often resorted to this answer when talking about things of this sort. He knew that he was truly not a boaster but a sincere lover of humility and that one can more efficaciously dissuade people from being overawed by such amazing events by indirect and artful objections than by direct explanations and so, by displaying a more praiseworthy humility, increase rather than diminish people's esteem. So, speaking from his own experience in the place, he said, "The truly humble man wishes to be thought of as of little worth, not to be spoken of as humble."

[8] There was also a very well-known thing that Bernard did while still alive in the flesh by appearing in the spirit to a brother and revealing to him the day of his death. This brother was a novice at Clairvaux, *living a good life** and *an industrious young man.*† Not long after his usual year of probation *he put on the new man,** though he had not yet removed the former. In effect, *being made perfect in a short space, he fulfilled a long time.** Then, five days before his last day, he was visited by a brother,[8] and the novice, being totally cheerful, said among other spiritual words, "Look, I am going to die in five days time. Today our

*1 Pet 2:12
†1 Kgs 11:28
*Eph 4:24

*Wis 4:13

---

[8] The critical edition here adds, "This was Br. Gerard, who is today the abbot of the monastery of Longpont."

holy father appeared with a great number of monks and, fired with gentle words of consolation, told me that I would die on the fifth day." *The saying spread abroad among the brothers,** and before it happened it was made known everywhere. Everyone was waiting for the day, but above all the blessed monk too was in expectation. Now the fifth day was drawing to a close at Vespers, and his spirit was more and more lifted up to the Lord.

*John 21:23

Finally, around the eleventh hour, suffering the agony of death and closing his eyes to the light of day as is usual, while no one was aware of it, he hastened to his death. Meanwhile, the holy father visited him, as to a person waking up from a deep sleep, as if bringing back the one passing from this world and not allowing him to go without bidding him farewell. When the brother heard his voice, he opened his eyes and looked at him with a serene gaze in a miraculous way. Everybody was in awe that a mortal man who was dying should so triumph over death that at the very moment of death he should be overcome with joy and exhibit to us that beautiful saying of the poet: "Begin, young lad, to show with a smile you know your mother."[9] Then the holy father encouraged him with kind words and bade him not to be afraid but to resume at once his journey to the Lord Jesus Christ, and to offer him the humble greetings of his own poor family. On hearing these words the brother acknowledged them with a motion of his lips as far as he could, and once more closing his eyes he straightaway *slept in peace.*[10]

---

[9] *Incipe, parve puer, risu cognoscere matrem* (Virgil, *Eclogue* 4.60). Virgil, *Eclogues, Georgics, Aeneid 1–6*, trans. H. Rushton Fairclough, rev. G. P. Goold, Loeb Classical Library 63 (1916; Cambridge, MA, and London: Harvard University Press, 1999), 52–53.

[10] *Requiescat in pace*, Office of the Dead.

A REVELATION GIVEN TO HERVÉ OF BEAUGENCY

[9] Many things were revealed to this servant of God through the Spirit; we know of many other things that he predicted in a wonderful fashion without a previous revelation. From these we will add a few examples. The holy father was once in the city of Noyon in the residence of the bishop, Simon,[11] when Hervé of Beaugency,[12] still a fine lad, born of royal blood and nephew of that bishop, was brought to him.[13] On the following night Christ showed to his servant what would come about after a long time. Indeed, it seemed to him while he was celebrating Mass that he gave to a certain angel the kiss of peace, which was then passed on to the boy. Now, there is no doubt that because of this revelation, this Hervé would renounce the world and later promised to become a devout servant of Christ. This promise became famous and known far and wide. And as Hervé later told us, during his adolescence, against every other argument it kept stirring his conscience that it would be impossible after such a promise from the holy man for him to remain in a secular garb. Nor was this hope denied him.

In fact, the venerable Walléran, the first abbot of Ourscamp,[14] gave Hervé the habit of a monk, and when he was performing this angelic duty he received the peace from the mouth of the holy father and handed it on to Hervé. Afterward his way of life seemed worthy of such prophecy, for he succeeded Walléran in the administration of the monastery of

---

[11] Simon de Vermandois, bishop of Noyon, 1122–1147, founder of Ourscamp.

[12] Monk at Ourscamp; became abbot in 1142, d. 1143.

[13] See *Fragm* I.57 (VP 302–3; *Notes* 169–71).

[14] Founded in 1129 near Noyon.

Ourscamp. Much later, Hervé foresaw and predicted his own death to this same Walléran, through a revelation he received that foretold his own imminent death while he was still healthy and sound in body.[15]

[10] What we add here is similar. When the holy father was traveling in the vicinity of Paris, the bishop of the city, Stephen,[16] and all the others who were also present asked him to make a detour and come to the city, but they could not obtain their wish. Unless a serious cause prompted Bernard, he declined to attend public meetings, with some strong feelings on the matter. In the evening he had proposed to go elsewhere, but the next morning when he first spoke to the brothers, he told them to say to the bishop, "We will go to Paris as he asked." So when a great group of clergy had gathered, as they always did to hear the word of God, at once three of them were struck with compunction and turned away from their inane studies to engage in true wisdom, renouncing the world and keeping close to the servant of God.

Looking intently at the first of these, Bernard suddenly started to interrogate him and asked him to follow him. He leaned over a little to the brother who was sitting close by and whispered in his ear, "I see him now just as he is, and I foresaw him in a vision by night coming here, which is why the Lord has brought us here." Indeed, this man changed and afterward became a novice with great purity and devotion; in many ways *he was acceptable to God and to men.** After many years in Clairvaux, he rested in a blessed end.

*Sir 45:1

Gaudry* and Gerard appeared once to the man of God, who was staying in the city of Troyes. They were his venerable sons but are now released from

*Gaudry de Touillon

---

[15] *Fragm* I.55, 57 (VP 301–3; *Notes* 169–71).
[16] Stephen of Senlis, bishop 1124–1142.

the flesh. One of them was his uncle, the other, his brother by blood. Since they were going past quickly, he wanted to call them back and retain them, but they replied to him that they had to go to their brother Geoffrey, the monk,[17] who had been their companion from the time of their conversion and had fought strenuously on the side of God* in building many monasteries. Immediately the holy father ordered the hurrying brothers to hasten on their way, and returning to the monastery at the very moment that he had foretold to them, he found Geoffrey now lying at the point of death.[18]

*RB Prol. 2

Count Theobald Released and Peace Restored

*count of Champagne
†Neh 9:37

*Heb 2:18

[12] The Lord had released that trustworthy prince, Count Theobald,* *proved in many trials*,† with great mercy and in a wonderful way. He was the most powerful person in the kingdom, second only to the king,[19] and he was totally dedicated to giving alms and known for his deep piety to all the servants of God, but especially as a loving friend of Bernard's. *God had allowed him** to be calumniated and afflicted by the king and likewise almost all the neighboring potentates, all of them conniving against him, so that he despaired of avoiding their attacks, for they publicly derided his religious way of life, belittled his gracious devotion, and sneered at his almsgiving. The

---

[17] Geoffrey d'Aignay, one of Bernard's original companions. See Marc Debuisson, "La provenance des premiers cisterciens d'après les lettres et les *vitae* de Bernard de Clairvaux," *Cîteaux* 43 (1992): 5–118, here 70.

[18] See *Fragm* I.41 (VP 296–97; *Notes* 150).

[19] Louis VI le Gros, 1108–1137.

monks and lay brothers were called useless knights and archers. This persecution took place not only outside his territory, but even within his cities and castles people resorted to these insults.

Finally, when many of the bishops and other people were gathered together and the man of God was also there, while they were speaking about these things and discussing them, one of the bishops, a man of authority and well-known for his prudent views, spoke up and said, "Count Theobald is in the hand of the king and cannot be wrested from him." But another prelate replied, "There is someone who can free him." Everyone there was astonished and wanted to know what he meant. Then, when he heard that God who could do all things could free Theobald, the bishop was annoyed. "Yes, he can," he said, "if he manifests himself, if he holds a cudgel, if he strikes out everywhere, but so far he has not done that." In this desperate situation, when those outside his realm were strongly insisting to the prince that almost all the powerful men among them had fallen away from him and that the few men who seemed to remain on his side were suspected of defecting to the others, all this insistence left him in a state of torment.

The bishop of Langres, Geoffrey,[20] frequently and personally consulted the man of God, asking him what the Lord had revealed to him about these matters. To these inquiries Bernard replied as he often did, that nothing had come to his attention except troubles upon troubles. There was a civil war between King Louis and Count Theobald, a very complicated situation during which Bernard strongly

---

[20] Geoffrey de la Roche-Vanneau, cousin of Bernard, monk of Clairvaux; abbot of Fontenay 1118, prior of Clairvaux 1128–1138, bishop of Langres 1138–1163. Debuisson, "La provenance," 79.

reprimanded the king for his outrageous behavior.[21] But then, when he eventually inquired further, Bernard said, "After five months there will be peace." Then peace was again restored on the last day of the fifth month, as Bernard himself was praying and working toward it, and because of his careful application, credit, and unambiguous charisma, the devout prince was freed from these dangers that were so severe and threatening.[22]

BERNARD IN GERMANY

[14] Later the servant of Christ went to the kingdom of Germany and quickly came to those parts of Mainz where he wanted to restore peace between the king, Lothair,[23] and the nephews of Henry the emperor,* namely, Conrad,[24] who afterward succeeded Lothair in the kingdom, and Frederick,* the father of this Frederick,[25] who, elected after Conrad, became today's prince. The venerable metropolitan of Mainz, Albert,[26] sent a worthy cleric named Mascelin to meet the man of God. This Mascelin, when he was sent by his lord, said that he was sent to serve him, and as soon as the man of God saw him, he said, "Another lord has sent you to serve himself."

The Teutonic knight was taken aback and wondered what this meant; he asserted firmly that he had been sent by his lord, the archbishop of Mainz. "On

*Henry V

*Duke
Frederick II

---

[21] Ailbe J. Luddy, *Life and Teaching of St. Bernard* (Dublin: M. H. Gill & Son, 1927), 474–77.

[22] See *Fragm* I.49 (VP 299–300; *Notes* 160–61).

[23] King of the Romans 1125–1137, crowned emperor 1132.

[24] Conrad III of Staufen, emperor 1138–1152.

[25] Emperor Frederick III/I Barbarossa, r. 1152–1190.

[26] Albert of Saarbrücken, archbishop of Mainz 1111–1137.

the contrary," said the servant of Christ, "you are mistaken. Christ, the greater lord, is *he who has sent you*."* Then the man understood the implications of these words. "Do you mean," he said, "that I should become a monk? God forbid; I haven't even thought of it, it hasn't entered my mind."* Nevertheless the servant of God contradicted him and affirmed what should happen in so many words, not because he himself had thought about it, but because God had disposed it that way about him.[27] So on that journey *he was converted to the Lord*;* he bade farewell to the world, and with many other highly educated and distinguished persons whom the servant of God had gathered at the same time, *he also followed him*,* as Bernard had predicted.

*Jdt 11:20

*Jer 44:21

*Sir 5:8

*Matt 9:9;
Mark 2:14

HENRY, BROTHER OF THE KING OF FRANCE

[15] By a similar conversion the Lord also changed the brother of the king of France, Henry, who today adorns the see of Beauvais.[28] It so happened that this Henry came to the man of God to speak to him about some secular business while he was visiting the brothers in the monastery, commending himself to their prayers. The holy father said to him in the course of his words of exhortation, "*I am confident in the Lord** that you will in no way die in the post you now hold. But the prayer you have just requested from the brothers will be answered quickly, and you will experience the strength of it to prove it to you." This in fact happened not long afterward, to the surprise of many people, and

*Rom 14:14

---

[27] See *Fragm* I.58 (VP 303–4; *Notes* 173–74).

[28] Henry of France, brother of Louis VII, bishop of Beauvais 1149–1162, archbishop of Reims 1162–1175; see Bernard, Ep 403 (SBOp 8:383–84; James #435).

the conversion of such an important youth filled the monastery with the greatest joy.

Henry's companions were mourning him, however, and his whole family was bewailing him as if he were already dead. Above all, Andrew of Paris[29] treated Henry as drunk and completely mad, not sparing violent insults and dire reproaches. Henry himself on the contrary begged the man of God to pray for them, especially for Andrew's conversion. The man of God said to all those listening, "Leave it awhile. At present his soul is full of bitterness, so do not be overly solicitous for him, for he is close to you." But when Henry insisted further with this hope he had conceived that Bernard should speak to Andrew, the man of God looked at him severely. "What is this?" he said. "Have I not told you, he is yours?" Hearing this, Andrew who was standing there, was violently opposed to the idea of his own conversion and revolted at it, saying, "Because of what you have just said I know you are a false prophet. I am quite certain that what you have predicted will not come about. I say this to you in front of the king and the princes in this distinguished monastery, and I do not spare you this accusation, namely, that your lying words are known to everyone."

Well, *how marvelous is God** in his counsels over the sons of men,** smiling at their vain efforts so that he may fulfill *his proposals** when and as he himself wills. Indeed, a little later Andrew went away swearing all sorts of evil things on the monastery where his lord dwelt, desiring to demolish the valley where the monastery was founded, along with all those living there. Those who had heard the prediction of the holy man about him were greatly moved and

*Ps 67:36
*Ps 65:5
*2 Tim 1:9

---

[29] A member of Henry's retinue.

wondered, since he was seen to go away in such a manner. But God did not allow their weakness and lack of faith to be tried for long. On the very day that Andrew went on his way, rejecting the grace of God in that manner, the following night he was overcome and, as it were, drawn by the Spirit of God using force, so that he could not wait for the day, but rising up before daylight, he returned to the monastery as quickly as he could, and he showed himself to us like another Saul, or rather like another Saul changing into another Paul.

[16] Among the others whom Christ wrested from the vain way of life of this world through the ministry of his servant in the region of Flanders were many noblemen, many sagacious men, and many learned men who made their sacred profession in his monastery. The first of these seems to have been Geoffrey de Péronne,[30] who afterward took up the office of prior of Clairvaux* and died as prior.[31]   *1140
Evidently the gospel was so thoroughly fulfilled in these men that *many will say to you, Look, here is the Christ; look, he is there.** Now a number of ways were   *Matt 24:23
found in which they chose to make their profession, some in one place, some in another, until the servant of God met those on the point of being dispersed and, from the gracious words that *proceeded out of his mouth,** he openly put aside their former hesitation   *Rev 19:15
and likewise with a strong and unchangeable will agreed with their decision. This was done, though not without a sudden and unexpected change of mind from some of them.

When this Geoffrey followed the man of God, he began to be struck with a violent temptation. One of

---

[30] Treasurer of the church of Saint Quentin.
[31] See *Fragm* I.58 (VP 170–71; *Notes* 173–74).

the brothers looked at him carefully: "Why is it that
your face has a downcast and sad expression and looks
as if it is enveloped in a thick dark cloud?" Geoffrey
replied, "I know, I know that I will never again be
happy." When the brother rather anxiously related
this statement to the servant of God, he looked up at
the basilica near the road along which he was walking, and he turned aside and entered it and prayed.
Geoffrey, weighed down with depression, standing
with the others who were waiting outside, rested on
a rock. Then they both rose up, one from his prayer,
the other from his sleep, and Geoffrey appeared as
much more joyful and cheerful than the others as he
had previously been sadder. And when the brother
we just mentioned started in a friendly fashion to ask
him about his former downcast expression, he replied,
"Although I said then that I would never be happy
again, now I tell you I will never again be depressed."

BERNARD'S PREDICTION
CONCERNING GEOFFREY'S FATHER

[17] During the first year of his novitiate this Geoffrey prayed to the Lord fervently for the conversion
of his father, a powerful nobleman whom he had left
behind in the world, yet for whom he was solicitous
with filial concern. The man of God said to him, "Do
not worry. I will personally bury him with my own
hands here at Clairvaux as a tried and tested monk."
Both these things came about: he became a perfect
monk, and, as Bernard had predicted, he was buried
at Clairvaux.[32] While Bernard was absent, the father

---

[32] The text is not clear, but presumably the writer is referring
to Geoffrey's father.

could not die, so for five months he was sick and had in himself the growing and continual feeling of dying, but he waited until the holy father returned, when, as he had once promised, he laid him in the tomb.[33]

[19] The lord abbot of Cîteaux, Rainard,[34] whom the holy father embraced as a son at Clairvaux and as his father when he was raised up, came to those parts of the Provence for the purpose of establishing some monasteries. Concerning this trip, the man of God, still residing at Clairvaux, was suddenly moved by an inspiration and said to one of the brothers, "The lord of Cîteaux is either already dead or just about to die." The brother was not a little put out when he heard these words. He was, however, even more taken aback when after a few days he heard the death of the abbot announced.

[20][35] Once the servant of God remained all night in prayer in his monastery at Clairvaux, and he offered prayers to the Lord, as was his custom. But it happened that at the same moment a poor man, truly a man poor in spirit, lay dying in a cell in the guesthouse. His soul was carried up to heaven with the sound of the chant, while the holy father was listening. The following morning he interrogated the brothers who were there at the moment of his death and found that it had occurred at the precise time that the sound of the choir rose up into the heights.

---

[33] In *Fragm* I.58 (VP 303; *Notes* 173–74) Geoffrey's father is named as Matthew. More details are given there about this prediction and its results. Bernard also wrote two letters regarding Geoffrey's conversion, Ep 109 to Geoffrey himself and Ep 110 to his parents, reassuring them about his well-being as a new monk of Clairvaux (SBOp 7:280–83; James ##111–12).

[34] Rainald de Bar, monk of Clairvaux and fifth abbot of Cîteaux, 1133–1150.

[35] The first portion of this paragraph in Recension A is omitted in MSB MS. 1.

Blessed Malachy, Bishop

[21] When the bishop Blessed Malachy[36] rendered his holy soul to heaven, the venerable abbot offered the saving victim* for his departure, which he† had desired with all his heart to be at Clairvaux. The holy man, Bernard, had studiously written Malachy's life,[37] a book that was full of spiritual value. He recognized the glory of the man through a divine revelation, and at the end of the sacrifice he changed the form of the prayer and took the collect prayer from the feast of holy pontiffs rather than from the Office of the Dead, saying, "O God, who has made blessed Malachy co-equal in merit to your saints, grant, we beseech you, that we who offer this feast for his precious death may imitate the example of his life." Then, approaching with reverence, he kissed Malachy's sacred feet with the utmost devotion. He did not, however, agree to write about the nature or time of this vision in his *Life of Malachy*,[38] nor did he tell anyone about it, but when pressed by those who asked him about it, he was content to agree that it was just too personal, too emotional for him.

*i.e., a Mass

†Malachy

Examples of Bernard's Healing Gifts

[22] Regarding those many signs that pertain to the grace of healing that Christ worked through this his servant and seemed to show forth in him, John

---

[36] Saint Malachy O'Morgair, archbishop of Armagh, 1134–1148.

[37] Fol. 125ᵛ of MS. MSB 1 has the rubric *Incipit prephacio dompni bernardi clareuallis abbatis in uita malachie dunensi episcopi et apostolice* [sic] *in hybernia legati*.

[38] Bernard, VMal (SBOp 3:295–378).

the Evangelist witnesses: *Were every one of them to be written down, I suppose that the whole world could not contain the books that would be written.** We can proffer, however, at least a few examples from so many.

*John 21:25

The castle called Château-Villain was almost six miles from Clairvaux. A pregnant woman had gone past the time of her term, and several months had gone by, so she wondered that she had not yet given birth to her child. Her period of bearing was so delayed that it seemed that she was ill, and she began to believe she had a tumor rather than being pregnant. Who would believe that an infant could remain for a whole year within the womb of its mother? In a desperate state, the woman was brought to the monastery of the man of God just as she was. Feeling wretched, she sat down near the door and made known privately to the brother porter the cause that made her so unhappy.

When he was told of this and felt compassion at this unheard-of difficulty, he came to the abbot, entreating him, explaining to him truthfully the woman's emergency, and unfolding to him the matter of his errand. O, how wonderful the work of the divine power, marvelously speeding up what had been marvelously delayed. After she had for such a long time expected that infant to be born, *the woman brought forth a son at that very moment,** and when the porter, who had gone off for medicine, came back to the door, he did not find the distressed woman there.

*2 Kgs 4:17

[23] At another time in the territory of Auxerre, close to a town called Cosne,[39] a woman was in great danger for a long time because her son had come to the point of being born, but she did not have the

---

[39] Ferruccio Gastaldelli, "La piu antiche testimonianze biografiche su san Bernardo," *Analecta* 45 (1989): 3–80; see *Fragm* I.54 (VP 301; *Notes* 167). Identified with Cosne-sur-Loire in the Nièvre.

strength to give birth. When the servant of Christ came to the place and was asked for a blessing, he sent blessed water. The woman tasted it, and immediately her boy was born. The venerable bishop of Chartres, Geoffrey,[40] baptized the boy and gave him the name Bernard.[41]

BLESSED BREAD

On the same journey and in the same territory, when a great number of people with fever asked for blessed bread from the man of God, as was customary everywhere, a certain Gerard from the town called Clamecy, an ignorant and scornful chap, derided the faith of the people. While he was actually using these words of derision, he was taken with a violent fever and was forced to follow the man of God as far as Auxerre. Asking for a penance from him whom he had slandered, he obtained a blessing after many prayers.[42]

Now this blessed bread, once tasted, gave health back to many people, so that they were healed by God's power alone and were able to know this and understand it. **[24]** We have seen in the region of Meaux a knight giving astonishingly devout thanks to the man of God, because as soon as he had tasted the bread blessed by him he was fully healed from the quartan fever under which he had labored so seriously for almost eighteen months, and from the mo-

[40] Geoffrey de Lèves, bishop 1116–1149; see Bernard, Epp 55, 56, 57 (SBOp 7:147–49; James ##58, 59, 60).

[41] This story is taken almost verbatim from *Fragm* I.43 (VP 297; *Notes* 154).

[42] *Fragm* I.47 (VP 299; *Notes* 160).

ment he had been subject to it, he was so demented that he could not even recognize his own mother.[43]

We have also heard that venerable man Gérald, bishop of Limoges,[44] bear witness of a young man of his family who was lethally wounded in the head and lay frothing in the mouth and mentally deranged, who when a small piece of bread blessed by the man of God was put into his mouth, he quickly felt its power and rose up cured at that very instant.

Nor should we keep quiet about the blessing that rendered the substance of the bread untouched by the slightest corruption, so that we have often seen several loaves preserved for seven years or more without any change of color or taste.

A few days before, the venerable abbots Gerard[45] and Henry,[46] who came from somewhere in Sweden, bore witness to us when we were talking about these things that the bread signed by Bernard with a blessing eleven years before still remained completely incorrupt among them. This is similar to what we have learned from those among us still here today and that we also believe to have occurred to many others.

[43] See *Fragm* I.59 (VP 304; *Notes* 175), where the Latin varies considerably but the miracle is the same.

[44] Gérald-Hector de Cher, bishop of Limoges 1138–1177; see Bernard, Ep 329 (SBOp 8:265–66; James #382).

[45] Monk of Clairvaux and second abbot of Alvasta, Sweden, the first Cistercian abbot in Scandinavia, 1153–1193; he resigned and returned to Clairvaux, where he died in 1193. See *Exordium* 4.28–29 (CCCM 138:258–62; *Beginning*, 374–80); Debuisson, "La provenance," 76–78; and James France, *The Cistercians in Scandinavia*, CS 131 (Kalamazoo, MI: Cistercian Publications, 1992), 110–15, 495.

[46] Henry, monk of Clairvaux, first abbot of Varnhem, Sweden, daughter of Alvasta, 1150–1158, then first abbot of Vitskol (*Vitae Schola*), Denmark, until ca. 1163. See *Exordium* 6.10 (CCCM 138:366; *Beginning*, 541–49); Debuisson, "La provenance," 89; France, *The Cistercians in Scandinavia*, 39, 63–64, 499, 508.

ARCHBISHOP ESKIL FROM DENMARK AND HIS LACK OF FAITH

We now offer evident and dependable proof of this fact. **[25]** A great Danish man who was honored with magnificent prestige, Archbishop Eskil,[47] had a special affection for the holy father and cherished him with a particularly strong devotion. He was not satisfied with seeing him in his sons, for he built a new monastery and begged from Bernard a crowd from the sacred congregation. His very strong desire prevailed, and this man with such authority in his far-off islands, who was powerful in both ecclesiastical and secular circles, left behind his goods and exposed himself to many dangers in taking on his laborious journey to Clairvaux. The expenses he went to were not just immense; rather we have heard someone protesting that he spent more than six hundred marks of silver on the journey. As humble and sublime a person as he was, he came to Clairvaux *from the ends of the earth*, not out of curiosity *to hear words of wisdom** but drawn by zeal for the faith and an overpowering devotion.

How great was his flood of tears and how humbly he showed himself, not only toward him who received him marvelously well but even to the least of the brothers, it is not easy to say. In the end he returned to his own land, able to take back with him some bread blessed by the servant of God. For a long time he kept it and then ordered it as a human

*Matt 12:42;
see 1 Kgs 10:1-8

---

[47] Eskil, bishop of Roskilde, Denmark, 1134, then archbishop of Lund (Denmark, now Sweden), 1138. Exiled for some years, he returned in 1168, resigned in 1177, and retired to Clairvaux, where he died in 1181. See Bernard, Ep 390 (SBOp 8:358–59; James #424); *Exordium* 3.27 (CCCM 138:219–24; *Beginning,* 300–306); France, *The Cistercians in Scandinavia,* 32–42, 63–69.

precaution to be cooked again in the oven, just as those who cross the sea have their bread twice cooked. Hearing of this act, the holy man did not allow such a devout person to go astray but rebuked him in a friendly fashion for his lack of faith, which he disclosed in this way: "Is not the blessing able to preserve the bread better than a second cooking?" And he did not agree to bless the bread, but, ordering some ordinary bread to be brought, he blessed it and said, "See, take this with you; do not be concerned from now on about corruption."[48] He took it, went back home, and to this day takes delight in the fact that his lack of faith was overcome by the evident truth of the outcome. He could not be prevented from visiting the sepulcher of the holy father. Neither is his love for Bernard now less than it was, nor is his trust in Bernard less than when he was living; rather, he does not doubt that Bernard now lives an altogether better life. He has also confessed to us that the bread that he had retained is even now, after three years have gone by, just as wholesome as when the faith and blessing of the holy man preserved it.

[26] A certain religious told us a story, when he came to this archbishop, of a miracle worthy of remembrance once enacted in the monastery that he himself founded, which we have mentioned above:

> There was, he said, in that region a certain young nobleman* who was closely related to the archbishop, but because of his many shameful actions not at all dear to him. Struck down by a serious illness he could hardly ask the archbishop to visit him, and so he betook himself to the monastery that the archbishop

*Count Niels, kinsman of Eskil

[48] No doubt Bernard was thinking here not just about the corruption of bread but also about the corruption of morals.

had founded. While he was there he renounced the world with extreme compunction of heart, and though he persevered for a
number of days in this humble and most
faithful sorrow for his sins, he became more
and more painfully sick.

Finally, he became so sick that he realized
that his end was near. He embraced the abbot
and the brothers who were present with a
warm and loving affection, and he warned
them with his admirable devotion that they
should take up spiritual weapons and, as soon
as his soul departed, commend his soul con-
fided to their care. They should also show
themselves faithful in giving him safe and
necessary guidance among the piercingly
cruel arrows of the enemy who was on hand.
When he had been strengthened by the divine sacraments and by his prayers and filled
with the most kind and loving devotion of
these servants of God, he abandoned himself
to the faithfulness of all those who were
standing nearby, and he died. So the brothers
offered prayers for the commendation of his
soul and devoutly received the saving host of
the Body of the Lord.

[27] Then suddenly the enemy of human
salvation, who without doubt believed that
the nobleman's soul was going to be freed
from his power, the soul that he had irretriev-
ably occupied for a long time, was infuriated,
and God allowed him to exert himself cruelly,
so he pursued one of the brothers with an
unexpected fury. The wretched man cried out
with a horrible noise and could hardly be
restrained by all those there. In the end he
was carried away with great effort and laid in
a bed, so troubled that he tried with his teeth
to viciously tear his own limbs and those of
others. He no longer knew his own language

but began speaking in another tongue that those standing there did not know. Since nothing that he said made sense to them, but still they heard him giving out unknown words without the slightest hesitation, they concluded that he was almost certainly using another language.

After a few hours when the brothers were still confused, they anxiously thought and carefully considered what they might do about the man's speaking. One of them, conceiving a healing counsel, inspired by the Lord, ordered that the tooth of the blessed Bernard be brought and placed on the man's breast. This tooth was among the sacred tokens, namely, from our father's hair and beard, that I myself had recently entrusted to the archbishop. When this was done, the German language began to pour out of the man's mouth in horrible words, and the evil spirit proclaimed, "Take it away, take it away! Remove Bernard." And he went on, "Woe is me! What a great burden you have become, O Bernard, what a dire and intolerable weight you have become to me!" He kept crying out like this and shouting out for some time.

Then a brief silence, and suddenly the brother, cleansed by a stroke of divine mercy, opened his eyes and as though waking from a deep sleep looked around in astonishment at the brothers who were there, saw his chains and, totally mortified, wanted to know where he was and what had happened to him. From that moment, through the merits of the blessed father, he received back his former health of both mind and body and could not remember anything that had happened to him during his grave plight or what he had spoken about.

All this was told us by the reverend Eskil, archbishop of the Danes, on the occasion of the bread blessed by the man of God, though the event may have happened at a different time.

HEALING ANIMALS

[28] Bernard's blessing frequently went out not only to men but also to beasts of burden, as once when he harshly rebuked the cellarer of his monastery because without letting him know he had allowed animals to die that were meant to feed the poor. From then on, as was his custom, he blessed the salt and ordered it to be given to the animals, and at once any infection that had arisen ceased. We have seen this happening in other monasteries and we know about it, as when he heard about brothers' animals being left to die and even without being asked warned them beforehand and sent the same cure.

VARIOUS MIRACLES

The monks of Chézy[49] lived at a place called Gaude. The holy man was spending the night there when they showed him a young man who was crippled. With a prayer and a blessing he healed him, so that when he came back to the same place after a very few days the man was standing there in a healthy state, now a devout person.[50] In that same district near a town called Augour the people brought a deranged woman to Bernard, who was passing by.

---

[49] The Benedictine abbey of Chézy-sur-Marne; see Bernard, Ep 263 (SBOp 8:172; James #336).

[50] *Fragm* I.52 (VP 301; *Notes* 167).

He placed his hand on her, prayed, and sent her away cured, so that she went off.[51]

[29] Wherever the needs of the holy church drew him, even in remote regions, the gift of miracles followed him, and anyone who met the man of God did so with ardent thanksgiving. Near Verfeuil (such is the name of a castle in the territory of Toulouse, which, as we mentioned in the previous book,* the holy father once entered imbued with many virtues), a boy who was crippled in both feet and both hands from his mother's womb received healing in both feet and in one of his withered hands through prayers in memory of a local martyr. The other hand was still unusable, as if kept like that by divine disposition, so that when the holy father healed it with a blessing it should be clear that he partook of the power of the saints.

*bk. 3.16–20

In Aquitaine there is a city called Cahors, through which the man of God was making a journey at the time. There, apart from many other benefits that he did for many sick people, when Bernard laid his hands on one of the servants of the city's bishop, who had received a serious wound and lost the sight in one of his eyes, the man regained his sight.

In the vicinity of Angoulême at a place called Châtelard, after the offering of the sacred host, while the bishops Lambert of Angoulême* and Gerald of Limoges were standing by, they brought to the servant of God a boy who was lame and maimed from his mother's womb. He was severely deformed, with his legs twisted into a ball, his knees up to his navel, and his feet stuck to his buttocks. So Bernard first made the sign of the cross, then stretched out each of the limbs and with wonderful facility unfolded them. He then immediately restored the boy to health. Taking

*1137–1147

---

[51] *Fragm* I.54 (VP 301; *Notes* 167).

hold of his hand, he lifted him up and sent him off walking freely. The people praised the Lord with great shouts of joy for such a display of his might.

Then on the following day in the town of Limoges, in a village called Saint-Genis, many miracles shone out through him. Everywhere people suffering from various complaints gathered round him, and the power of the Lord was there to heal them. Among these was a lad who had been blind from birth, for almost ten years. He was presented to the man of God in front of all the people. Bernard spat on his fingers and, making a short prayer, *rubbed his eyes with the spittle** and *in the name of Christ† opened the eyes of the lad born blind.‡*

*John 9:6
†1 Pet 4:14
‡John 9:32

[30] When he entered the kingdom of Germany on one occasion, the man of God brought light to the place in such an excellent manner with the graces of healing that it can be neither expressed in words nor believed if spoken. From witnesses who were there in the territory of Constance near a town called Donningen—from those who carefully investigated and saw with their own eyes—we heard this: soon afterward, on one day Bernard laid his hands on eleven blind people, healing their sight, and he healed ten who were disabled, and he made eighteen walk who were lame. Apart from these, we are not able to recount the great number coming from so great a multitude, though we can at least commend a few to memory, of whom the facts are known in some of the more celebrated places.

When the man of God came to Constance and the fame of his powerful deeds was widespread, the abbot of Reichenau, a famous monastery within the ancient lake of Léman,[52] sent to him a blind man to whom he gave alms, and he received his sight.

---

[52] Lake Constance; in English, Lake Geneva.

There is a place called Heitersheim, belonging to the same diocese of that city but quite remote from the city. There too, just as in other places in that province through which Bernard was traveling, God was glorified in his servant through many miracles. It was there that a blind man received his sight when he laid his hand on him. And again, a man who was deaf and dumb from his birth was granted his hearing and began to speak.

Also in the city of Basel, after he had preached a sermon to the people, as was customary so that what they had read in the holy apostles might be fulfilled in that place (*for they went forth and preached everywhere, while the Lord worked with them and confirmed the message by the signs that attended it*),* a mute woman was presented to him, and when he prayed for her she immediately began to speak. A lame man was presented, and he walked, and a blind man too was presented, and he saw.

*Mark 16:20

[31] Near the city of Speyer, Conrad, the king of the Romans, was present. He led the man of God from the church to the guesthouse with great devotion and then brought a lame boy to him, asking him to consent *to lay his hand on him*.* As soon as he had made the sign of the cross, the boy got up, stood on his feet, and began to walk of his own accord, while everybody cried out in praise of God.

*Luke 4:40

The same thing happened in the chapel of the bishop of that city while the king himself was watching: Bernard gave sight to a blind woman there and made a man who was lame from birth walk. Christ performed many other signs by the hand of Bernard, but these few things will suffice as examples.

When the devout king also presented to him with his own hands some poor little boys, he merited to be granted the cure of many. Then again, near the town of Speyer, in the Diocese of Mainz at a place near Frankfurt-on-Main, the servant of God carried out innumerable powerful deeds. From everywhere in that region, whoever was suffering came to him, and such was the concourse that the king, unable to prevent the people from crowding around, took off his regal garment and, lifting the holy man in his arms, carried him out of the basilica.

Among the many people who wanted to be healed was an old man from the district who was paralyzed. He was well known and highly esteemed; after many prayers and much effort, he was brought to the man of God. After a very short prayer, as was customary, he stood up straight and was healed at once. Not only was he made well, but rather he appeared full of vigor, so that if you could see him you would believe he was not just altered in appearance but was another man. He was now so strong that when others were lifting up the bed he had been brought in, one of the bystanders, Hugh, the archdeacon of Toul, remembered that he was a paralytic and said, "Do not go back empty-handed:* *Take up your bed and walk.*"* Then Hugh placed the bed on the man's shoulders and sent him off walking tall, so that *all the people, when they saw it, gave praise to God.**

In the same place, a boy who had been deaf and dumb from his mother's womb was lifted up on a ladder into a window. When the man of God approached, the boy received his hearing from Bernard's hand and began to speak. There was also a paralyzed woman in the same region. A rich and honorable woman, she too received back her health, which she had lost a long time before. When she went out and was walking, all those who saw her rejoiced, but the knights who brought her and offered her to Bernard were more than the others over the moon, for they thought that their religious devotion had played some part in this miracle.

*see Isa 55:11
*John 5:8

*Luke 18:43

At the same time, while the holy man was passing close to the shore of the Rhine at a place called Boppard and curing sick people throughout the province, they brought to him a paralyzed man on a bed. When the account of Bernard's fame for performing miracles spread in the village just mentioned, the sick man was carried to him. Bernard placed his hand on the man in the midst of all the people and sent him off home, restored to health.

BERNARD AT TRIER

[32] That same year when the servant of Christ was going into the town of Trier, all the people there as usual rushed out to meet him. They brought two sisters to him, both of whom had lost the sight of their eyes four years before. He touched them, making the sign of the cross, and the sight of light returned to them. When they saw the man of God they followed him with all the rest.

In the basilica of that city, when this man imbued with apostolic grace was offering the immortal host at the altar of the blessed Peter, a lame man was brought to him who began to walk, a blind man was brought who saw, and a deaf woman was also brought who began to hear. This woman recounted that she had been advised in a dream about the man of God and instructed that if she sought him out, she would receive her hearing through his kindness.

Near Koblenz, a noble castle in the diocese of Trier, the servant of God passed over the River Mosel at the spot where it flows down into the Rhine. When he had gone not very far, a crippled man was brought to him, over whom he made the sign of the cross. He then ordered him to be set down and walk, but no one did so. At once, though, the cripple himself cried out that he could not relax the upper part of his leg. He did not know why, although he had tried before to extend it like his other knee, he could not release it however much he tried. As they were all wondering about this, all of a sudden, to prove what Bernard had said, he was put down in that place, began to walk, and found himself completely healed.

BERNARD AT COLOGNE

[33] We must not omit what was going to happen at Cologne. This is a great city, where great power came to the servant of God and the people showed him great devotion. To this very day is seen in the monastery of Blessed Peter, as we have recently heard from trustworthy persons, a young man, formerly crippled, now walking about freely. This man had been brought to the man of God to lay his hands on him. He then received the ability to walk and after that was publicly acknowledged as his son.[53]

Abbot Henry of Sweden, whom we have mentioned above, recently related this story to us: a noble woman, once the wife of his brother, fell into a frenzy of grief after the death of her husband, and for a long time she had to be restrained with chains. She was brought to the holy father in the same city. Among the great thronging crowd, hardly had he touched her with the sign of the cross than the chains fell away all at once and she fully recovered her senses, with complete healing.

In the same city the noble parents of a deaf girl brought her to the holy father. They told him that the girl had been dedicated in a monastery of holy

---

[53] I.e., presumably, "he became a devout follower of Bernard."

nuns and had lost her hearing while she was there; for several years she had gone about with this impediment. The holy father touched her ears and made the sign of the cross over them. At once she regained her hearing, and he gave her back to her parents.

Other things also happened in the city of Cologne. An honorable woman had lost the sight of one eye. For five years, she said, she spent a great deal on doctors in vain.* At once the blessed man by the sign of the cross gave her light, for *what he had received freely he gave freely*.* When another matron was brought to the servant of Christ on a bed in the Basilica of Blessed Peter, he ordered her to get up at once and go away on her feet, completely healed, though for a very long time her leg had been contracted in such a way that she could neither get out of bed nor stand on her feet.

*Luke 8:43

*Matt 10:8

Other people who carefully observed the prayers of the man of God verified how he laid hands on the sick in that city during the three days that he was there. They attested that he made twelve cripples stand up, healed two who had been maimed, restored sight to fifteen blind people, and allowed three mute people to speak and ten deaf people to hear.

[34] Meanwhile at Aachen while the blessed man was celebrating a solemn Mass in the most famous chapel of kings in the whole Roman Empire, the King of kings and the Lord of lords with his almighty power restored the feet of a crippled man and gave sight to four blind people through the hand of his servant.

A Remarkable Miracle at Liège

At the same time within the territory of Liège, apart from the numerous other things that we must pass over for the sake of brevity, near the town of Fontaine,* while praying he opened the eyes of a boy

*Chaudfontaine

born blind. He was not only blind, but his eyelids were closed, and he was practically dead. Opening the boy's eyes with his sacred fingers, by a divine gift the blessed man gave strength to his eyelids and clarity to the pupils of his eyes. At once the boy, marveling at this previously unexperienced light, cried out loudly in exulting joy, "I can see, I can see the day, I can see all the men with their beards!" He started to clap his hands and jump up and down, and he said: "O God, from now on *I will not dash my foot* against a stone."*[54]

*Ps 90:12

In the town of Cambrai, while the man of God was celebrating solemn Mass, someone brought to him a boy deaf and mute from birth, and at once he began to hear and speak. Those present mounted Bernard onto a wooden step so that he could address the people with a new sermon from that elevated position. No wonder the astounding devotion of the crowds followed, giving a marvelous cry of admiration. These things happened in the kingdom of Germany, where God worked in a wonderful way through the hand of his servant.

[35] Even in Spain, where Bernard was not present, indications of his sanctity blazed abroad. When *the faithful and prudent servant** had gathered the precious fruit of the Lord's cross from all sides and propagated it everywhere, he sent some of his sons to Spain,[55] for he desired fruit there as among other

*Matt 24:45

---

[54] Although the boy and Geoffrey of Auxerre are obviously quoting this psalm, used by Satan in the temptations of Jesus (Matt 5:6; Luke 4:11), the fact does not seem to have been noticed before. The singular *stone* here is surely more correct than the plural reading of the manuscript, *lapides*, since it is singular in all those places in the Vulgate.

[55] To Sobrado, near Santiago de Compostella, founded 1142, and Poblet in Catalonia, founded 1150.

peoples. One of them was Albert, a carpenter in a place called Sobrado. He was overcome with a serious illness and for a long time lay in bed paralyzed. Meanwhile his abbot told the holy father of Albert's sickness, beseeching him to have mercy on Albert. On the same day that the blessed man of Clairvaux had prayed for this paralytic at his abbot's request, *since the word of his power* had run swiftly,†* the power of his prayer immediately healed the Spanish brother, who felt it like a vase full of water being poured over his head. When his abbot returned home, he inquired diligently from the healed brother the manner and time of his being freed and discovered that he was cured in Spain at exactly the time that the servant of God was praying in France.

*Heb 1:3
†Ps 147:15

[36] And because we are writing about Spain,[56] we should describe what happened to the reverend Peter, bishop of Asturia.[57] This Peter was of a noble family, by profession a monk and a devout person in his monastery, which he ruled at that time, but he labored under a severe pain in his head, so that he could not observe the rule of fasting or stand up without a fur covering. Hearing of the man of God's fame for his deeds of power, he sent a brother to petition Bernard for help and to implore his holy intercession.

The holy man sent him a woolly fur cloak, which he himself had formerly worn, and he promised by the power of the Lord a remedy for the sickness in Peter's head. Peter received the blessing sent to him with the utmost reverence and devotion. He made confession as carefully as he could for his sins, and putting on his priestly stole as if he were touching the fringe of Christ's garments,* he put on the fur

*Matt 9:20;
14:36;
Mark 6:56

---

[56] *Ad Hispanias vertimus stylum,* lit. "we turn our pen to Spain."
[57] First abbot of Moreruela, a daughter house of Clairvaux; he became a Cistercian in 1158; see VP 230, n. to 874.

cloak of the servant of Christ and covered his head. The fruit of his faith was not slow in coming, but he himself was amazed when he at once felt the effect of the medicine. From then until the present day he has asserted to all comers that he was healed and relieved of all pain, for he had been found worthy to experience this supernatural healing power. When he was made bishop he divided the precious gift in two, carrying one part with him into the trea- sury with the greatest honor and placing the other in the monastery with the same veneration, so that neither the see to which he had been elevated nor the monastery to which he had been called should be deprived of such a blessing.

Miracles Near Clairvaux

[37] From now on we must return to those things that happened in a marvelous way in our own region. Here, he seemed perhaps to be called more than a prophet, for one called a prophet is *not without honor except in his own country*.* The town called Mussy† on the River Seine is only a short distance from Clair- vaux. From there they brought a man with dropsy to the man of God, who placed his hands on the man, prayed, and placed his own belt around the man's stomach, which was enormously swollen, telling him to restore the belt when he was healed. Nor was his healing slow in coming, for the swelling gradually disappeared. So after about twenty days he returned, looking graceful and in fine form, and he gave the belt back with thanksgiving to Bernard, his curer.

At another time, when Bernard was going from his monastery, they took him to an elderly man who was paralyzed, from a local town called Meurville. Passing that way, he touched the man and prayed

*Matt 13:57;
Mark 6:4
(*ne . . . nisi*, Vulg)
†Mussy-l'Évêque

for him briefly, then ordered him to go on his way on foot, now cured. While he was walking away, a great crowd of people converged on the holy man and praised the Lord with tears in their eyes. Again, when he was returning along the way outside the monastery, they brought him a boy who was deaf and mute. *Spitting, he touched his tongue and placed his fingers in his ears.** Immediately the obstacle in the boy's ears came out in front of everybody, and the chain binding his mouth was released.

*Mark 7:33

[38] Maranville is a place about three miles from the monastery. The blessed man was once passing by when he touched a lame girl and cured her. She is still now on her feet, and we have recently seen her in good health.

At that same time in the vicinity of a castle called Bourlemont, two knights were speaking about the virtues of the blessed father, but one of them did not believe what he heard and said, "If he heals a boy here, then I will firmly believe." He mentioned that there was a deaf and mute boy there who ate with them but could not speak or hear. After a few days, when the holy father was going nearby, the two knights brought the boy to him. He laid his hand on the boy, made the sign of the cross on his mouth and ears, and spoke to him, and at once he sent him away, able to speak and hear. Near Reynel, a town in the same region, a well-known young man called Simon may be seen. He was brought to the servant of God crippled. When Bernard laid his hand on him, he received the ability to walk.

Bar-sur-Aube* is a town three leagues, as they say, from the monastery of Clairvaux. There, the works of divine power often shone out through the man of God. Besides those things that we have paid little attention to, our curiosity was overcome by many miracles, four of them for cripples, whom Christ had

**Barrum super Albam*

lifted up at different times through Bernard's prayers and his laying on of hands, and for two blind men to whose eyes he brought light, and for two deaf and mute men to whom he gave the power of hearing and speech. Then near the other Bar-sur-Seine,[58] at his touch a blind man was given sight, a paralytic was healed, and a boy lame from his mother's womb was made able to walk.

[39] When our most reverend Pope Eugenius III[59] was taken from being a monk at Clairvaux and became abbot of Saint Anastasia in the city of Rome and from there transferred to the cathedral of the apostles, he went to France, and the holy man went with him. Bernard was no less preeminent in the virtue of an apostle than was Eugenius in apostolic dignity, such was the gathering of those suffering various sicknesses coming to the blessed man. At one point the supreme pontiff devoutly entered the basilica where Bernard was celebrating solemn Mass. When he had completed the sacrifice and many came forward as usual, desiring to be healed, the pope was besieged by the crowd, and the efforts of his ministers were hardly able to get him clear. Among the many miracles done among those who gathered around the apostolic man,* we write of two that we witnessed. The great joy that they excited should not be forgotten.

Charlette is a village situated between the Castle Provins and the River Seine. There, since the previous year, a child nearly ten years old had lain paralyzed, hardly able to move his head unless someone else helped him. His mother and other neighbors carried him on a mattress and brought him to the

*i.e., Bernard

---

[58] *Alteram Barrum super Sequanam.*

[59] Bernard Paganelli, monk of Clairvaux, abbot of Saint Vincent and Saint Anastasia, elected pope February 1145.

holy man, who was going through that area by a public road. When he made the sign of the cross, the boy stood up on his feet; then Bernard ordered him to walk. Without any delay the boy jumped up and started to walk, giving glory to God. For a long time he followed the saint while he was on his way, until he was unwilling to let the boy go any farther and told him to return home. This event caused great wonder and great rejoicing to all who saw it, but more than all the others, the boy's younger brother fell upon him with kisses as if he had been raised from the dead. Many others were moved to tears. After four years in the village the mother brought this same boy to the blessed man, offering to kiss his sacred feet, saying, "This is your father, who gave you back your life and gave you to me."

BERNARD AT CÎTEAUX

[40] In that same year,* at Cîteaux, where the abbots had come together† as was the custom, the aforesaid venerable pope‡ was present, not presiding with apostolic authority but rather sitting among them as one of them. When the servant of God had gone aside to his cell in which he rested after Vespers and the assembly had gone out, they brought him a boy who was deaf. This boy had come from nearby; as we learned afterward, a long time previously while watching over his flock, he had been struck with terror and had as a result completely lost his hearing. The holy father prayed over him, laying his hands on him, and asked him if he could hear. With tremendous fervor, affirming, "Yes, my lord, I do hear, I do hear," he embraced Bernard with such vigor that they could hardly be separated. When people heard what had happened, the boy was brought to the

*1147
†for the general chapter
‡Pope Eugenius

supreme pontiff and others, and this miracle became famous everywhere.

The holy father came to a monastery in the diocese of Besançon called Cherlieu.[60] Many other abbots of the Order were with him. While he was there, a matron of the district who had been lame for a long time was brought to him, lying in a carriage. He made a short prayer over her; when he gave her a blessing in the name of the Lord, she rose up and was healed, at once returning home in a healthy condition.

At the same time in the monastery of Morimond,[61] which is one of the first abbeys of the Cistercian Order, a monk was so paralyzed that almost all his limbs had lost their function; he could move neither hand nor foot. The blessed man on his arrival visited this man, and when he was asked to, he placed his hand on him. Immediately the sick man felt the effect. But for the grace of the miracle to work more effectively, the man recovered slowly, first one hand and then the other. Just as Bernard was about to go on his way, however, he covered the sick man with his cloak, and suddenly, in a very short time, he obtained the complete healing of the rest of his body.

In the monastery of Auberive[62] there was a young monk who had lost the use of his voice, so he could not join his brothers in singing the psalms or make anyone understand what he was saying unless they were very close to him. When the holy man visited the monastery, he gave him a drink of water mixed with wine, blessing it, and after a while the restricting fluid in the young monk's breast spurted out with an astonishing sweetness. On that very day he was

---

[60] =Carus locus; founded 1131 by Clairvaux.

[61] Daughter of Cîteaux, founded 1115, the same year as Clairvaux.

[62] Near Langres, founded by Clairvaux 1135.

freed from his affliction and began to sing the psalms as one of the brothers. This high favor perseveres to this day.

[41] When on another occasion the holy father was visiting the monastery of Trois Fontaines,[63] a certain cleric was brought to him from among the Regular Canons, an elderly man who was blind. Bernard placed his hand on the cleric and made a short prayer, at once sending him off to the church able to see.

MIRACLES IN THE CITY OF TROYES

In the city of Troyes many miracles made the servant of God shine out in splendor. From among these we must commemorate two done in the presence of Bishop Geoffrey of Langres[64] and Bishop Henry of Troyes.[65] People brought to Bernard a girl who was bent over, praying for her to be healed.* She lived in the house of the bishop of Troyes, being related to him and well known. Such was the immense concourse of people present that although when the servant of God made the sign of the cross it was as if a soft ball of potter's clay formed in his sacred hands. When he ordered her to stand up straight, a place could not be found. At last they got her to stand on a large table that was near; she climbed up onto it,

*Luke 13:11; *et erat inclinata,* Vulg

---

[63] Founded 1118, first daughter of Clairvaux. See Louis J. Lekai, *The Cistercians: Ideals and Reality* (Kent, OH: Kent State University Press, 1977), 34.

[64] Among the first monks of Clairvaux, first abbot of Fontenay 1118, prior of Clairvaux 1128–1138, bishop of Langres 1138–1163.

[65] Henry of Spanheim, monk of Morimond, abbot of Villers-Bettnach, bishop of Troyes 1145–1169.

standing erect, while everybody praised the Lord with shouts of joy. We have recently heard from those who know her that she is still alive.

In the same city a mother brought a mute girl to the holy father. She had the sickness of epilepsy, which prevented her from speaking. Without any delay the servant of Christ placed his hands on her, and the bond that fastened her mouth was loosened and she spoke normally. In the diocese of the same city called Donnement, when the holy man had celebrated solemn Mass, a father brought his blind son to him. Bernard, spitting on his fingers, stroked the boy's eyelids, at once giving him back to his father with his sight restored.

Not far from that same place, near the town Arzillières, again after the celebration of Mass, a lame woman who had lived there for a long time as a beggar came to Bernard. Going out of the basilica and making the sign of the cross over her, he healed her. A great number of people who had gathered there from all around were filled with admiration and rejoicing. Again, when he was leaving the town called Rosnay, they brought to the man of God as he was passing a man who was paralyzed and stretched out so flat that he seemed to be but an image of the pallor of death laid out on a cart. Bernard, after making the sign of the cross, had the man set down and ordered him to walk. He got up from his cart onto his feet and eagerly followed Bernard, while all the people around were stupefied and shouting the praises of God.

[42] At another time near the castle called Brienne, while passing along he met a lot of people, as they always gathered together in a huge number to meet him. When they were all looking at a lame girl from the town, he touched her, and she stood up. Since then we have seen her running to him with the

others and giving more thanks than any of them. In the village of Sens near the castle called Trainel, during the holy solemnity of the Mass, a blind woman who had lived there for ten years and was known to everybody received her sight back by the hand of the man of God while all looked on with amazement.

Near Montereau, where the Yonne and the Seine flow together, when the most pious Prince Theobald and others were present with a number of noteworthy men, some people brought a paralyzed woman to the man of God while the divine sacrifice was being offered. Having finished the Mass, he touched her; she straightaway got up healed and returned home, walking on her own two feet. We saw the bed she had been carried in left empty there in the basilica.

At the castle of Joigny in the same diocese, when the servant of Christ was passing that way, they brought a blind woman to him in a public highway. He stood there, made a short prayer, and placed his hands on the woman, and the Lord opened her eyes. When it was noticed that she could see, a great up-welling of praise followed from all those there as they shouted to one another, "Anna, sees, Anna sees!" (That was the name of the woman.) Many people gathered round her from everywhere. **[43]** Meanwhile the holy man was hurrying away from the crowds when a young man, blind in one eye from the time of his birth, caught up with him. He at once received the sight of his eyes at the holy man's blessing, and the joy of the people following him was redoubled.

Chablis is the name of the village that possesses the famous Basilica of Saint Martin. He was its founder and also the founder of the church of Tours, as its glorious confessor of the faith. When the servant of God was passing by the village, the people brought him a lame young man. When he offered a prayer for the young man, he stood up, and when he started to walk freely without assistance, they led him to the Basilica of Saint Martin while all praised the Lord who had raised up the spirit of this Martin in Bernard.

[44] Christ did many marvelous healings by the hand of his faithful servant and acted even more marvelously in the visions he showed him. He felt within himself many others by the power traced in his mind when they were done. He did others at the suggestion of the Holy Spirit, healing without being asked. From these we have selected a few examples. But we fear that in relating them we might seem to pass over the immense number, so we warn you now that there are perhaps too many works to be marveled at because all too briefly written about. Indeed, many of these we have seen were done so quickly that however hastily we write we cannot keep up with them. And although it is customary to say that nothing is easier than saying, through the grace that the man of God received he seemed to do his miracles more easily than we can relate them.

On one occasion when the man of God was going out of the monastery, a certain man from the district brought his son to be healed. Within the monastery itself, Bernard would not easily agree to lay his hand on the sick, lest the concourse of people there should disturb the quiet of the house and destroy its discipline. But the boy we have just mentioned was mentally deranged and weak-minded; he was also lame and deaf and mute. When Bernard prayed over him and laid his hand on him, he was freed at once from all these infirmities; he heard and spoke and walked, and he became sound in mind, so that his former restlessness and frenzy just ceased. When the devout father took his son, now healed, to the oratory of the Blessed Mother of God with thanksgiving, the brothers spoke together, arguing about the many sicknesses of the one boy. **[45]** The holy father replied, "It was

a scourge of God and the awful vexation of the evil
spirit. Last night I had a vision in this very place, near
the River Aube, where the boy was healed." He went
on, "I saw a boy like this brought to me, in such a way
that the evil spirit went out of him, and at once he
received his health and the use of his limbs."

Concerning that same vision the blessed man added,
"When I went on a little farther on the same road that
we are now walking along, near the village that is called
Longchamp, a little girl was presented to me, and the
Lord gave back to her the ability to walk." The brothers
heard this and were astonished, more astonished at the
miracles still to come than the ones past. Has the world
ever heard the like? You come to a place: there a lame
girl is waiting for him, expecting the man of God to be
going to pass that way, and he is found immediately and
at the same time by those who are passing by, according to the word that Bernard himself had predicted.
Presented to him by those who brought her, she was
given the sign of the cross by the man of God, just as
predicted. From the gift of God she received the ability
to walk and went away giving thanks.

[46] The following year* a quarrel arose between   *probably 1138
the bishop and the clergy of the city of Langres, so
the man of God was obliged to go there. It was a
serious case, causing a great deal of friction. When on
the first day he had labored without effect and in the
morning was getting ready to go away, he said to the
brothers, "In a vision I saw myself at night entering
the church, where they brought a lame woman and
she was healed." About an hour later, when the clergy
had come together again because they all hoped to
make peace, they urged him with many prayers to
enter the cathedral of the blessed martyr Mamert.[66]

---

[66] The third-century Saint Mammès or Mamas of Caesarea.

Because a famine was pressing on them, he exhorted the people to give alms. While they were talking, a lame woman was presented to him, as he had predicted, and she stood up erect while everyone there was astonished, especially those who saw it and recalled that they had heard what was going to happen.

A Woman Healed at Gontran de Sura

[47] In the district of Trier is an ancient monastery that is called Rutina. When the man of God was once celebrating solemn Mass there, a great number of people came to him. Meanwhile at Gontran de Sura,[67] which is a town near the monastery, he had a woman brought to him who was deprived of the use of her legs. Having for a very long time had to creep along the ground, she was utterly unable to get up; pulling in her hands a little cart, she used to drag her paralyzed limbs on it. Because of the huge number of people present, the woman could not be brought to the man of God, so he suddenly healed her in the middle of the basilica, and she went out walking, giving thanks to God and weeping profusely. The jubilant people at once took her little cart to the altar so that they could leave it there to the honor of the Lord and his servant Bernard.

The holy father later confessed to us that this cure had been foretold to him on the previous night, when it seemed to him that in the same basilica in the midst of people standing around, he touched this woman and passed on. Although in a way unknown to himself, he saw her healed immediately, and he was full of joy because no one had recognized him.

---

[67] In 1169, at Saarberg, near Trier (VP 231).

On that very day at Rutina, in the presence of the blessed man, a light from heaven shone out brightly, and the blessing from it returned the power of walking to two crippled women and sight to two who were blind.

There is no doubt that while praying, the servant of God wisely acknowledged the presence of divine power. **[48]** But he also confessed that he could not possibly express this manner of knowing in words. Sometimes, he said, he made the sign of the cross over people and then passed on having healed them; then, if someone who heard about it mentioned it to him and he returned there, he found that it had happened just as it had been said.

Once when he had left the city of Basel, he had made the sign of the cross over a deaf man and then moved on. Soon afterward he spoke to Alexander of Cologne,[68] saying, "Go back and find out whether the man can hear." Alexander returned and found that he could hear very well.[69] On the same day, when the man of God had made the sign of the cross over another man blind in one eye and gone on, he said, "God has opened his eye." When Alexander returned along the road, he asked about this healing, too, and so Bernard came to know about it. This is the same Alexander who in those days at the sacred admonitions of the man of God, having seen his powerful works, left the world with almost thirty others and followed him. After a short time the man of God sent him from there* to a monastery in the diocese of Toulouse called Grandselve.[70]

*presumably Clairvaux

[68] Abbot of Grandselve 1149, abbot of Cîteaux 1166, canon of Cologne; d. 1175.

[69] VP 232, n. to 1193.

[70] Founded 1114 by Gerald of Sales; he became Cistercian in 1145 at Clairvaux.

While on the road in the Diocese of Constance, near the castle of Freiberg, when he had placed his hand on a blind man, he sent back a person who had seen him, and the blind man was found to be able to see. Again, in the town of Cologne near the monastery called Braunweiler,[71] Bernard did the same with two other blind men; when they announced that they could see, he confessed that he himself had also felt that power.

[49] In the region of Sens, in a town called Saint-Florentin, people brought a deaf woman to the man of God. He placed his hands on her and sensed the gift through the Spirit, but when she was still senseless and agitated, as is customary with that type of sickness, which she herself was used to, she cried out at the top of her voice that she could hear nothing. On the following morning, when she did not return and no one else indicated anything about her, the holy man, knowing that divine mercy had been granted her, ordered that she be brought back. When she discovered that she had received her hearing, she came back glorifying God and giving thanks to the servant of God.

As the father was going out of the city of Metz, devout people were as usual accompanying him, along with their bishop Stephen[72] and his brother Rainald, count of Bar, and other persons, both clergymen and members of the Military Order of Knights.* Meanwhile, Bernard asked the nobleman Henry of Salm about something that the bishop and others who had come together had put to him, namely, to bring peace to the city of Metz and the people, toward whom he was at total enmity. But Henry absolutely

*i.e., the Knights Templar

---

[71] Brumvillers or Brauweiller, near Cologne (VP 232, n. to 1206).

[72] Stephen de Bar, bishop of Metz 1120–1163.

refused, turning his back on them, and would not yield to their entreaties.

While this was going on, they brought a deaf man to the blessed man, asking him to lay his hand on him. But the man of God, filled with zeal because he was dealing with these demanding cases, looked Henry in the face and, reddening with zeal and with authority, turned to the knight, saying, "You have contemptuously refused to listen to us, but this deaf man will at once hear us in your presence." Placing his hands on the man, he made the sign of the cross over him and placed his fingers in his ears. Immediately the man began to hear. Then Henry was so alarmed and shaken that he threw himself at the feet of the man of God and, making humble satisfaction, freely agreed that he would do anything he asked.

[50] The servant of Christ was at one time passing by the town of Brienne when he saw a blind woman begging there. He looked at her for a little while as she was requesting alms from those walking by. "You are asking for money," he said; "God will give you your sight." Going up to her he touched her and opened her eyes. She felt within herself this unexpected gift and was amazed at it no less for the greatness of the mercy she had been given than for the unaccustomed light of day.

Among the first offspring that this extremely abundant vine sent out, the monastery of Igny[73] successfully took root in the parish of Reims. Once when the holy man was visiting it, he passed by a village called Rivolles near the River Marne. A very wealthy and devout friend, Samson, archbishop of Reims,[74] accompanied the man of God and took

---

[73] Founded in 1128 from Clairvaux.
[74] Samson de Mauvoisin, archbishop 1140–1161.

him about with his usual veneration. An elderly lame man was sitting by the road begging, and one of the brothers gave him alms. The holy abbot, who was following, turned around after he had passed the man and, looking at him for a moment or two, asked those nearby what he was suffering from. He then ordered the man to be shown to him. The men suspected that he was going to give him something extra, so they said, "Sir, he is crippled and cannot be moved. We will take him whatever you want to give him." As soon as Bernard heard this, he said, "Lift him up and bring him to me." They first looked at one another with astonishment, not knowing what he was about to do. But at last they recognized him and shouted to one another, "It is the abbot of Clairvaux; he is going to heal him right away!"

[51] Now it was Bernard's custom when he was going to do anything not to be recognized in the villages, and he forbade his companions to make him known to those he met or to say anything about him, but to those inquiring who was going with them, they should just say they were monks or name one of the persons accompanying them. So when these men recognized the servant of God, they ran off and, lifting up the lame man, they brought him along and presented him to Bernard. He placed both hands on the man's head and, looking up to heaven and making a short prayer, he insisted that the man should be put down and allowed to walk. But the lame man excused himself and said, "I cannot do so." So Bernard said, "I order you in the name of the Lord and with his power: get up and go. Be healed now from this very moment." What more can be said? The man was immediately set down, he was immediately healed, he began immediately to walk, and he was filled with complete stupor and cried in ecstasy at what had happened to him. But his com-

panions and those who knew him praised the Lord and gave thinks to God, who out of the abundance of his goodness had exceeded the merits and even the hopes of this wretched man.

So it is that to this day locals show the place where such a clear sign of divine power shone out in glory, where this elderly crippled man, who had for many years been half dead in his lower limbs and destitute of all functioning from his waist down, asked for alms but received complete healing. This was the last time that the holy man went into the district of Reims, and it was one year before the sacred yielding of his body to death.

Now this is the most happy ending for us of his most blessed deeds, but we have spoken about them in another narrative. But anyone who thinks he can relate all the marvelous things done by this most holy man will be mistaken. It is necessary to be silent about many of them, for it is quite impossible to comprehend them all.

The end of the second book.

Book 5

BY GEOFFREY OF AUXERRE
(CALLED BY GEOFFREY BOOK 3)[1]

The beginning of the third

Bernard's Last Days

When after so many labors the Lord resolved to give the sleep of a precious death to his beloved Bernard, for a long time abbot of Clairvaux, and bring his faithful servant into his eternal rest, his spirit began to progress more and more strongly in him, while his flesh began to fail. The holy man knew that the prize was drawing near and ran more swiftly than ever, feeling in himself that the unfolding of this earthly dwelling was imminent. He aspired with all the more longing for the dwelling of God, *to a house not made with hands, eternal in the heavens.** In his most pure breast there broke out by frequent signs the flame of a sacred desire unable to be restrained, and the *flaming word** showed forth the vigor of internal fervor, just like the holy living creatures described by the

*2 Cor 5:1

*Ps 118:140

---

[1] In this book MS. MSB 1 omits sections 2 and 22 from Recension A as found in the critical edition.

prophet, where among others things he said, *they*
*Ezek 1:7
sparkled like burnished brass.*

Lying on his bed, Bernard's body was beset with
many ailments, but his soul was nonetheless free and
*Sir 18:1
powerful through God, who claimed the victory.* In
the midst of all his suffering, Bernard did not cease to
meditate on or to dictate sacred matters, to pray with
loving fervor, and to exhort his brethren with kindly
care. When he offered the holy sacrifice of Mass, which
he hardly ever missed right up to his last moment, he
sustained the vigor of his spirit, strongly forcing and
offering himself as an acceptable sacrifice to God *in*
*Eph 5:2
the sweet-smelling odor of holiness.* During that time he
wrote a letter to his uncle Andrew, a Knight of the
Temple who was in charge of one of the chief columns
*2 Tim 4:6
in the region of Jerusalem, and told him, "*I am failing;**
I do not think I have long to remain on this earth."[2]

BERNARD AT METZ BRINGS PEACE
TO A CITY AT WAR

[3] While the holy father was still in the monastery at Clairvaux vigorously finishing the race of
*2 Tim 4:7
life* though lying in bed, a serious calamity came on
the people of Metz. This great city went out with
an imposing force against the neighboring princes,
who had so provoked them that they were unable
any longer to tolerate their condition, but many were
given into the hands of a very few. Those fighting the
princes were enclosed within the restricted confined
gorges of Froidmont,[3] as it is called, and of the River
Mosel. Forced into this position, they were grappling

[2] Bernard, Ep 288 (SBOp 8.204; James #410).
[3] *Frigidi Montis*, later the site of the Cistercian monastery of
Froidmont, founded 1134.

with one another, and in one hour, it is said, more than two thousand perished, some cut down by the sword and many others drowned in the deep river.

Therefore that noble city, seized with massive fury, prepared itself with all its strength for revenge, while on the other side the outcome made the stronger forces bolder and more insistent in looking for greater booty. The devastation of the whole province looked certain and imminent when the venerable metropolitan, Hillin, archbishop of Trier,[4] overcome with utmost grief and anxiety at what had happened and fearing the worst in this pressing necessity, sought the only path left to him, appealing to the man of God. Coming therefore to Clairvaux, with total humility he prostrated himself at the feet of Bernard and all the brothers, entreating and imploring him that he might deign to oppose such evils, since it seemed that no one else could possibly do anything.

The Lord then, as always, directed the ways of his faithful servant, in these most difficult cases using him as a most appropriate tool. So for a few days he relieved him of his bodily sicknesses. After a while Bernard wrote to the venerable Hugh, bishop of Ostia,[5] saying, "It is true what you have heard. *I was ill, near to death,** but now I feel myself called back to death, yet as I am aware, not for long."[6] Reckoning this mortal life to be death rather than life, he felt that he had not been called back from death but to death, though it would not retain him much longer. **[4]** Divine Providence, in whose hands *his soul was pleasing to him,**   *Wis 4:14

*Phil 2:27

---

[4] Hillin de Fallemaigne, archbishop 1152–1169.

[5] Hugh, abbot of Trois Fontaines, bishop 1150–1158. For Bernard's letters to Hugh, see Epp 287, 290, 296, 306, 307 (SBOp 8:202, 207, 213, 223–25, 226–27; James ##414, 355, 361, 373, 372).

[6] Bernard, Ep 307 (SBOp 8:227; James #372).

disposed things for him in such a way that as often as a serious necessity came about, he swept aside all his weakness and the powers of his body did not submit to his mental state, though everyone who saw him marveled at it; he overcame his fatigue when more robust men would reckon it intolerable.

Once these affairs had been completed, Bernard returned to himself; he so labored under his many infirmities that when he was at rest he could hardly go on living, but when he was occupied in some way could not fail. The power of God was with him in this last of his works in such an open and magnificent way that he seemed to gain strength from his labors. It so happened that when this faithful mediator asked those residing on the shores of the River Mosel what would make for peace, one part, furious from the great carnage brought about by the enemy, with obstinate ill feeling refused to give what Bernard demanded. Suddenly, then, they went off, so agitated were they with fury, without even greeting the man of God, leaving to all the others only a feeling of despair for the possibility of peace. This flight was however not out of contempt for him, but rather from their reverence for him; indeed, they were afraid that he might easily change their shameless minds toward the enemies who were present, not considering what he could do in their absence by the Spirit, who was nowhere absent.

Now the whole place was caught up in a great commotion, and both sides thought about having recourse to arms, with only a ruinous omen like a cloud overshadowing them, when the holy man came and consoled those who were with him with the words, "My brothers, do not be disturbed." He told them, "Although you are now going through great difficulties, still the peace you desire will come." He revealed to those inquiring how he knew it, saying, "It was shown to me in a dream at night that I should celebrate a solemn Mass. When I had finished the first part of the prayer, I remembered the angelic canticle, that is to say, the 'Glory be to God in the Highest,' which ought to be said earlier, as is the custom. I blushed and, beginning the canticle I had forgotten, I completed it with you to the end." Then after midnight, when the holy man was still repenting from what he had done, he received a delegation of princes and, jokingly, turning to his brethren, he said, "Now recognize the promise made to us that we must prepare to sing the Glory be, the canticle of peace."

Meanwhile the two parties had come together for a few days to deal with peace talks. On account of the great problems on either side, both parties had utterly despaired of finding a solution, except that the holy abbot had quietly given all of them the promise of finding peace, and it would be fulfilled. The delay was of little profit, especially to those who were laboring under a variety of misfortunes and seeking remedies of a merely human sort, or even to those who were looking to be built up in their faith. Such was the crowd that the angry hordes and their disagreements prevented finding a peaceful agreement, leading almost to despair. But when the leaders of both parties saw the island in the middle of the river, they approached it in their skiffs. When they were all gathered there, they eventually came to an agreement devised by Bernard, the faithful arbiter. They shook hands with one another and were soon reconciled with the kiss of peace.

A Celebrated Cure

[5] Among all those healings that the Lord displayed through the hand of his servant, one was the

celebrated cure of a woman who had suffered a grave illness for eight years. All her limbs were shaking with violent trembling and severe movements. Since it seemed that all hope of relief was taken away from her because of these serious afflictions, and that the Lord had disposed things in that way, the woman came to Bernard in this badly stricken state, horrible to look at and wretched to endure. The crowd gathered round her to see what would happen. In front of them all the servant of God prayed. Gradually her agitation ceased, and she soon regained perfect health.

This miracle moved even the most intransigent with such astonishment that they acclaimed it with tears in their eyes, beating their breasts for almost half an hour. Such was the surge and crush of those who came hurrying along and kissing the sacred feet of the man of God that he was nearly crushed to death until the brothers lifted him, carried him into a boat, and settled him down a little way off. When the princes approached him, as he had asked them to do, to sue for peace, they sighed, saying, "We simply must listen to him without reserve since, as we have seen for ourselves, God loves him and listens to him, and *having heard him he did many things*,* for he has done many *great things in our eyes*."* As always, he was cautious about accepting this sort of glory, so he said to them, "God has done this not on my account, but for you."

[6] Now a like miracle and similar opportunity arose on that same day when the Lord turned the minds of the citizens of Metz toward peace. The holy man had entered the city of Metz and was vigorously trying to persuade the bishop* and the people *to agree on terms of peace*.* The offense the people had received burned fiercely within them, and they resented being forced to grant forgiveness when they were only thinking of repaying with force of arms.

*Mark 6:20
*Matt 21:42

*Stephen, bishop
1120–1163
*Luke 14:32

At that moment a paralyzed woman from the city was brought to the man of God. He placed his hands on her and prayed, and he deigned to place on her his own little cape and extended it over her. Holding it, he gave it to the bishop standing near and touched her sickly limbs under it. When he had finished this prayer and given her a blessing, he raised her up, and, in the sight of all those who had brought her on a bed, while they were still marveling, she went away healed.

Also, in the River Mosel, when the blessed man was sailing in a little boat because of the huge and unruly crowd of people, one of those who wanted a cure, a blind man, called out from the shore to take him to Bernard. While Bernard was sailing past, the blind man, hearing a fisherman in another boat sailing along after him, took off the cloak he was wearing and threw it to the fisherman so that he might be taken into his boat. It then happened that with immense faith the blind man went to the holy man as quickly as he could. When Bernard laid his hands on the blind man, he received his sight. In his amazement he cried out that he could see the hills, *could see the people, could see the trees** and everything else.

*Mark 8:24

AT SAINT BENEDICT'S MONASTERY NEAR MOSEL RIVER

[7] A few miles from there is a monastery called Saint Benedict.* A lame boy there was almost deprived of the use of his limbs from the waist downward; he could only use his hands and his thighs to move at all, and he dragged his feet uselessly after him. His father had carried him from a district in Burgundy four years previously and left him there, and from that time on he was kept alive on the alms of the brothers. When the blessed father arrived there

*Saint Arnoul Abbey

and the Lord did works of power in him throughout all the surrounding province, so making known his fame, the brothers of the aforesaid monastery took the boy to him on a trolley, asking him to help the distressed lad with his customary piety. He agreed and prayed for him, laying his hands on him, and straightaway he was restored to healthy mobility, so that he stood up straight, walking firmly on his feet. Since then, as we have recently learned from the abbot of the place, right up to the present, the boy, still in good health, follows and looks after the flocks, and if you want to know, *his name is John.**

*Luke 1:63

Another lame man lived in the vicinity of the same monastery. He was healed at the same time when brought for a blessing to the holy father, and he too received the gift of walking. Also, near the town of Toul there is a place called Gondreville, where the man of God gave sight to a blind woman in the presence of many people who had come together from the whole region. Indeed it is very difficult, if not almost impossible, to cover the whole range of marvelous things he did on this journey. In fact, we do not propose to put down in writing the signs of this sort or to give an account of the works of power done there.

Bernard's Last Days

Here we come, O most dear father, to the blessed end of your journeys, here to your final work. In this work the *King of Glory,** *the Lord your God,*† who has always magnificently brought to an end your journey and granted that peace which was so very valuable, so difficult, so desperate yet so necessary, now gives you glory in his own name and glorifies his name in you.

*Ps 23:7–10
†Ps 44:12

[8] Now with the reconciliation between the people of Metz completed and peace brought to that

province, the holy abbot returned to his monastery.
His body was failing and at this moment in a serious condition, so that his spirit with such sweetness
and gentleness of his mind was coming near to its
departure, and as if gradually sailing into the harbor,
it would remove the slender veil. To his brethren he
spoke quite openly: "*These are the words that I spoke** to   *John 14:10
you before I fell ill in this winter just past. What you
feared has not yet come to us. Summer is near at hand
and, believe me, the dissolution of this body." We
have learned by our own experience what the sacred
gospels witness about the holy apostles, that when
the Lord foretold to them his passion, *this saying was
hidden from them, and they did not grasp what was said.**   *Luke 18:34

Indeed, what the mind strongly rejects is not so
easily accepted or believed, especially when he, so
compassionate toward his brothers, suppresses words
of this sort. Besides, the facts themselves seem to cry
out in some way—*I have accomplished the work that
the Father has given to me that I should do*—* for more   *John 17:4
and more he failed to act in his normal fashion. He
withdrew his affections and the bonds of his sacred
desires, which he had previously showed with such
careful attention, and he set his thoughts more firmly
on the nearby shore. When, however, the venerable
bishop of the see of Langres, Geoffrey,[7] urged him to
deal with urgent matters and wondered that he no
longer applied his mind to them, he said, "Do not
wonder; *I am not of this world.*"*   *John 17:14, 16

[9] When the holy father saw that his dearest
sons were now miserable and depressed, wilting away
with dismay and on tenterhooks* at the solemn and   *Latin: *arescentes*
lamentable bereavement and desolation coming to

---

[7] Geoffrey de la Roche-Vanneau, first abbot of Fontenay
(1118), then prior of Clairvaux 1128–1138; bishop 1138–1163.

them, he was overcome with compassion and mercy toward them, so he sought to refresh them with his most tender consolations. He admonished them to be firmly rooted and anchored by indestructible love, faith, and hope in the bosom of divine clemency, and he promised that after his death he would not fail them in their need.

With more feeling than my words can express, he made every effort to imprint on our minds his pleading for love of purity and total perfection. Yet he also warned us with tears and charged us that if he had commended anything to us either by virtue or example, anything that we should strive after, we should hold on to it firmly. He used many other words in the same spirit of the apostle who said, *We beseech and exhort you in the Lord Jesus that you learn from us how you ought to live and to please God in all things; just as you are doing, do so more and more.** Would that he could persuade us to do effectively what he coaxed us to with such affection.

*1 Thess 4:1

If anyone wants to know the progress of his illness, there is a letter that he dictated to a special friend a very few days before his sacred passing from us. This must now be inserted into our narrative that we have brought to you so far, for although these words are strange coming from him, nevertheless they move us with emotion, all the more since they are his own words.

[10] The letter to Arnold, abbot of Bonneval,[8] who had sent him a gift and inquired with solicitude about his health:

> We have received your charitable gift with love but without pleasure. What pleasure can a person have when bitterness has totally over-

---

[8] Author of Book 2 of *Vita prima*.

whelmed him—except that being able to eat nothing is itself a delight. Sleep has fled from me, but pain is never far away, not even the benefit of release from feeling. The failings of my stomach are almost all that I am suffering. Frequently both day and night I am obliged to take a small amount of some liquid, but anything solid is out of the question. Even the slightest amount causes me great discomfort, but it is even more severe if it is altogether removed. Yet when I agree to take a very little occasionally, it causes grievous pain. My feet and legs are swollen, as is usual for a person with dropsy. Yet in all these things I would not hide from the concern of a friend: *According to the interior man, I speak less wisely;** the spirit is willing but the flesh is weak.*† Pray to the Savior, who does not will *the death of a sinner;*‡ pray to him not to put off the tempestuous moment of departure but to take care of me in it. Care for me with the promise of your strength, so that he who lies in wait may not find in my naked heel* a place to sink his fangs or a wound to strike me. I have written these things just as I am, so that you may know from this note by hand the love I have for you."[9]

*Rom 7:22; 2 Cor 11:23

†Matt 26:41; Mark 14:38

‡Ezek 33:11; RB Prol. 38

*Gen 3:15

[11] This is the exact letter that, as we have said and as his own words make clear, the holy father dictated when his death was imminent.[10] The careful reader will realize to some extent from the tenor of

---

[9] Bernard, Ep 310 (SBOp 8:230, James #469).

[10] Adriaan H. Bredero argues against the authenticity of this letter in "Études sur la 'Vita Prima' de Saint Bernard," *Analecta* 17 (1961): no. 1:3–72, no. 2:215–60, no. 3:3–59, here no. 2:254–56. See also Adriaan H. Bredero, *Bernard of Clairvaux: Between Cult and History* (Grand Rapids, MI: William B. Eerdmans Publishing, 1996), 104–8.

this letter how in the holy breast of this man, even while his body was failing, tranquility was in his mind, serenity in his mental powers, and sweetness in his spirit, and how great was the ground of his humility and his trust in the Lord right up to the end.

But it may be permitted for us to open to him our own thoughts, the pale visage of our grief, our frequent sighs, our anxious thoughts. This was the father who seemed to be leaving us. Indeed while such a treasure, so lovable a man, was still with us, yet the hope of keeping him for long had gone, and we did not have the means of traveling with him; we might not weep over him any longer, for he had entered so happily into the joy of the Lord God who had called him. Now what was left us but a life of weariness and death to fear. Now to you, *O good servant, that word "Well done" is said by the good Lord.** But in this separation our own condition was fraught with emptiness after such marvelous light, as we entered with misgiving after such golden times into the world that succeeds it, heavier, harder to bear.

[12] Those who came to their father before his departure, these sons of his to whom he gave birth through the gospel, came sorrowfully with tears and supplications to seek the mind of this man so dear to them, saying, "Father, have you no pity on this monastery, have you no compassion on us whom you suckled with milk from your motherly breasts with such keen and loving affection? How can you leave exposed to ruin those works of yours that you have labored so hard to accomplish in this place? How can you think now of leaving your sons so dear to you?"

Then, with tears and weeping, he raised his dove-like eyes to heaven, and, bringing forth in his mind the witness to that total apostolic spirit he found in himself, he was *hard-pressed between the two, and which to choose he could not tell,** leaving everything to the

*Matt 25:21

*Phil 1:23, 22

will of God. His paternal love persuaded him to agree to the desires of his children and remain here below, while *his desire to be with Christ drew him to depart.* **Phil 1:23* The humility rooted for so long and so powerfully in his heart persuaded him that from the intimate love of his heart he should call himself *a useless servant* **Luke 17:10* and reckon himself *a sterile tree,** from whose life no **Job 24:21* fruit could come, no good could come to anyone.

Then too, he was accustomed to confess, when speaking in familiar conversation, that he could hardly believe that people could trust him as being as useful as they said. He admitted that when thinking about this, he sometimes found himself in no little conflict within himself about whether such true and honest men could be so mistaken, whether such prudent men could seem able to be deceived, since he could not excuse anyone. While the whole world marveled, he alone was unable to see the wonders he had done, namely, the splendor of his works or of his counsel, like that simple and righteous man Job, who *did not see the sun when it shone nor the moon in its brightness.** **Job 31:26*

Bernard's Death

[13] Finally, when the bond of this exterior dwelling was dissolved and the free passage showed itself to a desiring soul, a great day shone bright in which the perpetual *day now arose.** As the moment drew near, **Job 14:7* the local bishops with a great number of abbots and brothers congregated around him. It was almost the third hour of the day, and the holy and truly blessed Abbot Bernard, that outstanding light of his generation, took flight happily from his mortal body into the land of the living, led there by Christ. He took flight from the choir of those singing the psalms and

from those of his sons standing close by, lamenting with grief and copious tears, to be transported to the joyful company of that multitude whom he had foreseen, to the ranks of the angels sent to meet him, to the welcoming embrace of the saints.

Happy that soul, so uplifted by the high privileges of his merits, where the desires of his lowly sons follow him, where the sacred desires of the heavenly beings drew him. Happy and truly serene is that day for him on which the resplendent midday, Christ, blazed out—a day long awaited by him all the days of his life with such longing, sought with sighs, frequented in his meditations, foreshadowed in his prayers. Happy the transition from labor to rest, from waiting until *gaining the prize,** from agony to victory, from death to life, *from this world to the Father.**

*Phil 3:14

*John 13:1

From this transition we know that so many things have appeared, so many by no means unworthy of being related, but it would be too difficult to describe every one of them, too long to write the story of them all. To this day *in many and various ways** his fatherly love has deigned truly to console his sons, even now, or rather more so now, since he is living and vigorously revealing their sorrows to them with many revelations, so that they may rejoice in him more gently and be less anxious and sorrowful over him. If the reader wishes a fuller narrative about these things, however, and especially those that do not demand a lengthy tale, we believe they should be reserved to their own final chapter.

*Heb 1:1

[14] Meanwhile, pushing on with the rest insofar as we can, we turn our minds away from violent things and, with deep sighs and sorrow, to those things about which the miserable flock cries out now that the shepherd has departed. We spare this page* and as much as possible close our eyes, strike our eyelids together against those tears that since he has gone

*paginae

away flow in our clear valley, drinking the whole church's chalice of sorrow—the valley that until now always dropped sweetness,* poured out joy, flowed with consolations.†

*Joel 3:18;
Amos 9:13

†Ps 93:19

Lying in State

When the faithful minister and priest of the Most High entered the place of the wonderful tabernacle† to the altar of God,‡ to offer to him the acceptable sacrifice of his spirit,§ his body, prepared with the rites of the church and clothed in his priestly vestments, was borne into the oratory of the Blessed Mother of God. Many of the nobles and others in the locality and from other places came together in mourning as quickly as they could, so that the whole valley was filled with weeping and wailing. More bitterly than the men, the forlorn sex of women wept over him outside the monastery, because while men were allowed to approach the remains of the blessed man, the discipline of the monastic order inexorably denied entry to women.

†Ps 41:5
‡Ps 42:4
§1 Pet 2:5

For two days the deceased shepherd of the flock lay in state, his countenance still with its innate gentleness, not lessened at all but rather growing in appeal to all. And still the vast concourse of people grew, so that the rush of those coming there was becoming intolerable, and so too their desire to touch his feet, to kiss his hand, to bring loaves to touch him with, or belts or coins and other things so that they might bring a blessing on themselves and keep those objects as souvenirs for their future needs.

They especially expected the great number of crowds to gather from far and wide throughout the local places on the third solemn day, as they prepared for the hour of the burial of his sacred body. But on the second day at noon so huge was the gathering of people, and so zealous was their piety, that they besieged his body on every side, thus showing hardly any reverence to bishops or to the brothers. Accordingly, fearing that something similar or even worse should happen on the third day, those taking part in Matins advanced the time for the internment and, having as on the two previous days completed the divine sacrifice, the celebration of Masses, and the psalmody with due ceremony, they then committed that most pure balm to its vessel, replacing that precious stone,* the best of pearls, in the stone sepulcher.

*1 Pet 2:6

Bernard's Burial

[15] Having happily completed the days of his life, about sixty-three years,[11] the beloved of the Lord, Bernard of Clairvaux, the first abbot of the monastery and the father of more than one hundred sixty monasteries, slept in Christ on the thirteenth Kalends of September* in the presence of his sons. He was buried on the eleventh Kalends* of the same month before the holy altar of the Blessed Virgin Mary, whose most devout priest he had been. On his breast in the tomb was placed a capsule that contained the relics of the Blessed Apostle Thaddeus.* When it was sent from Jerusalem in the same year, having such great trust and devotion to the saint, he ordered that it be placed on his body so that he might cleave to that apostle on the day of their common resurrection.

*August 20
*August 22

*=Jude the apostle

[11] MSB MS. 1 has, strangely, *Lxxxiii*, i.e., eighty-three, though Bernard was sixty-three years old when he died; the critical edition correctly here reads *annis circiter sexaginta tribus expletis* (VP 209).

[16] These things happened during the same year that our blessed Pope Eugenius,[12] the son of our holy father during his holy religious life, went from this light, or rather from this dark valley, into light. His merits shone out with many miracles in the city of Rome, which he ruled so gloriously. His successor Anastasius[13] presided over the church of Rome while the emperor of the Romans, the illustrious Frederick,[14] was ruling, and during the reign of King Louis in France,[15] the son of Louis.[16] The throne of the universal church and the monarchy of all creatures both visible and invisible was occupied by Jesus Christ, Son of God, in the year of the incarnation 1153, who with the Father and the Holy Spirit lives and reigns.

AFTERWARD

[17] Now, having written about these revelations that we already dealt with, we take up again what had been predicted about seven years before and that then came to pass. Two brothers in a monastery were talking about the life of the blessed father and his wondrous acts. One of them, brought up[17] since his early youth, said to the other, "Do you know how many years our blessed father has got to live?" "No, I do not," replied the other. The former said, "I know that he has six or seven years still to live in the flesh." How this religious acquired this knowledge

---

[12] Eugenius III, d. July 8, 1153.

[13] Pope Anastase IV (1153–1154).

[14] Frederick I Barbarossa, Holy Roman Emperor 1152–1190.

[15] Louis VII le Jeune (1137–1180).

[16] Louis VI le Gros.

[17] *Educatus*; i.e., reared at Clairvaux?

we do not know, nor can we know it now, because he did not indicate it then, and he died before the holy father.

The other religious, who is still living, took note of this prediction and was more amazed when he found out what had happened than when he had heard the words before. Because of this eyewitness account and the report of others who knew the speaker, we certainly have to believe him. Nor was this all, but what seems to be even more worthy of astonishment is the name and the person of Bernard's successor, which the surviving monk said he already knew from what the other monk had predicted. For at the same time as that brother predicted Bernard's death, he also predicted, "Dom Robert,[18] who is today the abbot of Les Dunes, is the future abbot of Clairvaux after this blessed father abbot."[19] And what that monk said would come about at some indeterminate time in six or seven years was seen to indicate what actually occurred, for Bernard died after the end of the sixth year and within the seventh year.

[18] The time had now arrived, and the holy father hurried to the final end. He was ill, as we have told you in the beginning of the book, so that now in that sickness virtue might be perfected and give warning of his imminent departure. Meanwhile the brothers implored with prayers and supplication to God as earnestly as they could. The holy man now realized that by their prayers they were putting off his desire, because he began to feel better in his body. So while the brothers gathered round him, he spoke

---

[18] See Marc Debuisson, "La provenance des premiers cisterciens d'après les lettres et les *vitae* de Bernard de Clairvaux," *Cîteaux* 43 (1992): 5–118, here 103–4.

[19] Robert of Bruges, first abbot of Les Dunes 1138, succeeded Bernard as abbot of Clairvaux.

these words: "Why do you hold back this sorrowful man? You are so strong, and you prevail. Spare me, I beg you, leave me be. Allow me to depart."

Just before this, when all the brothers were humbling their souls at this time of peril and fear, one of them had a vision. He saw a great multitude of people coming with great exultation to greet the man of God outside the cloister of the monastery. Leading that procession, four came before the others. The brother who was watching recognized that greatly beloved one whom Bernard himself had remembered with praise in the fourth book of *On Consideration*,* Geoffrey the bishop of Chartres,[20] as well as Humbert,[21] who was the first abbot of Igny,[22] and Bernard's two blood-brothers Guy* and Gerard.[23] Having received them reverently, after the kiss of peace, the holy father stayed with these four for a long time in conversation, waiting for the many others coming along.

*SBOp 3:448–66

*d. 1141 or 1142

Finally bidding him farewell, these men said that he must return from there by himself. But then he turned pale and, encompassed with interior pain, declared his agony of mind: "Why are you going without me?" he asked. They replied, "It is not possible as yet to satisfy your desires and ours until the time of New*[24] comes." They said "the time of New," when the new fruits are gathered; this meaning was clearly proved afterward by the event, when he died in the month of August. In the morning, then, that

*Exod 34:18; Sir 24:35

---

[20] Geoffrey de Lèves, bishop 1116–1149.

[21] Debuisson, "La provenance," 92–93.

[22] Humbert, monk of Clairvaux 1117, prior 1125, and first abbot of Igny 1128–1138, returned to Clairvaux and died ca. 1148; see S "In Obitu Domni Humberti" (SBOp 5:440–47; CF 54).

[23] D. 1138; see Bernard, SC 26:3–14 (SBOp 1:171–81).

[24] *Novorum*, i.e., New Fruits.

brother to whom this was shown told the others what he had seen and heard, and he consoled the others, who were now dreading the imminent death of the father. It was still winter.

[19] At the same time another vision of the former brother was confirmed. Indeed, the complete truth of the matter has now evidently been proved for both visions. A certain brother was looking and—see!— the most blessed man was preparing to ascend to Jerusalem and was now clothed for the journey. The venerable Odo,* who from his first years had vigorously led a holy way of life in a praiseworthy manner in the monastery, where he was accustomed to fill in for absent superiors, now approached him with reverence and asked him if he could go first. The truth of this vision is demonstrated in this way: this man Odo, who was worthy in the sight of God, was preparing to go to the celestial Jerusalem, where is the true *vision of peace*,* and he was going to follow a little after the holy father. He had by now fittingly discharged his function on earth, and he went before the father.

[20] But just a few days before the happy death of the father, another abbot who was quite near him in both place and affection saw him adorned in precious priestly vestments, suffused with eminent glory, and being led to the altar with most striking solemnity. When the holy father entered the great church, it burst forth with resounding voices: *"a child has been born to us."**[25] That child was truly *meek and humble of heart*,* receiving *the kingdom of God*,† before whom a multitude of angels and likewise the church of all the saints resounded with joy at his most felicitous birth, though to us it seems to be his death. For him it was his birth when he finished his life here on earth and

*subprior of Clairvaux

*Ezek 13:16

*Isa 9:6
*Matt 11:29
†Mark 10:14

[25] Second Mass for Christmas Day.

began it there in heaven. They were in exultation not with the sound of their voices but with the songs of their unanimous desires.

For if the whole celestial region learns to rejoice *in one sinner doing penance,** how much more must that joy be revealed in him by whom that region received such immense joy at the conversion and penance of so many sinners? Who can estimate how many there are still remaining in this earthly condition and way of life, and how great they will be when the Lord grants them repentance for salvation on transferring them to those other congregations of men and women through the ministry of this faithful servant? Or who can enumerate the number of those who under his loving care have been brought *to repentance through the goodness of God** in those hundred and sixty monasteries?

*Luke 15:7, 10

*Rom 2:4

For from those alone who are seen to be his special sons, apart from those who have already happily finished the course of their lives and those propagated through other places, on that day on which the most happy father merited to ascend from Clairvaux to that resplendent mountain, he left almost seven hundred souls serving the Lord and dwelling in those houses. Why wonder if we believe him, so dear to the heavenly court, so acceptable to the King, to be received with joy and exultation in heaven? In him *the grace of God was not given in vain,** since he labored so faithfully and efficaciously after all he did in his time and before. For he multiplied the talent given to him* so copiously, and finally he was given such a reward for what he had done.

*1 Cor 15:10

*Matt 25:14-23

But that is quite enough on that subject, for fear that anyone should complain that we have gone beyond the boundaries of the brevity we promised.

[21] In the morning, in the monastery of the aforesaid abbot who foresaw his birthday, on the very night when the holy father appearing to this prelate was going to die, the father bade farewell to this abbot and said, "You know that I am going away, nor will I remain here any longer." When he indicated his departure to the abbot, the abbot made haste and, coming to Clairvaux on that very day, found that the holy abbot had already gone, just as he said he would.

WILLIAM OF GRANDSELVE[26]

[22] William of Montpellier, the abbot we mentioned above, was a highly respected man while he was living in the world but even more magnificent when he fled from the world. Here in the monastery of Grandselve where he became a monk, he visited the holy father in a very devout way. He was about to return, but he was in tears and lamented that he would no longer see him. The man of God said to him: "Do not be afraid; without doubt you will still see me." William, a devout man, was waiting for the result of this promise, and on the very night that the blessed father departed from this life, he merited to see him, appearing to him in the monastery of Grandselve, where he said, "Brother William." And he: "Yes! It is I, my lord." "Come with me," he said. They went off together, and then they came to a very high mountain. The holy man asked him, "Do you know where we have come?" He confessed that he did not know. He replied: "We have come to the foot of Mount Lebanon.* Now, you will remain here, but I am going up the mountain."

*Sir 50:13

When William asked why Bernard wanted to ascend the mountain, he replied: "I want to learn." He

---

[26] Section 22 is missing from the critical edition.

was taken aback, "What, I ask you, do you want to learn, father? We believe that today you are second to none in knowledge." The holy man said to him: "Here there is no knowledge, no true understanding; up there is the very fullness of knowledge, up there is the true and full knowledge of the Truth." With this word he sent him off and went up the very high mountain before his eyes. When William saw him going, he was amazed, and at once there came to him the word that John once sang about heaven: *Blessed are they who die in the Lord.** The next morning he spoke to his abbot and his brothers. He told them that the holy father had departed from this life. When they noted the exact day and made a careful enquiry, they found that it was exactly as they had heard.

*Rev 14:13

O holy father, *you have disposed in your heart to ascend by steps, in this vale of tears;** now you have ascended from Clairvaux onto Mount Lebanon, the mountain of pure whiteness, the plenitude of light, the height of bewildering brightness. *Pure are your hands and clean your heart;** you have *ascended into the mountain of the Lord;*† you have arrived at *the riches of salvation,*‡ at *the treasures of wisdom and knowledge,*§ where pure as you are, you see pure Truth, where for you with all the saints there is one Master, the Christ, *where all are taught by God.** *Draw us after you,*† we beseech you, and from that high mountain look down with mercy on this your vale; be with those who labor still, stand by those who are in danger, stretch out your hand to those who climb that height. Give confidence to us as once you did; do not empty us of it now, but with your great and kind goodness, or more than that, may that vision by which we are bound to you not be taken from us because of our presumption.

*Ps 83:6-7

*Matt 5:8
†Ps 23:3
‡Isa 33:6
§Col 2:3

*Ps 23:4;
John 6:45;
see Isa 54:13
†Song 1:3

[23] The following night, after the sacred body had been laid in the tomb, the holy father, still engaged in solicitude for his sons and for his love for them in

*John 13:1

this world—*he loved them to the end**—showed this in a striking fashion. He appeared to one of the brothers, his clothes and his face shining in stupendous glory, like a flash of lightning, but when the brother desired to take hold of him, he moved on past and said to him, "I come for a certain simple brother." When the brothers heard this and were wondering about it, at about the time for Tierce the truth of the vision was confirmed. A certain brother had died. He was praiseworthy for his simplicity, and it should be believed that he said that Bernard had come for him and his soul was happy to have such a leader, and Bernard took him away.

After a few days had been completed, Bernard appeared in splendor to another brother and told us who were weeping over his departure, after some words of a quite consoling nature and the promise of eternal happiness to those who persevered in obedience and in the faith, "Know this and tell the brethren that there is buried in the oratory the body of a saint, and I have his clothing." He said that it was the bishop Malachy.[27] The tunic in which the saint had been happily buried and had been used at the celebration of the Mass, he had ordered that he be buried in it, just as he had been buried in his own clothing. This was altogether unknown to the brother until he saw this vision.

Happy is that bishop whose merits the holy father proclaimed both while he was living and after his death. Happy is that love that did not die with his death. Happy too the society that was not rent apart by that so cruel divorce.* Glorious indeed are these

*of soul and
body

[27] Malachy O'Morgair, archbishop of Armagh, died All Saints' Day 1148.

fathers who loved one another in their lives, so *that they were not separated in death.*[28]

[24] After about forty days a certain abbot from the island of Greater Britain joyfully merited to experience in himself the power of this holy society. He, at that time with some other fellow abbots, was seeking the Cistercian Order, as was customary. He was seized with a double illness and was desperately sick, with pleurisy and with a daily fever. For a long time he lay sick with this trouble so that the brothers who never left him were watching only for the departure of his soul. And when his mind was tortured not so much with the desire for this present life but with the desolation of his absent children whom he had left behind on his pilgrimage, he asked very earnestly to be carried to the tomb of the holy abbot.

There, when he had prayed with all the devotion he could muster, he thought of visiting the tomb of the blessed Bishop Malachy, placed on the west side of the oratory, and to elicit the help of this saint. But fearing his fatigue and as it were now secure from harm, they did not fulfill his request. So, another day, calling together the brothers, he came to the oratory and begged to be shown what he needed to see. While they were arguing about this, for they feared some danger, he said, "It is quite essential that I should seek the tomb of Saint Malachy. When during the past night I had hardly slept at all, I was suddenly awakened and heard a voice saying to me, 'You are healed of your sickness; if you wish to be healed of the other one, ask to be taken to the bishop.'" This

---

[28] *The Life of St. Benedict by Gregory the Great: Translation and Commentary*, ed. and trans. Terrence G. Kardong (Collegeville, MN: Liturgical Press, 2009), chap. 34, p. 125: "In this way it came about that those who had always been of one mind in the Lord were not even bodily separated in the tomb."

they did for him as he wished, and it was immediately done for him just as it was said to him. On that day he was healed, and after a few more days he took up his journey and returned home unharmed.

GEOFFREY'S LOVING EULOGY

[25] In this work, O most gentle Father, we recognize your Spirit, your zeal, your kindly attention. It is in your gift to delegate it to your coworker, so that you may also communicate to him the love by which you are more truly and more happily honored in heaven. Or rather, O God, giver of all your gifts, yours are all these works. You have filled everything since the beginning of time with the presence of your Godhead; everything overflows with the glory of your Majesty, visiting those parts and places with your eternal counsel, and filling them too with the special grace of your holiness. Make, O Lord, this valley abound always with spiritual fruit, which as you have made it clear in reality as in name, consent to enlighten those settling here with two kinds of outstanding brightness. Keep the house in which this your so precious jewel was kept, and *make it with us according to your word,** that *where your treasure is, there your heart may be,†* and there *grace and mercy,‡* and to all those present the sight of your untiring and heartfelt vigilance, and this also to all those *gathered here in your name,** which is above every name, *just as you are over all, God blessed forever.†* Amen.

The end of the sermon of the same on the anniversary of his deposition.

*Luke 1:38
†Matt 6:21
‡Est 2:17; Dan 1:9

*1 Cor 5:4
†Rom 9:5

Bibliography

Abelard. "Historia Calamitatum." In *The Letters of Abelard and Heloise*, translated by Betty Radice. Revised by Michael Clanchy. 1974. Reprint, London: Penguin Books, 2003.

Ambroise de Milan. *Hymnes*. Edited and translated by Jacques Fontaine, et al. Paris: Les Éditions du Cerf, 1992.

Bell, David N. "From Molesme to Cîteaux: The Earliest 'Cistercian' 'Spirituality.'" CSQ 34 (1999): 469–82.

Bernard of Clairvaux. *Epistolae*. Edited by Jean Leclercq and H. M. Rochais. SBOp 7–8. Rome: Editiones Cistercienses, 1974. Reprint, 1997.

———. *Five Books on Consideration: Advice to a Pope*. Translated by John D. Anderson and Elizabeth T. Kennan. Bernard of Clairvaux, vol. 13. CF 37. Kalamazoo, MI: Cistercian Publications, 1976.

———. *The Letters of St Bernard of Clairvaux*. Translated by Bruno Scott James. London: Burns and Oates, 1953.

———. *Magnificat: Homilies in Praise of the Blessed Virgin Mary*. Translated by Marie-Bernard Saïd. CF 18. Kalamazoo, MI: Cistercian Publications, 1979.

———. *On Loving God*. Translated by Robert Walton. CF 13B. 1973; Kalamazoo, MI: Cistercian Publications, 1995.

———. *Sancti Bernardi Opera* [SBOp]. Edited by Jean Leclercq and H. M. Rochais. 9 vols. Rome: Editiones Cistercienses, 1957–1977.

———. *Sermons on the Song of Songs*. 4 vols. Translated by Kilian Walsh and Irene Edmonds. CF 4, 7, 31, 40. Kalamazoo, MI: Cistercian Publications, 1976, 1979, 1980.

Bollermann, Karen, and Cary J. Nederman. "Standing in Abelard's Shadow: Gilbert of Poiters, the 1148 Council of Rheims, and the Politics of Ideas." In *Religion, Power, and Resistance from the Eleventh to the Sixteenth Centuries: Playing the Heresy Card*, edited by Karen Bollermann, et al. New York: Palgrave Macmillan, 2014. 13–36.

Bredero, Adriaan H. *Bernard of Clairvaux: Between Cult and History*. Grand Rapids, MI: William B. Eerdmans Publishing, 1996.

———. "The Canonization of Saint Bernard and the Rewriting of His Life." In *Cistercian Ideals and Reality*, edited by John R. Sommerfeldt. CS 60. Kalamazoo, MI: Cistercian Publications, 1978. 80–105.

————. "Études sur la 'Vita prima' de Saint Bernard." *Analecta* 17, nos. 1, 2 (1961): 3–72, 215–60; and 18, no. 3 (1962): 3–59.

Casey, Michael. "Towards a Methodology for the *Vita prima*:Translating the First Life into Biography." In Bernardus Magister: *Papers Presented at the Nonacentenary Celebration of the Birth of Bernard of Clairvaux, Kalamazoo, Michigan*, edited by John R. Sommerfeldt. CS 135. Kalamazoo, MI: Cistercian Publications, and Cîteaux, 1992. 55–70.

Conrad of Eberbach. *Exordium Magnum Cisterciense sive Narratio de Initio Cisterciensis Ordinis*. Edited by Bruno Griesser. CCCM 138.Turnhout: Brepols Publishers, 1994.

————. *The Great Beginning of Cîteaux: A Narrative of the Beginning of Cîteaux: The* Exordium Magnum *of Conrad of Eberbach*. Translated by Benedicta Ward and Paul Savage. Edited by E. Rozanne Elder. CF 72. Kalamazoo, MI: Cistercian Publications, 2011.

Daniel-Rops, Henri. *Cathedral and Crusade*.Translated by John Warrington. London: J. M. Dent and Sons, 1957.

Debuisson, Marc. "La provenance des premiers cisterciens d'après les lettres et les *vitae* de Bernard de Clairvaux." *Cîteaux* 43 (1992): 5–118.

Dimier, Anselme. "Le miracle des mouches de Foigny." *Cîteaux* 8 (1957): 57–62.

Elder, E. Rozanne. "Bernard and William of Saint Thierry." In *A Companion to Bernard of Clairvaux*, edited by Brian Patrick McGuire. Leiden: Brill Academic Publishers, 2011. 108–32.

————. "Making Virtues of Vexing Habits." In *Studiosorum Speculum: Studies in Honor of Louis J. Lekai, O. Cist*, edited by Francis Swietek and John R. Sommerfeldt. CS 141. Kalamazoo, MI: Cistercian Publications, 1993. 75–94.

Fragmenta Gavfridi. Edited by Christine Vande Veire. In *Vita prima Sancti Bernardi Claraevallis Abbatis*, edited by Paul Verdeyen. CCCM 89B. Turnhout: Brepols Publishers, 2011. 235–307.

France, James. *The Cistercians in Medieval Art*. Thrupp [UK]: Sutton Publishing, 1998.

————. *The Cistercians in Scandinavia*. CS 131. Kalamazoo, MI: Cistercian Publications, 1992.

————. *Medieval Images of Saint Bernard of Clairvaux*. CS 210. Kalamazoo, MI: Cistercian Publications, 2007.

Gastaldelli, Ferruccio. "La più antiche testimonianze biografiche su San Bernardo. Studio storico-critico sui *Fragmenta Gaufridi*." *Analecta* 45 (1989): 3–80. Reprint in Ferruccio Gastaldelli. *Studi su San Bernardo e Goffredo di Auxerre*. Millennio Medievale, 30; Reprint, 3. Florence: Sismel. Edizioni del Galluzzo, 2001. 43–127.

Geoffroy d'Auxerre. *Notes sur la vie et les miracles de saint Bernard, Fragmenta I [Précédé de] Fragmenta II*, by Raynaud de Foigny. Edited and translated by Raffaele Fassetta. SCh 548. Paris: Les Éditions du Cerf, 2011.

Goodrich, W. E. "The Reliability of the *Vita Prima Sancti Bernardi*." CSQ 21, no. 3 (1986): 213–27.

———. "The Reliability of the *Vita prima Sancti Bernardi*: The Image of Bernard in Book 1 of the *Vita Prima* and his Own Letters, A Comparison." *Analecta* 43 (1987): 153–80.

Gregory the Great. *The Life of St. Benedict by Gregory the Great: Translation and Commentary*. Edited and translated by Terrence G. Kardong. Collegeville, MN: Liturgical Press, 2009.

Hayen, André. "Le concile de Reims et l'erreur théologique de Gilbert de la Porrée." *Archives d'histoire doctrinale et littéraire du moyen âge* 10 (1935–1936): 1–23.

Heffernan, Thomas. *Sacred Biography: Saints and Their Biographers in the Middle Ages*. New York: Oxford University Press, 1988.

Holdsworth, Christopher. "The Affiliation of Savigny." In *Truth as Gift: Studies in Medieval Cistercian History in Honor of John R. Sommerfeldt*, edited by Marsha L. Dutton, et al. CS 204. Kalamazoo, MI: Cistercian Publications, 2004. 43–88.

———. "The Early Writings of Bernard of Clairvaux." *Cîteaux* 45, no. 1–2 (1944): 21–61.

Horace. *Epistles*. In *Satires, Epistles, and Ars Poetica*. Translated by H. Rushton Fairclough. Loeb Classical Library 194. 1926. Reprint edition, Cambridge, MA: Harvard University Press, 1929. 248–441.

[Kingsmill], Sister Edmée. "Bernard and Abelard." In *The Influence of Saint Bernard*, edited by Benedicta Ward. Fairacres Publication 60. Oxford: SLG Press, 1976. 89–134.

La Vie de Saint Bernard, par Guillaume de Saint-Thierry; Continuée par Arnauld de Bonneval et Geoffroi de Clairvaux. Translated by François Guizot. Paris: Éditions Paleo, 2010.

Leclercq, Jean. "Études sur Saint Bernard et le texte de ses écrits." *Analecta* 9 (1953): 3–245.

Lekai, Louis J. *The Cistercians: Ideals and Reality*. Kent, OH: Kent State University Press, 1977.

Lucan. *The Civil War [De Bello Civili]*. Edited by A. E. Housman. Translated by J. D. Duff. Loeb Classical Library 220. Cambridge, MA: Harvard University Press, 1928.

Luddy, Ailbe J. *Life and Teaching of St. Bernard*. Dublin: M. H. Gill & Son, Ltd., 1927.

Matarasso, Pauline, ed. and trans. *The Cistercian World: Monastic Writings of the Twelfth Century*. London: Penguin Books, 1993.

Mews, Constant J. "Bernard of Clairvaux and Peter Abelard." In *A Companion to Bernard of Clairvaux*, edited by Brian Patrick McGuire. Leiden: Brill Academic Publishers, 2011. 133–68.

———. "The Council of Sens (1141): Abelard, Bernard, and the Fear of Social Upheaval." *Speculum* 77, no. 2 (2002): 342–82.

Monagle, Clare. "The Trial of Ideas: Two Tellings of the Trial of Gilbert of Poitiers." *Viator: Medieval and Renaissance Studies* 35 (2004): 113–29.

Morson, John. "A Newly Found Bernardine Manuscript." *Collectanea Ordinis Cisterciensium Reformatorum* 16 (1954): 30–34, 214–21.

———. "Some Manuscripts of the Life of St. Bernard." *Bulletin of the John Rylands Library* 37 (1955): 476–502.

———. "Texts in a Bernardine Manuscript at Mount Saint Bernard Abbey." *Collectanea Ordinis Cisterciensium Reformatorum* 16 (1954): 214–21.

Murray, A. Victor. *Abelard and St Bernard: A Study in Twelfth Century "Modernism."* Manchester [UK]: Manchester University Press, 1967.

Otto of Freising. *The Deeds of Frederick Barbarossa* [*Gesta Friderici I Imperatoris*]. Translated by Charles Christopher Mierow. New York: Columbia University Press, 1953.

Picard, André, and Pierre Boglioni. "Miracle et Thaumaturgie dans la vie de Saint Bernard." In *Vie et légendes de Saint Bernard de Clairvaux. Création, diffusion, réception (XIIᵉ–XXᵉ Siècles). Actes des Rencontres de Dijon, 7–8 juin 1991*. Edited by Patrick Arabeyre, et al. Brecht and Cîteaux: *Cîteaux: Commentarii Cistercienses*, 1993. 36–59.

Regnard, Joël. "Saint Bernard and the New Monastery." CSQ 49, no. 4 (2014): 431–53.

The Rule of Saint Benedict. Translated by Abbot Parry. With introduction and commentary by Esther de Waal. Leominster [UK]: Gracewing Publishing, 2003.

Smith, Richard Upsher. "Arnold of Bonneval, Bernard of Clairvaux, and Bernard's Epistle 310." *Analecta* 49 (1993): 273–318.

Truax, Jean A. "*Miles Christi:* Count Theobald IV of Blois and Saint Bernard of Clairvaux." CSQ 44, no. 3 (2009): 299–320.

Vacandard, Elphège. *Vie de saint Bernard abbé de Clairvaux*. 2 vols., 4th ed. Paris: Librairie Victor LeCoffre, 1910.

Valente, Luisa. "Gilbert of Poitiers." *Encyclopedia of Medieval Philosophy*. Dordrecht: Springer Netherlands, 2011. 409–17.

Virgil. *Eclogues, Georgics, Aeneid 1–6*. Translated by H. Rushton Fairclough. Revised by G. P. Goold. Loeb Classical Library 63. 1916. Cambridge, MA, and London: Harvard University Press, 1999.

Vogüé, Adalbert de. *Grégoire le Grand: Dialogues.* Translated by P. Antin. SCh 260. Paris: Les Éditions du Cerf, 1979.

Waddell, Chrysogonus. *Narrative and Legislative Texts from Early Cîteaux*. Studia et Documenta vol. 9. Cîteaux: Commentarii Cistercienses, 1999.

William of St. Thierry, et al. *Bernard of Clairvaux: Early Biographies.* Translated by Martinus Cawley. One-volume edition, slightly revised. Guadalupe Translations. Lafayette, OR: Abbey of Our Lady of Guadalupe, 2000.

———. *La Vie de Saint Bernard, par Guillaume de Saint-Thierry; Continuée par Arnauld de Bonneval et Geoffroi de Clairvaux.* Translated by François Guizot. Paris: Éditions Paleo, 2010.

———. *St. Bernard of Clairvaux: The Story of His Life as Recorded in the Vita prima Bernardi by Certain of His Contemporaries, William of St. Thierry, Arnold of Bonnevaux, Geoffrey and Philip of Clairvaux, and Odo of Deuil*. Translated by Geoffrey Webb and Adrian Walker. London: A. R. Mowbray, 1960.

———. *Vita Prima Sancti Bernardi Claraevallis Abbatis, Liber Primus*. Edited by Paul Verdeyen. CCCM 89B. Turnhout: Brepols Publishers, 2011.

Williams, Watkin. *Saint Bernard of Clairvaux*. Manchester [UK]: Manchester University Press, 1935.

Scriptural Index

Scripture references in the five books of the *Life of Bernard* are cited by book and section number.

Acts

2:2	1.13
2:37	1.13
4:10	2.15
4:32	1.13, 1.15, 1.31, 3.3
5:12–13	1.15
6:10	3.14
7:22	1.37
7:51	1.37
8:18-19	2.41
9:5	2.13
9:15	1.19 (2x), 2.25, 3.32
10:10	1.57
12:11	1.57
13:3	1.58
13:48	1.13
20:26	3.26
26:14	1.10, 1.11
27:23	1.31

Amos

9:13	1.61, 5.14

Col

2:3	5.22

1 Cor

1:27	1.40
2:12	1.61
3:16-17	1.30
4:3	2.41
4:15	1.17
5:3	2.28
5:4	5:25
8:11	1.30
9:19	3.6
10:33	3.2
11:28	1.42
12:7	1.42
13:1	1.28
13:2	1.61
14:24–25	1.15
15:10	5:20

2 Cor

2:11	1.42
2:16	2.24
4:7	3.1
5:1	5.1
5:14	1.70, 3.26
6:2	2.25
6:14–15	1.28
10:11	3.4
11:23	5.10
11:27	1.25, 1.35
12:2	2.51
12:4	2.51
12:7	1.45, 2.54
12:9	1.41, 2.26, 2.54, 3.1
12:10	1.35

Dan

1:9	5.25
7:7	1.46

265

Titus		**Wis**	
2:12	3.12	4:13	4.8
		4:14	5.4
Tob		8:19–20	1.21
9:11	1.18	16:18	1.33

Index of Names

Items in the Acknowledgments (Ack), Introduction (Int), and Editor's Note (EN) are cited by page or note number; the five books of the *First Life of Bernard of Clairvaux* give book and section numbers or notes. The Appendix to Book 1 is cited as App, the Prefaces to Book 2 as Pref, and the Prologue to Book 3 as Prol. Bernard and the monastery of Clairvaux are not included in the index, though his works are listed under *Bernard of Clairvaux, works.*